Stefanie Knauss / Alexander D. Ornella (eds.)

# Reconfigurations

AF649656

# Theologie.Kultur.Ästhetik

Grazer fundamentaltheologische Schriftenreihe

herausgegeben von

Gerhard Larcher und
Christian Wessely

Band 3

LIT

Stefanie Knauss / Alexander D. Ornella (eds.)

# RECONFIGURATIONS

## Interdisciplinary Perspectives on Religion in a Post-Secular Society

LIT

Gedruckt mit Unterstützung durch:
Bundesministerium für Wissenschaft und Forschung, Wien
Amt der Steiermärkischen Landesregierung, Abt. Wissenschaft und Forschung
Styria-Fonds der Kath.-Theol. Fakultät der Karl-Franzens-Universität Graz

Das Land Steiermark
→ Wissenschaft

**Bibliographic information published by the Deutsche Nationalbibliothek**
The Deutsche Nationalbibliothek lists this publication in the Deutsche Nationalbibliografie; detailed bibliographic data are available in the Internet at http://dnb.d-nb.de.

Für die Bildrechte zeichnen die Autorinnen und Autoren der einzelnen Beiträge verantwortlich.

ISBN 978-3-7000-0739-5 (Österreich)
ISBN 978-3-8258-0775-7 (Deutschland)

Satz und Layout: Christian Wessely

Umschlagbild: Alexander D. Ornella

**A catalogue record for this book is available from the British Library**

© LIT VERLAG GmbH & Co. KG Wien 2007
Krotenthallergasse 10/8
A-1080 Wien
Tel. +43 (0) 1 / 409 56 61
Fax +43 (0) 1 / 409 56 97
e-Mail: wien@lit-verlag.at
http://www.lit-verlag.at

LIT VERLAG Dr. W. Hopf
Berlin 2007
Auslieferung/Verlagskontakt:
Fresnostr. 2
D-48159 Münster
Tel. +49 (0)251–62 03 20
Fax +49 (0)251–23 19 72
e-Mail: lit@lit-verlag.de
http://www.lit-verlag.de

**Auslieferung:**
Österreich: Medienlogistik Pichler-ÖBZ GmbH & Co KG
IZ-NÖ, Süd, Straße 1, Objekt 34, A-2355 Wiener Neudorf
Tel. +43 (0) 2236/63 535 - 290, Fax +43 (0) 2236/63 535 - 243, e-Mail: mlo@medien-logistik.at
Deutschland: LIT Verlag Fresnostr. 2, D-48159 Münster
Tel. +49 (0) 2 51/620 32 - 22, Fax +49 (0) 2 51/922 60 99, e-Mail: vertrieb@lit-verlag.de

Distributed in the UK by: Global Book Marketing, 99B Wallis Rd, London, E9 5LN
Phone: +44 (0) 20 8533 5800 – Fax: +44 (0) 1600 775 663
http://www.centralbooks.co.uk/acatalog/search.html

Distributed in North America by:

Transaction Publishers
New Brunswick (U.S.A.) and London (U.K.)

Transaction Publishers
Rutgers University
35 Berrue Circle
Piscataway, NJ 08854

Phone: +1 (732) 445 - 2280
Fax: + 1 (732) 445 - 3138
for orders (U. S. only):
toll free (888) 999 - 6778
e-mail:
orders@transactionspub.com

# Contents

Stefanie Knauss and Alexander Darius Ornella

# ./configure
## Introduction

Connections between religion and media studies have steadily grown in popularity both in the US and Europe over the past few decades, and have been increasing at a greater pace since the beginning of the 21st century. Academics from a wide variety of disciplines, such as religious studies, theology, sociology, cultural studies, science studies, and journalism, to mention but a few, have been exploring the relationship between media, religion and society. Several research centers and projects have emerged beginning in the mid to late 1990s, including, for example, the Center for Religion and Media at New York University,[1] the Center for Media, Religion and Culture at the University of Colorado Boulder,[2] the Network *New Visibility of Religion in Europe* located at the University of Manchester[3] (which includes universities and academics from all over Europe), and the International Study Group *Film and Theology*.[4]



This seemingly increasing interest in the relationship between media and religion raises interesting questions: why is this kind of interest on the increase now, and how did it come about, what does it say about society and culture, what kind of changes does it reflect, if it does, about society and culture and how can and should we – as academics interested in these phenomena – react to these changes. Yet these questions can be deceptively simple: religion is a deeply intricate part of culture and asking questions like the above leads to other even more complex questions. For example, the identification of that which we can call 'the religious' has changed significantly in the last few decades; investigations into 'the religious' are thus characterised as much by hermeneutical questions as by trying to quantify appearances of 'the religious;' the two are irretrievably intertwined. Equally important is the question of how to adapt our research methods and questions to these new trajectories of religious expression and intent. And most importantly: given the flexibility that 'religion' appears to be characterised by throughout the centuries, we should be careful of our own terminology as we seek to understand these new manifestations of an ancient way of seeing, reacting to, and shaping the world. If the conceptions of religion,

1 http://www.nyu.edu/fas/center/religionandmedia/.

2 http://www.colorado.edu/journalism/mcm/mrc/.

3 http://www.art.man.ac.uk/RELTHEOL/network/.

4 http://www.film-und-theologie.de/.

as well as their role and presence, have changed fundamentally in today's society, as this book proposes, then any research in this area has to take into account the fact that previous definitions of 'religion' as a term might no longer be as conceptually viable as they once were.

In the past few decades, there have been major trends, developments, and events in both academic discourse, society, and the media that have raised questions and furthered interest in the field of media-and-religion studies. In academic discourse, it has become evident that secularisation theory is in need of reevaluation, not least because thus far it has not been possible to draw coherent conclusions from the empirical data gathered.[5] Furthermore, we are witnessing the rise of various kinds of religious fundamentalism across the globe. 9/11 and the war in Iraq have certainly contributed to this rise, but the phenomenon is not limited to the Arab world: in the US and in Europe religious fundamentalism has also won ground, especially among Christian evangelicals, but also within other religions. Religion is on the daily agenda again in both the public and the political sphere. In the media itself, there is an omnipresence of religious imagery and the supernatural in large-scale film productions such as THE PASSION (Mel Gibson, USA 2004) or the LORD OF THE RINGS trilogy (Jackson, New Zealand/USA 2001/2002/2003), in various TV series, such as GILMORE GIRLS (Amy Sherman, USA 2000–ongoing)[6] as well as in minor and local productions (e.g. references to the Last Supper in Germany's current BIG BROTHER production). In both US and European book bestseller lists, books with a title borrowed from a religious tradition or dealing with religious and spiritual issues are a constant feature.



The strong presence of these phenomena in society, and the interest raised by them both in the general public and in academia suggests that we are facing a multi-dimensional and complex transformation process that affects various aspects of our lives (society, culture, religion, politics, and media). The former relatively monolithic religious composition of (western) society has given way to a global plurality of ideas, values, and religions.[7] All aspects of our lives, whether private or public, religious, political or economic, have become entangled with the media.

Given these major developments, it seems that the moment has come to reconsider approaches and methodologies in religion-and-media studies and their

5 Cf. Sweeney, James, Revising Secularization Theory, in: Ward, Graham, Hölzl, Michael (eds.), *New Visibility of Religion in European Democratic Culture*, London: Continuum, in preparation.

6 Cf. the title of Season 4, Episode 13: Nag Hammadi Is Where They Found the Gnostic Gospels, http://www.tv.com/gilmore-girls/nag-hammadi-is-where-they-found-the-gnostic-gospels/episode/290404/summary.html, accessed March 20, 2007.

7 Cf. Berger, Peter, Religion in a Globalizing World, Panel, Key West/Florida, Dec 4, 2006, http://pewforum.org/events/index.php?EventID=136, accessed March 2, 2007.

appropriateness for today's issues. In its attempts to explain the phenomenon of the relation of media and religion in a 'post-secular' society, most research has focused on the western context and dealt with various phenomena in individual, but not necessarily interconnected or interdependent, ways. One point of interest has been how religious communities use media to present or stage themselves, recruit new members, and broadcast their message. Thanks to its array of religious symbols, film has also attracted much attention among scholars. Many authors have identified religious motifs in media products, but their research has largely been limited to a comparison with a biblical or otherwise traditional prototype, often resulting in nothing but a denouncement of the film's representations. Psychoanalytical approaches have dealt primarily with issues of identification; studies of the socio-psychological effects of media on their audience have so far suffered from monocausal explanations and methodological weaknesses.[8] Another line of inquiry has focused on the question of the power of the media, often based either on Adorno's interpretation of the 'culture industry' or Fiske's theory of media power to the audience.[9] Both of those approaches are marked by a binary opposition between those in power and the disempowered and an inherent mistrust of 'the power' of media. Also, they do not take into account what the audience can – and does! – do with media products.

All these approaches can still provide valuable insights into the interaction between religion, media and society. Yet today, the interactions of these three aspects and the way these interactions are carried out has changed; they have become more interdependent, shaping and influencing each other in fundamental ways. The isolated view of a particular medium, media format, or media content of earlier approaches fails to explain this interdependence, the motivations and decisions of recipients as well as social shifts, such as the half-life of some but not other religious motifs in media.

It is obvious from the articles collected in this volume that religion, media, and society have come to interact and depend on each other. Media shape religious consciousness and expression; they might even acquire a transcendental status in doing so. The religious,[10] on the other hand, is present in media in multiple ways, providing recipients and consumers with a plurality of choices they can



8 Cf. Gauntlett, David, Media, *Gender and Identity. An Introduction*, London: Routledge, reprint 2006, 28f.

9 Cf. Gauntlett, Media, *Gender and Identity*, 20ff.

10 We are aware of the various meanings of the terms 'religion' and 'religious' and the ways they can be used. However, to account for the variety of ways in which religion enters the public sphere in post-secular society, we think it best to use the term 'religious.' The fact that the majority of contributions collected in this volume focuses on the jewish and christian traditions, reflects their strong influence on the European and Northern American context. We do hope, however, that our reflections on religion, media and society can be relevant for other contexts, too.

choose from. In the 21st century, media and religion have become highly mutually dependent – if there ever was a time in which they were autonomous at all.

The time has thus come for a metadiscourse on the theoretical and methodological approaches in the field. According to Nick Couldry, "the media are there, their trace caught inevitably in our image of what is happening to the social world, but the figure is blurred. So questions of what exactly media do, and why they matter, go partly unanswered, even unformulated."[11] Indeed, media (in the broadest sense) and technology 'do' something to us, even as we 'do' something with them.[12]

Therefore, it is particularly important for any further research in media-and-religion studies to take into account the participation of viewers in the meaning-making processes in the reception of a film or any other form of media or media product. Studies in religion/theology and media have started to move from the enumeration and interpretation of symbols and motifs, of media content, to trying to understand not only what these symbols but the overall media experience as well means for the individual, what the individual does with it and – going beyond the individual – to situating this experience within a larger social context. We are enmeshed in a web of media that constantly interacts with its agents, culture, society, and religion – with all participants becoming transformed in the process. Thus, fresh perspectives are necessary to study this interdependence, to comprehend the complex relations between media, society and religion, and to understand the transformation of society and religion as a result of this mediatisation and technologisation and the changes caused by the omnipresence of the (transformed and reconfigured) religious in the public sphere.



Given the pervasiveness of the media in today's world, it is not surprising that most articles in this volume take as their material 'texts' (in the broadest sense) that are not explicitly religious or meant for religious contexts. Yet these texts need to be considered by religious studies and theology as the very space where 'religion' is transformed and interacted with, and where the interdependence between religion, media, and society becomes most visible. In order to understand this presence of the religious in the public sphere better, traditionally important concepts of theology (such as iconology or the transcendentals) need to be reconsidered in their meaning for this new context; others need to be further developed where their importance in theology and religion has been neglected in the course of history (e.g. the notion of 'experience', subjectivity or the body and embodiment). Further, research has to reflect the symbolic

11 Couldry, Nick, *Listening Beyond the Echoes. Media, Ethics, and Agency in an Uncertain World*, Boulder: Paradigm Publishers, 2006, 4.

12 Cf. Marsh, Clive, *Cinema and Sentiment. Film's Challenge to Theology*, Waynesboro: Paternoster Press, 2004.

authority of religious concepts and figures and why they are still used by the media and authors to add value, meaning, authenticity and credibility to their works.

Given the global nature of media and media phenomena, this book does not focus on a single local context but takes into consideration both western (US and European) and non-western societies. Only in situating the phenomenon of the post-secular in a context that is truly global not only in its methodologies and disciplines, but also and most importantly in its social and cultural awareness and considerations, can one do justice to the questions that need to be posed today.

The articles collected in this volume reflect both the variety of phenomena and the interdisciplinarity of approaches that is necessary in the study of religion and media today. In editing the book and putting together the articles, the notions of both 'media' and 'religion' have been understood as broadly as possible, in order to be able to account for the interdependent tendencies and developments in society.

This broadness is reflected in both the structure of the book and the naming of the specific chapters. We have chosen to include the "./" symbol, a Linux command which simply means 'the current directory', as a prefix to our sections in order to emphasise the importance of contextual and local thinking and to point out the fact that such an approach, in our media society, exists only in a tension found within global perspectives, that is, the tension between global and local 'thinking' that characterises today's thinking by necessity.



The first section of this volume, `./blurrings`, brings together articles that analyse how traditional boundaries between media and religion, art and religion, religious and political authorities, gender roles and reality and fiction have become blurred. Binary distinctions have been thought to be useful for making the world and its multitude of impressions navigable to human beings, even though postmodern reflections have shown that they distort experience more than that they enhance it. Similarly, what has been thought to be a strict division between the sphere of media and religion has been realised, instead, as being rather blurred. But only when the deceptive impression of clear distinctions is allowed to be blurred somewhat are new perspectives allowed to emerge. Discourses about the media have been informed by aesthetics to a major degree, and media themselves are aesthetic objects (an iPod is bought not only for its technology, but also for its design and associated lifestyle). On the other hand, contemporary arts use media in innovative ways and at the same time introduce a meta-reflection on the use and abilities of media. Therefore, this first section opens with two articles that think about the fundamental relationship of aesthetics and theology. In his article titled "Foundational Theology, Art, and Aesthetics:

Methodological Interrelations," **Gerhard Larcher** reflects on the relationship between the arts and theology. He establishes a critical function of the arts for theology: they question assumptions about human existence in a way that might sometimes be shocking, but in this, changes being and motivates reflection. In a similar vein, **Leo Karrer** re-discovers the notion of 'experience' for theological reflections in his contribution titled "Experience as an Interpretative Framework for Art: Reflections on the Art of Theology (and its Failures)," and shows that the experience of art might be seen as an intensified way of encountering reality and, at the same time, of reflecting on and processing it. Thus art opens up a space for the experience of God's revelation, too.

**Robert M. Geraci** studies a different kind of blurring in his article "Cultural Prestige: Popular Science Robotics as Religion-Science Hybrid": that of the roles of religious and scientific authority. Looking at examples of popular robotics and artificial intelligence books, he shows how religious motifs and thus religious authority are used to promote the researcher's interests and stabilise their position in the public. Religious authority is also a theme in **Sofia Sjö's** contribution on "Are Female Messiahs Changing the Myth? Women, Religion and Power in Popular Culture and Society." Studying the use of messiah characters in popular TV series and films, she asks whether gender roles are truly becoming blurred with regard to the functions that men and women can take over in saving the world and how they go about doing that. Although she discovers aspects which have become 'unisex', others – and most prominently religious authority – have remained gender specific.



The blurring of boundaries between 'real' reality and 'virtual' reality is an important issue in media discourses. **Wolfgang J. Schöffmann** shows in his article, "Jesus, Luhmann, Marilyn: Iconoclasm Meets Media Society," that this distinction is one of the major arguments in both the classical iconoclastic debate of the 8th and 9th century, and in debates over the use and danger of media today. He points out that looking at classical patterns of argumentation can inform today's thinking about the relationship of media representations to reality and how to interact with them.

The title of the next section, `./make world`, refers to a basic command in the FreeBSD operating system to rebuild and upgrade a system.[13] It also associates the power of media and religion to create new realities, or at least, to change one's perspective on reality so that one sees it with new eyes. In "Religious Remediations: Pentecostal Views in Ghanaian Video-Movies," **Birgit Meyer** shows on the basis of a detailed ethnographic study of Ghanaian film productions that, far from standing apart from the realm of religious beliefs,

13 Cf. http://www.freebsd.org/doc/en_US.ISO8859-1/books/handbook/makeworld.html, accessed March 9, 2007.

video-films call upon audiovisual technologies as a way to remediate Pentecostal views of the invisible world around which Pentecostal-Charismatic Christianity evolves. Video-films invoke a 'techno-religious realism' that addresses spectators in such a way that they authorize video representations as authentic. Broadening the horizon and looking beyond the 'borders' of the west, she emphasizes that religion and media are global phenomena and can be dealt with adequately only if they are approached as such. Taking a similar empirical approach, **Charlotte Haines Lyon** and **Clive Marsh** survey what audiences do with films in their article "Film's Role in Contemporary Meaning-Making: A Theological Challenge to Cultural Studies." They show that the interaction between film and viewer might occur on an unconscious level, but nevertheless, the encounter between the two re-makes the viewer's world to a degree.

In **Michael Hölzl's** article "One God – One King: Political Theology in Sergej Eisenstein's ALEXANDER NEWSKI," the theme of religious authority is taken up again, this time from the perspective of political theology. Hölzl uses Eisenstein's film as his reference text to show how, in spite of the blatantly anti-religious stance of Stalinist Russia, religious imagery is used to establish a world of good and bad, friend and foe, and to reconfigure the political leader as a national saviour.

In "Japan. Manga! Religion? The New Myths of the Japanese Ninth Art," **Sebastian Schlöglmann** looks at the world established in manga and anime, a genre that steadily has gained in popularity in the west. He shows that they construct a very peculiar world made up of a variety of traditional and original motifs, inspired by both eastern and western traditions which works exactly through its familiarising and alienating effects. Schlöglmann, too, emphasises the importance of understanding media and religion as global phenomena with relevance beyond their original context of production. On the other hand, in "The Pleasure of Seduction: The Role of Christian Symbols in Advertising," **Raphael D. Wiener** and **Markus R. Löhnert** use advertisements from Austrian public broadcasting in order to understand how the use of religious imagery in advertisement not only invests products with an 'extra value', but also changes the world of religion, because important religious concepts, such as salvation or sin, are understood in a new way.



The section titled `./immersion` focuses on the interaction between viewers and media, yet from a different perspective than represented by previous contributions. The articles in this section point out that the viewer is immersed in a matrix of omnipresent media with a strong emotional impact. **Graham Ward** opens this section with "All You Need is Love: MOULIN ROUGE or Christian's Tragedy," a close reading of Luhrman's film MOULIN ROUGE, in which he shows how the viewer is immersed deeply in the world of the spectacular and the spectacle, both of the film and within the film. In this immersion, she or he is made to reflect – even more so to experience – issues fundamentally relevant to human existence, such as authenticity, love, beauty, truth. **Gerard Loughlin's** analysis of the process of film viewing as a religious experience, illustrated by an analysis of Tarkovsky's film MIRROR in "*Video Divina:* Viewing Tarkovsky," similarly shows how cinema becomes meaningful when it touches onto the viewer's inner life, when the viewer becomes immersed in the film. Yet in order not to 'drown' in the film images and their ideologies, the viewer needs to look for the 'other' in what is shown: this is the art of seeing the invisible in the visible, as it is taught in Tarkovsky's films.

Knauss and Ornella both consider the effects that the immersion in the media world has for the individual, yet each focuses on different dimensions of human existence: embodiment and subjectivity. In her article, "The Sensuality of Sense: Reflections on the Bodily Dimension of Filmic and Religious Experience," **Stefanie Knauss** argues that the viewer becomes a part of the world of the film through his or her bodily, physical reactions to it. Watching a film, she or he experiences a moment of transcendence, which, however, is always bound to the physical here and now of the body. Knauss illustrates her theory with a body-orientated analysis of Bigelow's film STRANGE DAYS. In "Networked – Subjectivity Revisited," **Alexander D. Ornella** considers how our subjective selves and sense of subjectivity is affected by our being 'networked' by the media and communication technologies. In arguing that this aspect of being networked and connected characterises today's life, Ornella emphasises the relational, intersubjective and dynamic aspect of subjectivity, thus contributing to a renewal of theological discourses on subjectivity.



**Florian Kröppel's** article "Different Rites of Initiations – Different Heroes" takes the aspect of immersion quite literally: starting with a scene of HIGHLANDER, in which the hero is 'baptised' into his saviour role by falling into a lake, Kröppel argues that rites of initiations are an important motif used by filmmakers both to involve the audience in the film and make it meaningful for them, and to make a statement about the content of their films. This approach shows how heavily filmmakers in the west still depend on an at least implicit understanding of religious concepts and rituals.

The final section, `./plug-ins`, presents a tool for video analysis and automated object recognition and its use for media-and-religion studies. **Herwig Rehatschek**, **Werner Bailer**, **Helmut Neuschmied**, **Sandra Ober** and **Horst Bischof** describe in their paper "A Tool Supporting Annotation and Analysis of Videos" the technical aspects of a semantic video annotation tool (SVAT) which enables film analysts to annotate efficiently video footage. The most innovative automatic module included as a plug-in into SVAT is an object recognition and search tool. In his paper “Theological Film Interpretation: Some Approaches to a Better Understanding of ‘Moving Images’,” **Christian Wessely** reflects on the use and limitations of such a tool for sequence analysis and object recognition in the process of film interpretation, especially from a theological perspective. He argues that they are the basic material of any interpretation, yet can only prepare, not replace the interpretative encounter of viewer and film. Nevertheless, the sequence analysis that is made available and simplified by SVAT makes the interpretation traceable to other viewers and protects the media product from being used for the interpreter’s own purposes (missionary or otherwise).

This volume has developed out of the research project “Theology in a Media Society” conducted by the Institute of Fundamental Theology at Graz University, Graz University of Technology and Joanneum Research Graz, funded by the Austrian Science Fund (FWF) in 2003–2007. All participants in the project were given the opportunity to present the results of their research in this volume. However, in order to show the breadth of research in this field at the moment, we invited other scholars from various disciplines, and we are grateful to all of them who have responded with interest to the questions we posed and agreed to contribute and enter into the discussion of the role of theology and religion in a media society.

We would like to thank the FWF for funding the research which made possible the preparation of this volume, and the College of Catholic Theology at Graz University (Katholisch-Theologische Fakultät der Universität Graz), the federal state of Styria and the Austrian Department of Science and Research for their financial support of the publication. We are grateful to Equinox Publishing for permission to reprint Birgit Meyer’s article “Religious Remediations: Pentecostal Views in Ghanaian Video-Movies.” Furthermore, we thank Barbara A. Emmel for her help with translating and editing and her detailed comments, and Christian Wessely for preparing the photo-ready copy of the text.

# ./blurrings

Gerhard Larcher

# Foundational Theology, Art, and Aesthetics

## Methodological Interrelations[1]

Thinking about the role and status of the experience of art and of aesthetic reflections within the framework of foundational theology, we exceed merely practical theological or liturgical considerations; it is also more than a dogmatic theological aesthetics 'from above', which talks, for example, about God's beauty or YHWH's garment of light (Ps 104:2); in our perspective on the relationship between art and theology, foundational theology is understood as a gateway or boundary discipline, as a crossover discipline whose task is the translation and mediation of internal and external perspectives.

For such a foundational theological reflection of its relation to art and aesthetic experience, I see three main topics that need to be considered:



## 1. The relevance of the experience of art and aesthetic reflections as diagnostic tools for our current situation: On locating foundational theological discourses in realised modernity

First of all, foundational theology has to ascertain its position in modernity as the context in which it finds its topics today, and to begin to develop a theory of modernity. In modernity, aesthetic discourses and the arts have played a major role, in particular from the 19th century on and up to our own time, including relationships to religion and (to a lesser degree) churches. This aesthetic 'hype' or boom has, however, (paradoxically) to be seen in the context of general processes of the deconstruction of religion, metaphysics and political ideology (although a fundamentalist revival of religion with its own appellative aesthetic can also be observed).

In view of these historical and contemporary aesthetic tendencies, one has to ask: are these phenomena a sign for a compensatory, (post)modern aestheticisation of the existential search for meaning, its relativisation or elimination, or are they rather an indicator of an authentic spiritual renewal? And taken as a diagnosis of our times, what does this mean for the methodological basis of

1 Translated by Stefanie Knauss and Barbara A. Emmel.

foundational theological discourses in contemporary cultures and globalized civilisations?

Heuristically, we presuppose the Romantic assumption (cf. *Ältestes Systemprogramm des Deutschen Idealismus*, Schleiermacher, Schlegel, Schelling) that art is potentially the language of religion and as such, has a corrective function with regard to the abstract rationality of Enlightenment. I also draw on Nietzsche's hypothesis that in modernity, metaphysics and religion are replaced by the *aesthetic* experience of reality: "only as an artistic phenomenon is existence still bearable for us;"[2] and further that "we have art so that we do not despair of truth."[3] Out of a prolonged process of deconstruction, we have seen the development of the so-called death of God,[4] which coincides with the curious end of an iconographic representation of the image of God[5] (cf. Hegel: "we bow our knee no longer"), an extremely high esteem of art and an aesthetic undercurrent in modern civilisation, reinforced by media. This leads, on the one hand, to concepts of *Kunstreligion* (art as religion), developed for example by Schopenhauer, Wagner and still noticeable in contemporary festival culture, and on the other hand, to a latent mistrust of art among the churches.

I think that rather than the 'either-or' of the end of religion or its complete overlap with art, a mediating position is more helpful (and more likely): religion has not been extinguished, but rather it has moved. In art of high quality, transformations of traditionally important metaphysical and religious questions can be discovered in new images (e.g. in landscapes by Friedrich, Runge, van Gogh, or in realistic human shapes, portraits or everyday scenes by Munch, Rouault, Ensor, Corinth, Nolde, Jawlenski, Picasso) or can be found as precipitates in today's general aesthetic undercurrents (e.g. images of Christ by Bacon, Wallinger, Viola, Reihms, Kattelan); only by establishing a coalition with authentic art can a religious discourse defend its questions in public against an aestheticising but simultaneous banal media civilisation and can rediscover these questions in society. Thus contemporary art can be a 'theological topos' because of its critical qualities.

In this contemporary art (since Duchamp, Warhol, Beuys), a certain process of self-correction of the project of modernity in science, technology and ideology, that is ideologically self-interpreting as immanent, becomes obvious. These



2 "[…] nur als ästhetisches Phänomen ist uns das Dasein immer noch erträglich" (*Fröhliche Wissenschaft* 107,3. 464, translation S.K. and B.A.E.).

3 "[…] wir haben die Kunst, damit wir an der Wahrheit nicht zugrunde gehen" (*Nachgelassene Fragmente* VIII, 3, 16, 296, translation S.K. and B.A.E.).

4 Cf. the famous § 125 in Nietzsche's *Fröhliche Wissenschaft*.

5 This corresponds to W. Schöne's hypothesis developed in: W. Schöne, Die Bildgeschichte der christlichen Gottesgestalten in der abendländischen Kunst, in: W. Schöne / J. Kollwitz / H. v. Campenhausen (eds.), *Das Gottesbild im Abendland*, Witten/Berlin 1959, 7–55.

self-corrective processes in art are particularly obvious with regard to the issue of images. Possibly ours is a time of a new iconoclasm (to the second power) which might provide the opportunity of a re-importing and re-configuration of elements of Christianity scattered throughout our culture. After having established a strong cultural distance to Christianity, this development means new freedom. Ours is also a time when the traditional separation of art and church is possibly becoming weaker. Today, in a total media civilisation, in which art and religion depend on each other for the rescue of authenticity and reality, the church's and theology's traditional mistrust of that extremely high esteem of art (in which *verum* and *bonum* were often overshadowed by *pulchrum*) should no longer weigh so heavy. In our post-ideological present, art and culture become, therefore, new spaces for a regeneration of meaning, for which theology and the church should be open beyond their own socio-moral paradigma.

## 2. The search for meaning and the experience of art in relation to revelation and faith: Some aspects of a renewed *(de)monstratio religiosa*



After the introductory 'time-diagnostic' question of the role that art and aesthetics play for foundational theology, I propose some thoughts on the other main task at hand, namely to lead, from the perspective of a theory of subjectivity, to the experience of revelation and the option of faith via the experience of art and aesthetic reflection (this equals the traditional *analysis fidei* problem). However, I want to do this not in any argumentative and coercive sense of neo-scholastic *demonstrationes* (i.e. proofs of God's existence and plausibility arguments), but rather in the sense of a *monstratio* (a presentation of internal and external conclusions drawn from convenience). These methodological considerations are indispensable in a time when subjectivity is not a popular topic in foundational theology.

The question, then, of how far art is methodologically important for this first step in foundational theology, is to be posed as the question of the constitution of the 'hearer of the word', of his/her openness to revelation and faith. Here, the main focus is the analysis of the structure of a finite, bodily, sensual, aesthetically open subjectivity being touched by the totally Other (a revelation figure) in the tradition of Kant (from Schleiermacher to Schelling and Kierkegaard) in the 19th century, and by Henrich, Schaeffler and Ricœur in our time. This includes the relationship between aesthetic, ethical and religious experiences, in the traditional sense of the interaction of the three transcendentals (the good, the true, the beautiful) and of the systematic interaction of the three Kantian critiques of reason in a philosophy of hope ("What may we hope?"). In general, the aesthetic experience touches the subject in its history of consciousness at the intersection of theoretical and practical reason in the mind's power of judgement (implying imagination) and articulates itself symbolically towards hope.

In my opinion, an aesthetic experience can play a twofold role in the process of the experience of subjectivity: on the one hand, it can be carried out on an elementary, non-normative level in dynamic attempts at self-realisation, that is the dynamic process of realizing one's potential and being, under the conditions of ontological difference and absolute meaning, i.e. on the level of a *désir de l'être*, which forever strives for the satisfaction of desire (cf. Kierkegaard's analysis of Don Giovanni, or the general postmodern tendency towards aestheticisation) while avoiding having to make an existential ethical decision. On the other hand, aesthetic experience plays a role on the symbolic level of the aporetisation of the ethical consciousness and its openness for the explicitly religious; the ethical consciousness which despairs of itself, is overcome and taken beyond itself by the self-evidence of the aesthetical and religious (for example in the sublime or the beautiful shape of the witness) in shape of a *Lebenskunst* (art of life) itself.

I will illustrate this interaction of aesthetic experience and a philosophy of consciousness (with its search for meaning) in Dieter Henrich's *Versuch über Kunst und Leben (An Essay on Art and Life)*.[6] As with Henrich, I assume that "subjectivity [is open to] the experience of art in the dynamics of life"[7] and that "the practice of art [is] related to the dynamic of life in a certain way."[8] Works of art, therefore, can internally and externally reflect subjectivity as an open, vulnerable and finite process. They can irritate our sense of subjectivity, can turn it around cathartically. Works of art can thus result in an infinite and unbridgeable sense of otherness, a consciousness of change that points towards an eschatology of subjectivity. I agree with Henrich when he states that there is a "potential of art" as a symbolic indicator for transcendence to "orientate life" and "to move, and, by means of shock effects, to liberate," which "cannot be understood" from the motivations of the everyday conditions of the world alone.[9] Here, art and life as subjectivity coincide in so far as subjectivity is understood as a process which "begins with a knowledge of oneself"[10] which "comes from a cause beyond oneself."[11] The dynamic of subjectivity can



6 D. Henrich, *Versuch über Kunst und Leben. Subjektivität – Weltverstehen – Kunst*, München/Wien 2001.

7 "die Subjektivität in ihrer Lebensbewegung der Erfahrung von Kunst" (Henrich, 170, this and all further quotes from this work are translated by S.K. and B.A.E.)

8 "die Kunstpraxis zur Dynamik der Lebensbewegung in ein bestimmtes Verhältnis" (Henrich, 162).

9 Henrich, 144.

10 Henrich, 146.

11 Henrich, 149.

open up to a degree of certainty "that one's own life is based in a dimension of absolute meaning and that, in all its processes, it is protected and supported by it [a dimension of absolute meaning]."[12] This is "what mysticism [calls] 'illumination' *[Erleuchtung]*."[13] This experience could be called "the experience of a 'redeeming consonance'"[14] in "remembrance of the cause of all which itself remains unrealized in the moment of the present."[15] It marks the status of the symbolic indication of meaning in works of art by way of a specific sensuality of reason, or reason of sensuality.

"If works of art are to make conscious the dynamics of life, their descriptions cannot be distanced ones."[16] Art finds a resonance in life "which is not fulfilled through mere observation."[17] There has to be "a perceiving process of imitation growing out of the dynamics of life itself"[18] in a symbolic correspondence of the dynamics of subjectivity and art. Art as a symbolic indicator of boundaries or limitations would have to take up the dynamic of subjectivity in order to bring about any critical changes. Time-bound forms of art (music, literature, theatre, dance, film), which have their own, internal, unfolding dynamics, are particularly suited in accomplishing this. In this context, the challenging and transformative structure of a work of art as a metaphorical process (its cathartic function) is important. The work of art does not enter into the process at any particular moment or in any static way, in a certain dimension of subjectivity, but rather takes up dynamically in its symbolism the whole dramatic and liberating process of subjectivity and recapitulates it as auto-implicative metaphorical processes in literature, theatre, opera, music, film.



This does not result in meaningless pleasure, but in an essential participation, as a form of an 'art of life' between theoretical certainty and ethical overload. The artist testifies for the 'cause', for the 'charm of grace'; s/he embodies more than an extrinsic reference in the sense of traditional plausibility argumentations; the cause itself appears in him or her. In some cases, this aesthetic experience can even be an anonymous form of religious experience.

Thus today works of art can be something akin to a critical sign of hope, standing in for the absolute Other, an anonymous sign of the spirit in an apparently completely secularised time (cf. section 1). Works of art are essential indicators for the question of the meaning of a finite existence faced with love

12 "[...] daß das eigene Leben in einer Dimension letzter Bedeutung verankert ist und daß es in seinem ganzen Gang von ihr her gedeckt und getragen wird " (Henrich, 151).

13 Henrich, 151.

14 Henrich, 151.

15 "Erinnerung an den nicht in Präsenz zu bringenden Grund" (Henrich, 153).

16 Henrich, 165f.

17 Henrich, 145.

18 Henrich, 165f.

or death or can contain an experience of an absolute ethical obligation (cf. Rilke, Dostojevski, Lévinas) and for the absolute commemoration of a (hi)story of suffering (cf. W. Benjamin). Works of art represent that which can be experienced by the artist and the recipient as potential hearers of the word: that their postulations of hope could be realised and fulfilled. Religion and all genres of art are not only phenomena of the superstructure but rather essentials of that superstructure , if life is to succeed in all its other aspects, too.

Such authentic aesthetic experience always contains elements of surprise and revelation, not least because its object, the work of art, is formally challenging and difficult. The apparition of meaning and salvation is always free and cannot be forced. Perhaps that is why "revelation as challenge, revelation as an indicator of otherness [is] in a surprising and new way a topic of art in the 20th century."[19] Both can provide important input leading to the pathway for a faithful acceptance of revelation. Art as an analogy of revelation can provide a first means of access to freedom as an experience of that which is always greater, incomprehensible and at times secretive. In contrast to the seeming plausibilities of immanence, this freedom appears bottomless, even abysmal in its implications of a different and at times inaccessible reality. At the same time, works of art present this secret as one of a hoped for and desired proximity by means of its irreplaceable materiality and its formal representation. Presence and incarnation of sense are the specific revelatory qualities of art, even if always in a fragmentary state. According to H. U. von Balthasar, "the shape we encounter is in itself convincing, because the light with which it illuminates [us], emanates from itself and proves itself to be one that is evidently emanating from the cause itself."[20]



The encounter with art and experience of autonomous art is not another form of traditional natural theology which appears able to explain everything about the mystery of God, but neither is it a merely external *praeambulum* whose surface is expected to sustain the essential. It functions simultaneously both as code and decipherment of a self-revealing holy mystery (much like a mirror unlocks backwards writing), perhaps even the anonymous form of a self-revelation of that theological mystery by virtue of its universal spirit, which reveals itself in an explicit manifestation in the glory of the passing, descending God.

Faith with its responsive character (as poetic consent) leading into a receptive history of life, is a *Lebenskunst* (art of life). Because the *Lebenskunst* is about the self of the subject, originating from an inaccessible cause (cf. Henrich), this life

19 E. Nordhofen, Eine andere Geschichte der Kunst, in: Schmidinger, H. (ed.), *Zeichen der Zeit: Erkennen und Handeln*, Innsbruck/Wien 1998, 310–362, 362 (translation S.K. and B.A.E.).

20 "Die begegnende Gestalt ist an sich selbst überzeugend, weil das Licht, wodurch sie einleuchtet, von ihr selbst ausstrahlt und sich evidentermassen als ein solches, von der Sache her leuchtendes erweist." (H.U. von Balthasar, *Herrlichkeit. Eine theologische Ästhetik*, Bd. I, Schau der Gestalt. Einsiedeln ³1988, 446, translation S.K. and B.A.E.).

is situated in between a theoretical certainty and an ethical overload and lived inside as it were the liberated freedom of grace.[21] Art can make this form of existence perceivable and liveable beyond a fictional 'as if'. Together with the consent of faith, art can help to mediate an ontological plus of reality, because it opens subjectivity for a decision in favour of an always greater meaning of reality.

Another component of that quality of aesthetic experience which mediates faith, is the fundamental disposition for an immediacy of feeling and intuition for what has been experienced directly. Works of art can mediate a certainty of the presence of meaning which illuminates the specificity of the certainty of faith, in particular in its character as an undeserved gift. In the mode of this art of life, faith becomes a habitus of practice, a form of life because of the interaction with the symbolically expressive qualities of art in liturgy, the architecture of churches or personal devotional images. Just as for Ignatius of Loyola, an emotional experiencing of the mystery of faith is important, for Pascal, the mind is turned towards faith through religious practice as symbolic, and a formation of faith in and through the interaction with art is existentially possible.

## 3. The tradition of revelation between history and art: Its meaning for a foundational-theological hermeneutics of tradition



Christian religion is based on the presence of the sovereign revelation of God in the flesh. The symbolic self-expression of revelation and the reaction of the consenting faith both involve art. In its specific sensuality, art can emphasise this presence while at the same time indicating its otherness, and can express the transgressivity of the testimony to revelation. In this third main question, foundational theology has to face this issue of the possibility of revelation and its being witnessed and transmitted.

A hermeneutics of Christian tradition can never be restricted to the meaning of a hermeneutics of texts or a pragmatics of ethical guidelines; hermeneutics cannot work text- or literature-critically, but instead has to analyse the unforeseeable reflexes of God's work in images in the multi-temporal art space of the church, in which the aesthetic testimonies of multiple generations, past and present, come together in their importance for a consciousness of faith; for these have influenced the consciousness of faith in the church beyond a strictly text-based consciousness of faith for centuries. It is somewhat paradoxical that a religion based on the revelation of the *word* of God, codified in a collection

[21] Cf. G. Larcher, Zeitgenössische Kunst als Anstoß und Vertiefung des Glaubens, in: A. van Hooff/P. Reifenberg/W. Seidel (ed.), *Glaubenserfahrungen im Denken und Handeln. Fundamentaltheologische Skizzen*. Würzburg 1998, 211 and elsewhere.

of books, has been transmitted throughout history mostly through images and art (at least, where Orthodoxy and Catholicism are concerned). The symbolic self-expression of revelation in the flesh of its witnesses and the poetry of language, and the reflex of a totally consenting faith, both need art. This is about experiencing and thinking about the word of God in and through images. The prohibition of images (Ex 20:4; Dtn 4:9ff.), which is still influential, is thus not a prohibition of art, but of idolatry: it criticises obsolete syntheses of art and religion and motivates the invention of new aesthetic expressions.

With respect to a theological tradition, art and ethos are quite comparable; in art, the reflection on faith is provided with both an indicator and sensorium for what is important, and a means of expression of nearly the same origin as itself with the help of which it can express itself in sensual reflections and schemata. It is not as if faith does not have something of its own to say, but rather what it does have to say is essentially realised in ethos and art, and can in some cases be expressed anonymously and made present through those. That is why the critical moments in the tradition of faith's answer to revelation are ethically tinted and aesthetically illuminated in and of themselves. And that is also why the word of scripture and preaching could lead – in spite of all the consequences of iconoclasm – to the concept of the icon and subsequently to a great wealth of figurative traditions. A broad tradition made up of cultic, proclamatory and devotional images, in which the sensual imagination of the mysteries of faith interact with the sacramental act and the proclamation of the word, testifies to this. Another part of this process of tradition is, of course, architecture (e.g. the cathedral), music, etc.: space as constructed theology.



This means, with relation to the specific hermeneutical dialogue, that with increasing distance from tradition, the chances increase for the renewing of some of its topics in modernity: these topics are picked up anew, transformed in relation to their history of reception: in contemporary art these are for example the *topoi* of mysticism, body, time, memory, etc., which are made a topic so frequently in contemporary art that the well-known French art critic Catherine Grenier has been induced to ask: "L'art contemporain, est-il chrétien?" ("Is contemporary art Christian?") This might be slightly exaggerated, but it should provoke the new configurations of meaning arising from the experimental creative encounters between modernity and the multiplicity and variety of traditions.

For example, liturgical service – in itself a *Gesamtkunstwerk* involving the aspects of 'body', 'time' and 'memory' – is the most concrete space of experience and dialogue in the church in which nearly all artistic genres are included; in its various performances, art theologically becomes a language and faith a presence which can be experienced aesthetically. Liturgy, in return, is related to a diaconal art of life.

Such a sensual tradition of faith principally includes the astounding variety of autonomous modern and contemporary art in the multi-temporal art space of the church, in particular in the European and American worlds, but at times also within the global context as well. In the contemporary situation, when the blurring of borders between artistic genres, their integration into life and the dissolution of the notion of a 'work of art' causes a new inner reflectivity of social reality, art becomes a resonant body of hope, an indispensable sign of the times, with the help of which "the joys and the hopes, the griefs and the anxieties of the men of this age" (*Gaudium et Spes* 1) can be integrated into the proclamation of the Gospel and theology.

Leo Karrer

# Experience as an Interpretative Framework for Art

## Reflections on the Art of Theology (and its Failures)[1]

For many people today, theology is a strangely 'unreal' discipline and far removed from real life: it is occupied with the transcendent, the immaterial, that which is beyond the boundaries of the world and concrete reality. This is in no small measure due to the approach theology has taken for many years in its reflection on these themes in what is often an abstract, non-contextualised way. Yet, in its essence, theology is concerned with nothing but the reality of human life, and how it relates to the reality of God as it is represented in the biblical message. In thinking about the relationship between theology and reality, the notion of 'experience' and how humans experience reality cannot be ignored, even if these subjects represent a very difficult and often misunderstood concept. It is through the creative process of experiencing (which is more than the passive consumption of facts and events) that one comes to understand reality, that is one's own relation to the world, to oneself, to other human beings.



Experience understood as the active encounter with reality is a dynamic process that emerges from the dialectical relationship between the two poles of the 'input of reality' and the 'processing of reality'. This dynamic relationship, which is often full of tension, is expressed in a unique way in art which therefore becomes itself a way of intensely encountering, experiencing, and understanding reality. Thus if theology takes seriously its experiential dimension, it must (re-)consider its relationship to the arts as a moment of, so to say, materialised experience which offers itself as the object of new experiences. In fact, I propose that theology itself – if understood from an experiential point of view – *is* art in that it is a reflection of reality and thus its authenticity depends on a communicative and dialogal encounter with reality as it is experienced. Theology – like art – provides a framework for the processing of reality into experience. Theology understood as art can then explore new ways of giving oneself up to the mystery of reality whenever rationality or materiality fail to make sense of the encounter with reality in all its dimensions.

1 Translation by Stefanie Knauss and Barbara A. Emmel

In order to develop this thesis, I will at first define more closely what experience means and how it emerges out of the interaction between the input of reality and the processing of reality. I will then take a look at possible obstacles at both poles which threaten the emergence of experience and pay particular attention to how these obstacles often are reinforced by religion or theology. Having discussed the relationship between art and theology in general, I will then elaborate in detail in which ways I see theology itself as an art, and how this contributes to thinking of experience as a central category of theology.

## 1. In Experience, Life Becomes Aware of Itself

In philosophy, following Hans-Georg Gadamer,[2] the term 'experience' is often taken to be "unenlightened." In order to be able to use the term 'experience' in theology, an understanding first needs to be developed which is appropriate to both the hermeneutical method of theology as well as experience in an everyday context. The definition of the term is capacious and even somewhat blurred precisely because it is a key term in human existence, linking our multitudinous attitudes and relations to reality, ourselves, the environment, other human beings.



### 1.1 Experience: Encounter with Reality

Reality is that entity on which human consciousness acts, or metaphorically, the palate with which human consciousness creates. This interaction with reality results in what we call experience.

Experience can be generally defined as a conscious encounter with 'reality', an awareness of the act and actions of perception. In the journey through life, humans have the capacity to explore, become conscious of their identity as explorers and become acquainted with the environments – their life – they explore. Humans also have the capacity to develop an inner awareness and to develop meanings for an inner understanding of reality. Experience therefore is a precondition for a reflective or intuitive encounter with the process and actions of life, of living.

The capacious meaning of the term 'exprience' is reflected in its Greek equivalent *aisthesis*, which connotes a broad range of ideas: perception, feeling, understanding and consciousness, all pointing towards the inner link between the encounter with the world and a conscious knowledge or understanding of that world.

2 Cf. Gadamer, Hans-Georg: *Wahrheit und Methode. Grundzüge einer philosophischen Hermeneutik*, Tübingen [2]1965, 329.

Experience is, of course, more than the addition of objective realities, more than a mute consumption of events and facts which disappear afterwards without leaving a trace. It is a process in which reality opens itself to the self, and the self opens him- or herself to reality. Only through an attitude of conscious or intuitive openness to reality is a perceptive and true encounter with reality possible, otherwise, the result of this encounter could not be stored and valued in memory.

Experience is, therefore, a subjective process which becomes aware of itself as one 'digests' and faces reality in processes that range from rudimentarily conscious up to systematically reflected upon. It is both a way of living which provides knowledge, and a reflective behaviour towards reality. The experiencing subject becomes the resonant body for that which reveals itself. In this encounter with reality, the subject becomes aware of itself, but both within and as part of the context of the experienced world.

Critical for this understanding of experience are two inter-related aspects or poles: an encounter with reality, on the one hand, and a reflection on this encounter on the other. Reality has to be mediated by way of individual experiences, in order to open oneself to the wide field of further experiences. Otherwise, reality cannot reach its potential in the experiencing subject. And only by coming to the world like this is the subject open to and ready for new experiences.



This polarity in the process of experience can be described as reality input *(Wirklichkeitszufuhr)* at the one end and the processing of reality *(Wirklichkeitsverarbeitung)* at the other.[3] Experience is defined by the dialectic process of input (encounter) and processing (understanding). It is more than an unreflective consumption of facts, more than a fleeting sequence of events which impersonally and thoughtlessly consume and exploit the possibilities of life. It is the subjective attitude of a person towards reality which makes reality accessible; in it, the subject opens itself to reality, and reality to the subject.

Experience as an attitude towards reality takes all the power of the body, mind and soul of a person, his or her senses, instincts, sensations, rationality, language and ability to abstract, intuition and psychological strengths, character, competences and even disposition (i.e. whether optimistic or pessimistic). All of these factors help the experiencing subject to mediate reality dynamically, but they can, of course, also manipulate the subject in his or her interaction with reality and how reality input is processed. But even an incurable persistence in illusionment reveals a certain attitude towards reality, namely that of the denial of the experiencing subject.

3 The terminology is adopted from a paper presented by Gregor Siefer, Glaube – Wirklichkeit – Erfahrung, in: *Dokumentation des BT des ND-Männerrings vom 16.–21. April 1979 in Ottobeuren.*

Experience as the process of mediating reality is nevertheless not in itself a linear or purposeful process. It contains a disordered array of constructive and destructive aspects and forms, biographical, social, cultural, economic, political, historical and religious factors; it emerges from success and failure, in the will to live, and the fate to die, in a dependency on nature, tensions between the self and others. It includes passivity and activity, empiricism and artistic creativity, common sense and technical pragmatics. This is why experience defies all categorisation and systematisation.

The two poles, reality input and processing of reality, allude to an inter-relationship between practice and theory which are interdependent, yet do not dissolve into each other, similar to the two focal points of an ellipsis. When reduced to one of the poles, experience can become diminished and impaired or even powerless. The consequences for durable life are obvious: the degree to which one or the other of the poles is privileged (isolated at the expense of the other) or split off from the other, the weaker the dialectic process becomes that qualifies experience and ultimately defines life itself.[4]

## 1.2 Obstacles to the Processing of Reality



Obstacles that hinder the processing of reality make it impossible for the subject to work with the input of reality creatively. These can occur in the shape of traditions, norms, ideologies, prejudices, disappointments, normative roles, authorities, value systems and dependencies. Then, reality cannot be experienced fully and creatively, unfolded freely so to speak, because the subject is fixated on established or external patterns of experience or authorities and thus resists a broadening of his or her horizons. Prejudices, fixed principles and teachings, values, consumer mentality or academic schematicisms can critically influence one's attitude to reality and restrict the reflective process or hinder it completely. These various factors function much like lenses which can make the image of reality more blurred, or can colour or blot out aspects of reality entirely. The image of reality as seen through these lenses says in this case more about the lenses or the person behind them than about reality itself. Of course, it is impossible to dismiss these 'lenses' through which reality is perceived entirely, but they need to be reflected and exposed as such, as a process which in itself is again an experience that can be described as the processing of reality, as learning, understanding, remembering and transmission. This is what we mean by culture, art and education or civilisation. When this kind of learning is impossible, people become dull and narrowed, remain closed in and both inexperienced and un-experienced.

4 Food might serve as a metaphor for this: it needs to be consumed in order to be digested. Only through this process does it become nutritious and valuable for the living organism.

To expose oneself to new experiences is both revolutionising and critical because it requires distance from former perceptions and interpretations. This is the case because each new experience will change one's perspective on and interpretation of former individual experiences or the communal repository of experience (of a culture, civilisation, society). New experiences – if they are accepted, i.e. processed – necesssarily lead to a crisis of old experiences; these new experiences transcend through a 'negating' dialectic of previously acquired experiences. This is why memory plays such an important role in this process, as long as it does not solidify into a traditionalism that blocks the freedom and dynamic necessary for new experiences.

If an ongoing and dynamic processing of reality is avoided, rejected or otherwise blocked, the subject will suffer from a loss of the richness and potential of reality, and of experiencing that reality. The value of experience is that insight which the subject gains in his or her encounter with reality and without which that person could not fully understand him- or herself or the world.

Religious life and religiousity, too, are marked by these dimensions of experience. Spirituality and religion depend upon the reflective search for the meaning of God and his message. The will to understand is indispensable, even when one cannot fully grasp the depth of the mystical message or import a full understanding of it. Faith itself as a human activity is marked by a certain tension that makes it possible for faith to be either insightful or static (and sometimes both). That is, on the one hand, faith wants to be understood and integrated into the experiences of humans in all languages around the world, and become itself a means of fuller experience. On the other hand, the words that define faith can be and are often misunderstood and abused. Only when taking account of this tension within experience is it possible to speak with faith and about faith without being irrelevant or fundamentalist. Fundamentalist, doctrinal, ritual or authoritarian forms of religious life can lead to the rejection of a process of religious maturation, resulting in a religious experience that would be diminished or even suffocated.



## 1.3 Obstacles to Reality Input

Reality input itself can reduce or inhibit experience as a process, if the amount of input takes on such dimensions that a reflective or creative attitude to reality becomes impossible. In such instances, the world of facts and the powers that determine them overrun the subject so intensively that he or she loses his or her capacity for reflective distance to the self and the environment. This can be caused by drugs and addiction; trauma, violence, and loss; poverty or wealth; deep emotions such as guilt; emotional susceptability; intelligence etc., but also by the media, environmental issues or the laws of the marketplace and capital which cause dependencies not just of individuals but of whole nations. These extremes of input become then so dominant that it becomes impossible for the self to process reality in any truly reflective way. The powerlessness of the individual against the force and often violence of facts shows that new forms of communication and new structures of solidarity are required in order to be able to negotiate the encounter with reality and its problems, such as the interplay between the individual and global developments. In order for the input to be processed and become experience, reflection and 'digestion' are needed; these can unfortunately be impeded by obstacles such as those above.

Experience grows bottom up, out of details. Life as a process of experience does not start with ideas, abstract ideals or information, but with an ever-present reality with its (as yet) unstructured, chaotic facts and a large, confusing 'residue' of uncertainties which a person cannot process or master, no matter how much effort is expended. Experiential intensity and a disparate wealth of detail which characterise human life can be gained only through ever new and still always fragmentary experiences; otherwise, retained and older experiences distance the subject from the immanence of real life as it is lived in all its wealth. Thus, experience has to do with sensual creativity, an immediacy and closeness to life and a mediated understanding. Experience is always contextual and can be analysed discursively only to a limited degree. But when realities reach such dimensions and force that a productive approach to reality is impossible, loss of reality and alienation are the consequence.



These obstacles can also inhibit religious processes. In an environment destitute of religion, faith can no longer offer guidelines for sense-making processes and the structuring of life. The falling away of religious education as a school subject makes it impossible from the outset to decide in favour of or against religious content and contexts, simply because one does not hear about them. Because of this religious inarticulateness, the liberating impulse of a religious interpretation of life may never come about or be attended to, and a preoccupation with materialistic attitudes towards life can end up blocking religious experience that could be liberating. On the other hand, bigotry, Pharisaism or fundamentalism can also hinder maturation processes, as can an atheism which prematurely does away with the question of God.

## 1.4 Experience as Communal Interaction

Experience is not an individual subject's isolated encounter with reality. Experience is a dialectic process between the individual perceptive process and the sum of experiences made by all humans (cultural, technical, social, historical, religious knowledge and that general knowledge which is required for structuring one's life). This repository of experience is transmitted in language, symbols, images, verbal and non-verbal communication and rituals, and the individual experience of the subject can be fulfilled only in the interrelationship with this communal experience. In this process, the individual realises that communal experience functions as the interpretative framework for his or her reflection and integration of experience *as* his or her *own* experience. Without this cultural memory, nobody can gain access to reality, nor, by way of identification with others, an identity of his or her own. Cultural memory as the result of previous experiences becomes the framework within which events, persons, facts and relationships as well as values and agreements are interpreted. It is the horizon within which experiences of groups, or individuals are evaluated, corrected, interpreted, but also forgotten, neglected or lost. Individual experience becomes possible when the subject opens the self to this communal experience without losing him- or herself as an individual in it.

Experience becomes a bridge from the present to the remembered repository of past experiences, and thus is a precondition for finding a reflective distance in one's relationship to the past, and for being open to new possibilities in one's life. Experience is, therefore, conditional, as well as potentially unlimited and open to revision. Each experience contains a larger promise of reality than the experiencing subject can ever realise. The question of the relationship between theory and praxis is embedded in this interpretative framework, i.e. they both depend on experience.



Experience is the sum of all that which has occurred to humans, i.e. that which has been experienced, understood and invested in the development of personal and social culture over the ages. Experience qualifies overall history and the individual history of humans. It is understandable that the term goes in and out of fashion repeatedly in philosophical discourses, but, at the same time, can still be a most undefined and indefinable term.

For religious experience, this social dimension is also crucial. From a religious perspective, the individual is neither a discrete entity nor autonomous. One does not become aware of one's faith without listening and being attentive to that what others say and proclaim via religious rituals and communities, communication and structures of solidarity, and ultimately through the church as the community of all those who accompany each other in the communal processing of religious experiences. Every religious community is fundamentally a community of interpretation. And religious experiences, too, require others in an existential way. Experience, therefore, has a transcendental character in various ways.

## 2. The 'Instrument' of Reality Input and Processing

From what has been said so far it is clear that the sum of the experiences of an individual can never exhaust all of reality's possibilities, otherwise reality input and its processing would have to be identical, which is a purely eschatological speculation. Rather, experience is only a very small intersection of input and processing of reality with all its potential. Any individual person is able, of necessity, to experience only a part of the world and to a limited degree.

But then the question arises as to how and why any one person can find his or her way in this paradox of confusing abundance and inexhaustible possibilities (nonetheless limited by space and time), without losing the self in the process? The answer is that experience is neither total distance nor total fusion, but the achievement of a certain attitude towards reality in the midst of one's own life.

Or, to put it another way, the individual experiences him- or herself as fragmented, in a life-long process, or – to put it metaphorically – in being on the way to becoming him- or herself, including bypasses and wrong turns. But, and this is specifically true only for human beings, their rationality allows them to step back from themselves reflectively. In taking oneself as an object of reflection,  one gains access to oneself, one's life and realities. Nevertheless, the object is always at the same time the subject which 'consumes' and 'digests' reality input. The human is not static and motionless, but always dynamic and in flux in relation to him-/herself and other subjects.

The subject is not just the recipient of stimuli which could be reduced to a psycho-physiological dimension by the humanities. None other than Viktor Frankl himself warns against a psychological and sociological reduction of the subject. By contrast, the human is a being with self-awareness, someone with the ability to find and follow the way to freedom, someone who can think creatively and reflectively in relation to the world, and who can think about the sense of existence, behaviour and the relevance of decisions. Thus, the subject is not just a responding being, but also a responsible being. And even the complete refusal of responsibility would have to be interpreted as an attitude towards reality.

Experience relates to the intellectuality of humans. It is condition and process, which is that state of and ability to abstract from the spatially and temporarily given. This points towards a transcendental dimension because, although the subject can never escape the fragmentary confines of space and time, he or she can nonetheless find ways and strategies to transcend them within and even through their limitations. This is the reason for a human propensity for culture and ultimately the capacity for artistic creativity. This is not only a sign of human dignity, but also of the capacity for love, self-sacrifice and the ability to perceive those meanings which may lie within the dimensions of life and especially the meaning of the whole which can be gained through its multitude of details. Seeing the fragmented parts leads to a vision of the dimensions of depth and opens the way to gratefulness and astonishment. These are steps in the maturation of experience that occurs as the result of both input and processing.

But reality control has to admit that the ability to abstract is the cause not only for any good proceeding from the human intelligence, but also for any wickedness and the fall into the bottomless abyss of evil. Industrialised mass murder with its terrible and awful consequences for so many individuals has also to do with this. I do not know any comparable capacity for evil in the animal kingdom that humans are capable of. Human experience also includes a dark side, mourning, confusion, hatred and violence, misery (the abyss) and existential darkness, emptiness and disconsolation.

## 3. Approaching Art (and Its Failures)

These last lines above were meant to point out the ambivalence of human perception, interpretations and constructs of reality. All cultural activity, in particular art, grows out of this tension. Does the understanding of experience outlined above give access to the world of art and its understanding? Or is art simply the highest expression of human education? An epistemological phenomenon? Or – quite in the sense of Hegel – a discrete form of human orientation? Is it not only an epistemological, but also a pragmatic phenomenon? Presumably, the many differing understandings of art can be located between these two poles.[5]



Against the background of the understanding of experience as a bipolar process between reality input and processing outlined above, art can be understood as the most expressive and concise way of giving shape to that which wants to show itself and be formed creatively. The more densely, fully and fitting the expression and communication of experiences, the more their artistic meaning is revealed. Where art fails, it falls short of this revelation (such as an instrumentalised art market or artists' self-performance). Art is an intensified way of reality perception, interpretation and constitution, and therefore, concepts and approaches of art theory require permanent critical revision between the poles of input and processing,[6] and new perspectives to avoid these shortcomings.

Art could be understood as one way of relating to or interacting with reality, or as an expressive form of structuring one's life. Its qualities, too, flow from a double origin: the approach to both realities, that is, as reality shows itself

5 Cf. Rainer Volp, Kunst und Religion VII + VIII, in: *Theologische Realenzyklopädie* XX (1990) 292–329, and: Günter Wohlfahrt, ibd. IX, 329–337.

6 The author has attempted to address this issue in: Warum sich Theologie für den Film interessiert, in: *Pastoraltheologische Informationen* 1–2(1997), 321–328.

(input), and the truthfulness of expression and communication (processing). Presumably, art then has to find the balance between two extremes: as a *symbol* of the act of relating to reality (input and processing), or as the *diabol* of alienation from reality and the experiencing subject.[7]

Objections to the above lead to the quite obvious question: but what is 'art'? Nothing but literature, music, architecture …? What is science? Is not the scientifically exact method superior to art? And what about solidarity among humans and its legal systems? Is art superior to that? But taking the concept of experience as one's point of departure, art cannot be measured quantitatively as one among other cultural institutions or institutionalised forms of expression, even if that understanding is suggested by the art market. Outside of all quantifiable and distinct fields of experience, art is part of a qualitative dimension in that in art, experience approaches the true relations and finds communicative conciseness. If this is true, art has its place potentially everywhere, and thus a coherent theory or technical mastery can be high art, whereas expensive commissioned artworks may be nothing more than bluff or kitsch. Nevertheless, art is probably closer to the bright and dark aspects of life and more concise in its expressions than any scientific hypothesis looking for watertight answers. Whether art is successful or fails depends on its success or failure to enable (or not) reality input and its processing, thus promoting (or not) the relation to and communication about reality inter-subjectively.



## 4. Art and Faith/Theology[8]

With regard to Christian faith and theology, it can now be asked in which form and how they are present in the world of art, as well as how they relate to art and how art as an expression of the dynamics of experience can relate to theology. There are volumes to be read on this subject. All we can attempt to reflect on in this context is the question of whether faith and theology do not show *in and of themselves* an artistic dimension or inclination. They are not only forms of expression closest to art (or perhaps at times even in opposition to art), but rather *are* themselves art. Historically, the church is often merely associated with the commission of artworks, as if it had instrumentalised and used art. It is easily overlooked how poor art history would be without the church. What is at issue is not that parts of the church have taken possession of art, but how artists or art give shape to their experiences authentically.

7 Cf. what has already been said about the obstacles at the poles of input and processing of reality above.

8 Cf. W. Fürst (ed.), *Pastoralästhetik. Die Kunst der Wahrnehmung und Gestaltung in Glaube und Kirche*. QD 199, Freiburg 2002.

How can real art and failed art in the world of faith and correspondingly in theology be recognised? To put it simply: the quality of art shows itself in a continuous process of communication in how art leads towards experience (as we understand it) and the reality of life with all its revelations, and gives shape to it creatively. Religious experience, too, solidifies into historical objects if it does not lead to new experiences. Previous faith experiences fossilise and become irrelevant if they are preserved but not understood as processes leading into the future of new reality input and processing. Tradition, understood in the context of this sense of experience, would not be the normative look into the past, but a promise to engage actively, in hope and with openness, with new experiences and to accept experience as a process – and as an ever new venture.

In this context, it should be mentioned how in the celebration of the sacraments, e.g. the Eucharist, incredibly high forms of art can be brought together. Faith finds in the tension between the level of reality and symbolism an aesthetic expression which can hardly be surpassed. On the other hand, failures can be discovered in the same context: there are such careless forms of worship that it speaks to the psychological health and aesthetic sensibilities of those who do not (or no longer) attend.

The task of theology in the plurality of its disciplines is an academic reflection of life and reality in the light of the experiences with the God of Israel and Jesus. Theology is to be understood as art because it communicates these experiences in the context of a particular time. The trapdoors of failure open up where the twofold origins of theology are betrayed: reality with all its constructive and destructive aspects, and the experience of the God of Jesus who wants salvation for all. In this tension, theology as art is put to test. It has to understand itself as art in a dynamic and uncompromised way, with all its messiness, power, and the kind of in-your-face confrontation that can bring about positive change. Any discourses about art and the debates about how it is to be understood are invaluable not only because it opens the understanding of theology to the world of art and so-called modernity, but also because of the self-perception of theology itself.



It is understandable that the cessation of many traditions, with an accompanying complexity and insecurity of life, causes anxieties and so-called fundamentalist reactions in the subject in spite of all the advances in communication technology today. The consequences can easily be seen in subjects who are overly burdened and overly strained in many respects. In the face of high rates of unemployment, difficulties in the education and health sectors and, not least, in the pressure to choose from a multitude of options, the system leaves the solution of many problems to the individual who has already reached his or her limits. In the church as well, problems accumulate at its heart while policy makers shy away from dealing with the problems caused within and by the system. Pastoral workers in their parishes have to struggle to reconcile concrete life with the system. The elation and optimism of the late 1960s and early 1970s has evolved towards a mood of disillusionment and disappointment in a shift from visions to the pragmatics of problem solving or subjective survival strategies. We have to deal with the delay of the conciliatory *Naherwartung*.

It seems as if after the 'Enlightenment' of the Second Vatican Council and the following period of 'Romanticism' with its emphasis on the individual subject, we are now in a phase that can be associated with *Biedermeier*: restoration; retreat into the private sphere and in anonymous communication channels (internet etc.); a quick and selective mode of problem solving; little interest in overarching conceptual schemes; taking oneself as the central topic (partly in the role of the victim); and – in the church, too – the withdrawal to the cultivation of one's own small backyard, where things are still 'OK for me'. One creates subjective and often self-centered 'worlds' and spiritualities which are characterised by a kind of 'aestheticism' that can be defined as a styling of desire so that immediate satisfaction is achieved. One is satisfied by an intense but usually contained and limited feeling of well-being or happiness. Intellectual discourse is replaced by a demand for events, symbols and communities that provide satisfaction, as well as associative metaphors, icons and allegories ('Life is for me *like* ...'). One does not argue about fundamental and existential questions ('Truth') or stand up for necessary changes – perhaps as a form of solidarity. But one does expect them, nevertheless. Organisations or institutions are seen as functional instruments, but nonetheless still contain no power of identification or credibility for which one would campaign 'politically'. More important is functional competence (supervision, management, consulting, customer orientation etc.).



The relation of theology to the real world is relevant here. Does one retreat into the theological ivory tower without realising that the roof is on fire? A historisising theology seems simply to copy past models for the future. And a systematic theology occasionally gives the impression that it does not care about the results of biblical exegesis or the experiences of people in society. Occasionally, I come across christological views against which not even the historical Jesus seems to be granted the right to veto. Given the many christological, ecclesiological and eschatological questions and paradoxes, one reverts to a theological metaphorology, sublimates theological topics into symbols and icons and cements by this the traditional system and doctrine. As in the 19th century, banality threatens over and again.

This is not the whole picture, of course, but theology can and does become banal, bland, boring and irrelevant when it no longer desires or wishes to keep up a tension between realities and message, and when it instead simply pampers the already-known. Then it is in danger of becoming a functional theology for office bearers alone. But theology should go on its way in and with the church responsibly, i.e. to do its duty both towards reality and the Christian message. Theology cannot escape from that tension if it does not want to end up either retreating from reality, or fusing with it and thus losing itself in it.

## 5. Faith and Theology as Art: In the Midst of Reality Open for the Mystery

An authentic expression (which reaches into the utopian and fictional) is critical for art (which cannot be defined in a way that is free from misunderstandings) in its struggle for appropriate formal representations of experienced reality.

Art, and also the art of theology, are at root a defense of life and experience. They both are or should be made accessible to all people, and not remain the privilege of elitist artists' colonies looking down at the so-called trivial art. Art is democratic, i.e. open to creative professionals and artistic lay people equally. As soon as women and men, adults and children begin to express themselves creatively and thus communicate their experiences and lives in meaningful ways, they become artists and are creative as artists even if it might not be called high art in the market's world. A concept of the world and of humanity which serves life and a living out of the hope for life in abundance (cf. John 10:10), cannot act differently than to promote, invite and inspire all that supports the creative expression of experience. In art, the reality of human experience shows and expresses itself as fragmented. But if what is concerned in the distinctly Christian is the humane, then it should be possible to find art in all its varieties within the frameworks of the church and theology, in order to enable us to become closer to life, more sensitive and open to its experiential dimensions and in this sense become more sensually 'at home' in life. On the other hand, however, some people in the church and theology may try to protect themselves, consciously or unconsciously, against the directness with which art, situated between ecstasy and morbidity, poses hard questions of happiness, sense, success, freedom and authenticity, evil, limitation and death, God and the diabolical. Theology and faith, and therefore the church, betray their art if they block access to reality in all its creative and destructive aspects, thereby betraying their very own field.[9] Failure is a necessary consequence. If the church and theology can themselves discover their own meanings in those approaches to life that leave an open space for un-instrumentalised experience, and if they themselves can develop their own identities within these new forms of expression, then they will them-



9 Cf. L. Karrer, Hütet das Feuer. Die öffentliche Verantwortung der Theologie, in: *Bulletin ET* 15 (2/2004) 208–223, in particular 216ff.

selves become the source of a renewing of experience for others. Thus church and theology will find that faith, as Christian existential hope, is more than an institution, more than centralised security blankets, more than doctrinal and academic theology based on hierarchies of 'who quotes whom', a copying of what has been said before. They will become the space where experience as a relation to reality will be risked and will stand the test, namely, as life open to discovery and surprise; life as that which is shocked, ripped open and disturbed, inflamed, enthusiastic and avid. The aesthetic law of theology is, ultimately, *how* it comes into play in the tension between human and God.

If the church and with it theology offer space and inspiration to artistic vitality, they will become art themselves, or at least creative in their everyday work, even within the framework of an ordinariness of life. Maybe they will learn from art the art of a boldness in seeking and audacity in questioning in the face of reality with its hard facts. The church and theology will have to learn that the art of faith, and of theology, in spite of the resistance put up by reality, can open and keep open the door to hope, vision and a unity of feeling for the whole of life beyond and in spite of its confusing details and fragmentary nature. They will find that the art of a faithful life, with all its glorious and unhappy moments, offers flexibility and curiosity, the courage to start afresh, and a readiness to become involved with one's own existence; the ability to distinguish sense from nonsense; the strength of modesty as truthfulness; and in all that an amazement which provides both a sense of happiness and gratitutde, even if these states of being are momentary ones. The only way there is dedication in trust: love.



If reality input and processing thus reach their limits, does not the art of life also mean to give oneself up to the incomprehensible, into the mystery we call God? Does not the mystic of this art give us a glimpse of that?

Robert M. Geraci

# Cultural Prestige

## Popular Science Robotics as Religion-Science Hybrid

### 1. Prestige and Institutional Roles

This volume documents many ways in which theological language permeates modern media, an omnipresence of the sacred which applies even when scientists take part in media life. Even atheist and agnostic scientists have absorbed religious language from broader culture and use the terms and conditions of that language in popular science publications to establish their social authority. In particular, roboticists and artificial intelligence (AI) advocates reconfigure the religious categories of jewish and christian apocalyptic traditions, combining those categories with the credence leant by technological success to justify their claims to popular authority.[1] This hybridization of religion and science creates a new public role, one with prestige grounded in both of its fundamental elements but which aspires to be more than either.



Neither scientists nor religious leaders have the same prestige that they once possessed, but religion as a cultural force continues to hold sway over many people's hearts and minds. According to a 2004 Harris poll, the prestige of scientists dropped a surprising 14% from its 1977 level.[2] In the same poll, priests/ministers/clergymen received their lowest ranking ever: 32% of respondents considered the position to possess "great prestige." It appears at first glance that the tactics of popular science writers – borrowing strategies from theology – do not make sense given the polled opinion of American citizens. Why draw on the power of religion if priests have so little prestige? Either the pollsters do not accurately reflect common opinion or public perception of priests, etc. is not commensurate with public opinion of religion. The latter appears to be

1 Not all roboticists and AI authors fit the apocalyptic mold. Rodney Brooks, for example, has resisted the theological promises of other authors in *Flesh and Blood: How Robots Will Change Us.* New York: Pantheon Books, 2002. See also Joseph Wiezenbaum's *Computer Power and Human Reason: From Judgment to Calculation.* San Francisco: W.H. Freeman and Company, 1976 for an insider's critique of AI aspirations. More recently, the Virtual Reality pioneer Jaron Lanier published "One half of a Manifesto" in the ezine *Edge* (Nov 11, 2000), http://www.edge.org/3rd_culture/lanier/lanier_index.html.

2 The Harris Poll #65, September 15, 2004.

the case; sex abuse scandals have damaged the reputation of clergymen without damaging the people's faith in religion. Another Harris poll, for example, indicates that 82% of Americans believe in God, 70% believe in the life of a soul after death, 70% believe in heaven and also 70% believe in miracles.[3] The Harris polls do not correspond if we are to believe that religion, itself, has lost its authority. While the prestige of scientists dropped 13% from 1977–2001, ministers' increased by 2%. Clearly, the Catholic sexual abuse scandal cannot be ignored in considering the relative prestige of the position as indicated in 2004 (11% lower). If we ignore post-sexual abuse scandal results, we find that over the past few decades, scientists' prestige has lessened in the U.S. while that of ministers has remained relatively constant. The prestige of religion, meanwhile, may be greater than ever. For example, opponents of evolution have increased over the past decade.[4] We must, therefore, distinguish between the prestige of religion and that of its chief spokespeople.

Twentieth century scientists have seen a wide array of attacks on their authority. Their difficulties include public dismay over the horrors of the World Wars, academic disputes over the nature of objective reality, and religious disputes over moral and divine agency. The wars (and atomic power, in particular) damaged scientific prestige when individuals found they could no longer clearly accept an identity between scientific progress and social amelioration.[5]



Furthermore, U.S. scientists have faced a new kind of battle since the landmark publication of Thomas Kuhn's *The Structure of Scientific Revolutions* (1962). Kuhn's work launched a series of analyses that demonstrate the social factors constitutive of scientific practice. Sociological approaches have threatened many scientists, who believe that they diminish scientific authority in the public mindset.

Scientists and their sociological analysts have engaged in the Science Wars[6] ever since Kuhn and subsequent scholars contended that science is fundamentally

3 Harris Poll #80, October 31, 2006.

4 From 46% to 54% from 1994 to 2005 (Harris Poll #52, July 6, 2005).

5 Gilbert, James. *Redeeming Culture: American Religion in an Age of Science.* Chicago: University of Chicago Press, 1997, 37–38. Schoepflin, Rennie B. Apocalypse in an Age of Science. *The Encyclopedia of Apocalypticism, Volume 3: Apocalypticism in the Modern Period and the Contemporary Age,* ed. Stein, New York: Continuum, 2000, 437.

6 For a succinct summary of the Science Wars, see Ziauddin Sardar's *Thomas Kuhn and the Science Wars.* New York: Totem Books, 2000. Key arguments for various social aspects of science can be found in Barry Barnes's, David Bloor's, and John Henry's *Scientific Knowledge: A Sociological Analysis.* Chicago: University of Chicago Press, 1996; Henry Collins's and Trevor Pinch's *The Golem: What You Should Know about Science.* New York: Cambridge University Press, 2001; N. Katherine Hayles's *How We Became Posthuman: Virtual Bodies in Cybernetics, Literature, and Informatics*. Chicago: University of Chicago Press, 1999; Donna Haraway's *Modest_Witness@Second_Millennium.Female_Man©_Meets_Oncomouse™*. New York: Routledge, 1997; Bruno Latour's *Science in Action: How to Follow Scientists and*

social, without correspondence to absolute, objective truth.[7] They stress the important fact that social institutions (publications, grant writing, government agencies, etc.) play a role in the establishment of scientific facts, which are not self-evidently true. Scientists, who fear a connection between research funding and public faith in the goodness and efficacy of scientific research, have hotly contested this position. For instance, in *Dreams of a Final Theory*, a popularization of modern physics, written in part to raise support for the Superconducting Super Collider, Noble prize winner Steven Weinberg claims that while no working scientists care about the "relativism" attributed to science by sociologists, those in charge of funding the scientists might be discouraged from supporting researchers whose data are "socially constructed."[8]

More recently, the Intelligent Design (I.D.) controversy has pushed scientists to reassert both their classroom autonomy and their right to determine what counts as important in wider U.S. culture. Intelligent Design advocates argue that some aspects of material life are too complex to have emerged through 'chance' natural selection; they believe that these aspects demonstrate intelligent action in the creation of the world (such action, presumably, comes from God[9]). Because they have met with little success within the scientific establishment, the I.D. movement utilizes a religious campaign for popular control over education, just like William Jennings Bryan and his followers did at the time of the Scopes Trial.[10] Advocates seek public support for legislative action requiring that I.D. theories be added to high school education despite widespread scientific resistance.



The debate over Intelligent Design moves fluidly between scientific, religious, and political sectors. I.D. advocates declare themselves fit competitors for Darwinian evolutionists (they claim to offer cogent criticisms of natural selection)

*Engineers Through Society*. Cambridge, MA: Harvard University Press, 1987 and Latour's and Steve Woolgar's *Laboratory Life: The Construction of Scientific Facts*. Princeton, NJ: Princeton University Press, 1986.

7 Although scientists often defend an absolutist view of scientific objectivity, a comparative approach to relational ontology demonstrates that knowledge should be seen in the transitions of objects rather than in their final grasping. See Bruno Latour's What is Iconoclash? Or Is There a World Beyond the Image Wars? in: *Iconoclash: Beyond the Image Wars in Science, Religion, and Art*, eds. Bruno Latour and Peter Weibel, Cambridge, MA: MIT Press, 2002, 14–37, and Geraci, Signaling Static: Artistic, Religious, and Scientific Truths in a Relational Ontology, *Zygon: Journal of Religion and Science* 40:4 (December 2005), 953–974.

8 *Dreams of a Final Theory: The Scientist's Search for the Ultimate Laws of Nature*. New York: Vintage, 1992, 190.

9 Theoretically, I.D. accepts the possibility of non-divine intelligent causes for life on earth but in all cases but that of gods, such a cause would only regress the argument. If aliens guided earthly evolution, for example, we would still wonder how aliens came about.

10 On the Scopes Trial, see Edward J. Larson, *Summer for the Gods: The Scopes Trial and America's Continuing Debate over Science and Religion*. Cambridge, MA: Harvard University Press. 1997.

while the latter assert that the former utterly fail to be scientific (I.D. offers no progressive research agenda, operates on the fallacious presumption that evolution is somehow a 'theory in crisis,' and relies upon supernatural agents, which are by definition not scientific explanations). In their approach to the public, I.D. advocates argue that Darwinian natural selection endangers moral law and the salvation of individuals; therefore, the public should be permitted to insist upon in-class criticisms of it. Intelligent Design pits scientists against theologians in a court of public appeal – who will be held as reliable? as authoritative? To further confuse matters, it is not always clear who is a theologian and who is a scientist. Neither group can be universally assumed to advocate any particular position. Though the vast majority of scientists oppose I.D., many theologians do as well. And there are, in fact, scientists who support I.D.

The I.D. debate illustrates the ongoing struggle for U.S. cultural hegemony being fought by scientists and theologians. Both groups consider themselves uniquely qualified to lead the public toward greater prosperity and a meaningful existence. I.D. advocates, ridiculed by the scientific establishment,[11] brought their battle to school boards and state assemblies.[12]



Just as Christian theologians have sought popular approval to move a legislative agenda, contemporary scientists turn to the 'lay public' for acceptance. The flurry of popular science publications circulated in the 1990s and the first decade of the 21st century illustrate scientists' concern that the everyday person come to appreciate the significance and authority of modern science and technology.

In response to the 19th century historian Andrew White, the first president of Cornell University, many scholars have argued that religion and science fight with one another continuously.[13] The White thesis has been soundly rejected

11 Scott, Eugenie C., *Evolution vs. Creationism: An Introduction.* Los Angeles: University of California Press, 2004, 117.

12 Intelligent Design advocates have given up on convincing scientists and have focused their efforts on a 'wedge' strategy to divide public opinion from the scientific establishment and force I.D. into the schools irrespective of its scientific merit. See Barbara Forrest, The Wedge at Work: How Intelligent Design Creationism Is Wedging Its Way into the Cultural and Academic Mainstream. *Intelligent Design Creationism and Its Critics: Philosophical, Theological, and Scientific Perspectives,* ed. Robert T. Pennock, Cambridge, MA: M.I.T. Press, 2001.

13 *History of the Warfare of Science with Theology in Christendom.* New York: D. Appleton and Company, (1894) 1923. White never actually argued that religion and science necessarily fought (quite the opposite – he felt that science aided religion when 'dogmatic theologians' were pushed out of the picture) but he has been the posthumous standard bearer for those who believe it themselves. The first powerful critique of the White thesis was offered by Robert K. Merton in his 1938 Ph.D. thesis, eventually published as *Science, Technology, and Society in 17th Century England.* New York: Howard Fertig, 1970. Merton believed that Protestant religion created a beneficial environment for the rise of modern science. The rather provocative Merton thesis has found adherents but fails to explain why many of the major figures in the Scientific Revolution were Catholic (e.g. Galileo, the 'father of modern science'). While White and others argued for static relationships between religion and science, they have been aptly

by historians, who find that for all of his brilliance, White relies upon simplistic historical accounts that omit the richness of religion-science politics. White's own political issues (whether Cornell should be a secular institution) overrode all other concerns in his writing on religion and science. Despite the general rejection of the White thesis, no one questions that conflicts between religion and science do occasionally occur. The U.S. court battles over Intelligent Design amply demonstrate this fact.

While both theologians and scientists aspire to gain privileged epistemic positions, the former have a decided advantage. Compared to the complicated truths of scientific progress (especially when viewed through sociological lenses), eternal revelation seems attainable and reliable by the average individual. In particular, Protestant Christianity, which asserts the individual's power to read and interpret the Bible, promotes an egalitarianism missing from modern science. While, in principle, every individual could learn any particular bit of scientific knowledge, in practice the acquisition of such knowledge is difficult and borders elitism (at a minimum, the required Ph.D. rules out most of the public). For many people, the perceived exclusivity of science combined with the easily acquired insight of theology[14] makes the latter preferable.

In order to combat the populist asymmetry, popular science books aspire to explain complicated scientific concepts in language comprehensible to the lay citizen. With varying degrees of success, authors write books that share scientific insights with the public. Often, the conclusions of such books build upon the authority established through successful technoscientific work to further the authors' political aims. For example, biologist E.O. Wilson's most recent book describes various contributions of biology before concluding with the importance of environmental protection and proper biology teaching (in clear opposition to I.D.).[15]



One group of popular science authors fights fire with fire – they absorb the concepts, strategies, and powers of theology in order to overwhelm theologians.

criticized by John Brooke and Geoffrey Cantor in *Reconstructing Nature: The Engagement of Science and Religion.* New York: Oxford University Press, 1998 and the various essays in *God and Nature: Historical Essays on the Encounter between Christianity and Science,* eds. Lindberg and Numbers, Los Angeles: University of California Press, 1986. In a further challenge to the conflict thesis, Mario Biagioli has demonstrated the importance of non-scientific political factors in religion-science conflict in *Galileo, Courtier: The Practice of Science in the Culture of Absolutism.* Chicago: University of Chicago Press, 1993. Historical scholarship on the matter is definitive: no eternal warfare exists but examples of conflict do recur from time to time.

14 I do not mean to indicate that theological insights are easily attained. Indeed, theology can be as challenging a discipline as any. Nevertheless, Protestant Christian theologians in the U.S. advocate the fundamental penetrability of the Bible by 'everyday' believers. The merits of their hermeneutics are not at stake, only the perceived immediacy of them for average citizens.

15 *The Creation: A Meeting of Science and Religion.* New York: Norton, 2006.

In writing books this way, scientists take on a new role, one which brings together the powers of theologians and scientists. Many, though certainly not all popular science books seek to discredit theologians and place a scientific pseudo-priesthood in their place.[16] Religion is not always overt in media society; occasionally it is the scientists who make use of its popular power while maintaining their allegiance to atheist or agnostic scientific practice.

## 2. Religious Claims in Popular Robotics and Artificial Intelligence

In their search for public acceptance, roboticists and AI advocates in the United States incorporate themes from their jewish and christian apocalyptic traditions into their pop science books.[17] Apocalyptic AI looks forward to a radical divide in history and the establishment of a heavenly new world where human beings will inhabit bodies relieved of the alienation that degrades their present existence.

Apocalyptic AI advocates decry the limitations of human life. Human beings learn slowly, forget much, and eventually die (which has the added disappointment of leaving much of their learning lost). Key figures in this movement include Hugo de Garis, Ray Kurzweil, Marvin Minsky, Hans Moravec, and Kevin Warwick. Alienated by their bodies, Apocalyptic AI advocates look forward to a time when their minds will reign over existence, living forever and learning whatever they deem worthy of their thought. Historical progress leads inexorably to that moment, when eternity will replace finite temporality. The end of the world—a radical division between present and future – will permit humankind to shed its finite existence. Eternity awaits us at the end of history. Just as God promises his followers that he plans to reward them with eternal life, evolution guarantees the Apocalyptic AI faithful that an eternal world awaits.[18]

Apocalyptic AI predicts that massively intelligent computers will arise in the first half of the 21st century. These computers will vastly exceed humankind



16 On the 'priesthood' of scientists, see Mary Midgley's *Science as Salvation.* New York: Routledge, 1992.

17 See Robert M. Geraci, Spiritual Robots: Religion and Our Scientific View of the Natural World, in *Theology and Science* 4:3 (November 2006) and Apocalyptic AI: Religion and the Promise of Artificial Intelligence, forthcoming.

18 The promised eternity is two-fold. First, human minds will be uploaded into machines, ostensibly gaining eternal life. Second, the massive intellectual powers of machines will enable them to recreate all possible historical moments in the present. Moravec makes this eternal co-presence of time and history a major characteristic of the future. See: Pigs in Cyberspace. *Thinking Robots, an Aware Internet, and Cyberpunk Librarians: The 1992 LITA President's Program,* eds. R. Bruce Miller and Milton T. Wolf. Chicago: Library and Information Technology Association, 1992, 20–21 and *Robot: Mere Machine to Transcendent Mind.* New York: Oxford University Press, 1999, 168.

in their abilities because protein-based neurons cannot compute as fast as or remember as well as silicon-based computers. Human beings will upload their consciousness into machines, thus leaving their mortal bodies behind and joining their mechanical progeny in the age to come.

What Ray Kurzweil calls a singularity, and which looks a great deal like the Judeo-Christian end of time, will not keep us waiting.[19] At the singularity, exponential increases in technological evolution will radically alter society, leaving a new world that bears only the vaguest relation to the one in which we presently live. Increases in computer speed are held in Apocalyptic AI to demonstrate the validity of their future predictions.[20]

Machine minds will cast off the concerns of this world; the future will be a time of scientific learning, of intellectual discovery.[21] Although Kurzweil, at least, retains some semblance of human emotion and religious transcendence in his account, he cannot really justify its significance and offers little assurance that it will remain relevant in the face of his spiritual quest: the advancement of scientific knowledge. In the new world, scientific problem solving and rational computation override the rest of human existence.

Just as human bodies limit human minds, embodied existence stands in the way of scientific progress. The new world of Apocalyptic AI will be a virtual world. A "Mind Fire," in Moravec's words, will sweep over the cosmos, bringing "meaningful computation" to every atom of existence.[22] In the Mind Fire, powerful computation will enable the simultaneous recreation of every moment past and present, thus dismantling time and assuring the apocalypticists that the virtual world will last an eternity. The virtual world will disembody all information and destroy time.

Of course, human minds need human bodies. Most early Jews and Christians left no doubt that their resurrection was a bodily resurrection.[23] The human soul requires a human body, it cannot exist without. But God transforms hu-



19 *The Singularity Is Near: When Humans Transcend Biology.* New York: Viking, 2005.

20 Moravec, *Mind Children: The Future of Robot and Human Intelligence.* Cambridge, MA: Harvard University Press, 1988, 68; Kurzweil, *The Age of Spiritual Machines: When Computers Exceed Human Intelligence.* New York: Viking, 1999, 3; de Garis, *The Artilect War: Cosmists vs. Terrans: A Bitter Controversy Concerning Whether Humanity Should Build Godlike Massively Intelligent Machines.* Palm Springs, CA: ETC Publications, 2005, 244–245; Warwick, *March of the Machines: The Breakthrough in Artificial Intelligence.* Chicago: University of Illinois Press, 1997, x.

21 Kurzweil, *The Age of Spiritual Machines*, 185; Moravec, *Robot*, 163–189. Hugo de Garis, *The Artilect War*, 91–99. For Kurzweil, this search for knowledge is an "essential spiritual quest" (185).

22 Moravec, Pigs in Cyberspace, 15; Moravec, *Robot*, 166.

23 Setzer, Claudia. *Resurrection of the Body in Early Judaism and Early Christianity: Doctrine, Community, and Self-Definition.* Boston: Brill Academic Publishers, 2004.

man bodies in Jewish and Christian apocalypticisms. The new bodies are sinless and eternally youthful; they are purified.[24] The bodily resurrection of Jewish and Christian apocalypticisms solves the problems inherent in the old, worldly bodies: though the soul requires a body, the new world requires a new kind of body.

Apocalyptic AI advocates argue that ordinary human bodies bear no real relation to the pattern of neuron firings in the brain that constitutes the essential human person.[25] Since the human person is a pattern, not a body, it can be instantiated anywhere one pleases (and has the technical prowess to accomplish). Thus the bodies to which we have become accustomed will be sloughed off, as we 'download' our consciousness into machines[26] or upgrade our physical brains with machines that house far more consciousness than does the old grey matter.[27]

The apocalyptic bodies of AI come in two varieties. Depending upon one's persuasion, one might like to have a nice compact, easily transportable body – like a human being's, only better. Otherwise, one might prefer to live in some sort of more-or-less traditional computer (it might be enormous) and have a virtual body. As the person is a translatable pattern, perhaps it will move back and forth, never settling down in any one physical object.



Humanoid bodies would be a necessity if adding computer hardware to our brains (making us cyborgs) is the only feasible option; but many believe we will transport our minds out of our bodies altogether. Hans Moravec spends more time than anyone else describing the robot bodies of the future. His robot bush machines, which he calls "heavenly bodies,"[28] would manipulate objects on a nanoscale. Just as a plant's roots and branches subdivide into smaller and smaller branches, each of the robot bush's limbs would branch into increasingly many and smaller appendages. The tiny 'fingers' at the end of the limb would operate with far greater precision that human digits allow. "As with no magician that ever was," says Moravec, "impossible things will simply *happen* around a robot bush. Imagine inhabiting such a body."[29]

Eventually, physical activity will become irrelevant and physical bodies will give way to illusory bodies. Human minds – the thing to be preserved – must be housed somewhere but they do not need physical bodies to do anything. That most celebrated electronic media – the Internet – promises to become more than

24 E.g. 2 Bar 51:3–10, Mark 12:25, 1 Cor 15:42–54.

25 Kurzweil, *The Age of Spiritual Machines*, 54; Moravec, Pigs in Cyberspace, 16; Moravec, *Mind Children*, 116–117.

26 Kurzweil, *The Age of Spiritual Machines*, 118–125; Moravec, Pigs in Cyberspace, 18; Moravec, *Mind Children*, 4–5, 118–119;

27 Warwick, *March of the Machines*, 267.

28 Moravec, *Robot*, 147.

29 Moravec, *Mind Children*, 108, emphasis original.

a means of communication; it will be home to the minds of the future. Virtual reality promises the ultimate in bodily satisfaction. With virtual bodies, minds will experience unmitigated joy.[30] The virtual world created to sustain these immortal bodies would be a New Jerusalem,[31] heaven come – not to earth, but close enough to be reached by unearthly minds.

The Virtual Kingdom is as transcendent, as 'other', as the Heavenly Kingdom in jewish and christian apocalyptic traditions, which rely upon the promise of a newly built heaven and earth.[32] The present world, riddled with sin, cannot inherit the fully eschatological Kingdom. Rather, God will destroy the world and bring the faithful to life in the new. Virtual reality promises an unblemished world over which human minds will reign. It would circumvent the primary causes of unhappiness in human life: want and death. Happiness would be always just around the virtual corner.

The religious promises of Apocalyptic AI (freedom from alienation, the kingdom come, perfect bodies to house eternal minds) lend their weight to scientific authority. Apocalyptic AI advocates probably draw on theological categories unthinkingly; that is, they probably do not sit down wondering "what could make my book authoritative? Aha! Religious promises of salvation!" More likely they have absorbed those kinds of categories from the traditions in which they live and find them authoritative – just as does their audience.[33] Apocalyptic AI is the inheritor of an entire tradition of Judeo-Christian apocalyptic thinking. Apocalyptic beliefs go beyond theological speculation, they run rampant in pop culture.[34] They have become part of the U.S. cultural landscape, part of the way in which Americans think.



Apocalyptic AI advocates are the latest in a string of recent U.S. scientists seeking public approbation. Unlike scientists involved in the 'Science Wars' or those defending biology curricula from Intelligent Design, however, Apocalyptic AI authors – whose work more than either of the other two groups targets a popular audience – emphasize the religious aspects of their scientific practice.

30 Moravec, *Robot*, 170–171; Kurzweil, *The Age of Spiritual Machines*, 142.

31 Benedikt, Michael. Introduction, *Cyberspace: First Steps*, ed. Benedikt, Cambridge, MA: M.I.T. Press, 1994, 14–15.

32 E.g. Isa 65:17, 1 En 94:16, Rev 21:1. Note that Isaiah probably did not have a literal interpretation in mind when he predicted the coming of a "new heaven and a new earth." Subsequently, however, an expectation that the world requires radical purification came to dominate in apocalyptic circles.

33 Cross-cultural comparison demonstrates the cultural inheritance of Apocalyptic AI. The religious worldview of Japanese robotics, for example, has an equally relevant – but different – effect in Japan's scientific practice (Geraci, Spiritual Robots).

34 Stephen D. O'Leary, Apocalypticism in American Culture, *The Encyclopedia of Apocalypticism*, 392–426; Paul Boyer, *When Time Shall Be No More: Prophecy Belief in Modern American Culture*. Cambridge, MA: Harvard University Press, 1992; Alex Heard, *Apocalypse Pretty Soon: Travels in End-Time America*. New York: Doubleday, 1999.

While the authors may prohibit questions of salvation from affecting their everyday research practices, they rely upon them to authorize their social practices.

## 3. Reinventing Religion, Reinventing Science

To bridge the gulf between themselves and the public, scientists write pop science. In doing so, they reinvent themselves, seeking a new identity in which technological achievements can be wedded to religious prestige. This process of reinvention closely resembles Joseph Ben-David's theory of 'role-hybridization' in the sociology of science.

Writing around the same time as Kuhn, Ben-David sought a different sociological explanation for scientific progress. While Kuhn counted upon the accumulation of anomalies within a paradigm to initiate change, Ben-David argued that the desire for prestige guaranteed that young scientists would step outside their predecessors' boundaries and redirect scientific research.

Prestige is the lynchpin of Ben-David's position. He believed that young scientists hoping to acquire prestige (and the academic positions to which it entitles) branch out from established lines of thought and practice. The most productive strategy for the acquisition of prestige is role hybridization. Ben-David argues that scientists who find themselves either unfit for or unable to find positions in more prestigious scientific roles will seek to bring some of those roles' prestige into less prestigious roles, thereby 'hybridizing' them. Role hybridization is the "process whereby a person in Role A is set to achieve the aims of Role B" through an attempt to "apply the usual means in Role A to achieve the goals of Role B."[35] Successful application leads to innovation and, thereafter, prestige.



For example, in order to address human illnesses, Louis Pasteur abandoned his "early work of great theoretical interest" and investigated bacteria, then out of vogue with medical scientists.[36] Pasteur, a chemist, adopted his criteria of relevance and success from medical practitioners rather than from medical scientists, who constituted a separate group in 19th century Germany. German medical scientists had monopolized research facilities[37] and fought the bacteriological theories of Semmelweis, Lister, and others.[38] Pasteur's approach applied bacteriology toward the prevention, not just the understanding, of illness.

35 Ben-David, Joseph. Roles and Innovation in Medicine, *Scientific Growth: Essays on the Social Organization and Ethos of Science,* ed. Gad Freudenthal, Berkeley: University of California Press. 1991, 33–48, 45.

36 Ibid., 41.

37 Ibid., 36.

38 Ibid., 39.

Bacteriology became a respectable specialization in medicine thanks, in part, to Pasteur's work. Bacteriological research was not an accepted element of medical research, which was separate from medical practice, but Pasteur's hybridization of chemistry and medical practice allowed him the freedom to make a scientific contribution impossible from the standpoint of the professional medical scientists. He "gave rise to bacteriology by maintaining his theoretical perspectives after moving into research on wine fermentation and elaborated his discovery into a new specialty."[39]

According to Ben-David, role hybridization is a way for scientists to gain jobs and recognition. For Apocalyptic AI advocates, role hybridization works toward social authority. The key figures already have jobs and scientific prestige; they are established figures in their fields. Despite their scientific credibility, Kurzweil, Moravec, de Garis, and Warwick all lack social authority. They lack the credentials to speak on behalf of all humankind – these are the credentials they seek in tying their technological innovations to religious categories.

Close ties between cultural authority and technology are nothing new. For example, in *Territorial Ambitions and the Gardens of Versailles*,[40] Chandra Mukerji carefully argues that the power of the French monarchy during the reign of Louis XIV was inscribed upon the land through technological prowess. The Sun King's vast prestige drew upon military engineering, waterworks, the textile industry, and horticulture. The scientific and technological achievements of French culture were synonymous with the power of the state.



Although technoscientific might and political power have been closely allied, technological and scientific knowledge have not, by themselves, provided scientists with social prominence. It was not the engineers who captivated the heart of Louis XIV but his finance minister, Colbert. Even the famous garden designer, André Le Nôtre, accepted little responsibility for Versailles, allowing it to remain the evidence of Louis' sovereign power.[41] The power of technology tends to assert the authority of some other figure. To gain social power of their own, scientists must step outside their traditional roles.

Popular science publishing is role hybridization. Pop science authors in robotics and AI use theological categories in order to ratify or guarantee scientific aims. In doing so, the scientists implicitly accept the prestige of those strategies while using them to acquire social authority the scientists previously lacked. The merger of religion and science in pop science books aims toward the cultural authority of scientists.

39 Ben-David, Joseph. Social Factors in the Origins of a New Science, *Scientific Growth*, ed. Gad Freudenthal, Berkeley: University of California Press. 1991, 49–70, 61.

40 New York: Cambridge University Press, 1997.

41 Mukerji, *Territorial Ambitions*, 270.

The religious categories (freedom from alienation, access to transcendent realms, immortal salvation) manipulated by Apocalyptic AI advocates situate robotics and AI in a continuum of faith that has preoccupied the western world.[42] The apocalyptic imagination emerged during the Second Temple period of Judaism (among both Jews and Christians) and has been of recurring significance throughout western history. Apocalypticism certainly exists in contemporary theology, particularly among fundamentalist groups, but mainstream Americans have adopted apocalyptic faith from the tenets of Christianity and given it free reign in literature, movies, and even science.

The use of religious strategies in pop science is subtly different from role hybridization, as described by Ben-David. Rather than step down from a position of theoretical strength to enhance a lesser discipline in which more room for professional growth exists, Apocalyptic AI advocates reach up to "the queen of the sciences" for strategies that will enhance the credentials of the fields in which they already hold prominent positions.[43]

Often, role hybridization occurs when scientific roles are particularly difficult to obtain. Scientific growth occurs "where and when persons become interested in the new idea, not only as intellectual content but also as a potential means of establishing a new intellectual identity and particularly a new conceptual role."[44] That is, role mobility occurs as a result of the desire for recognition, a job, a chance to make a remarkable contribution, etc. "Mobility of scholars from one field to another will occur when the chances of success [...] in one discipline are poor, often as a result of overcrowding [...] In such cases, many scholars will be likely to move into any related field in which the conditions of competition are better."[45]



In the case of Apocalyptic AI, however, advocates have already established themselves as prominent researchers. The limitations they feel are institutional and social structural, rather than personal. While they have already made contributions to their fields and earned reputations for successful research, they share a desire to enhance the social standing of their fields within the public mindset. They wish to be arbiters of social value, to determine when and how

42 For an overview of apocalyptic theology in the Western tradition, see *The Encyclopedia of Apocalypticism vol. 1–3*, eds. Bernard McGinn, John J. Collins, Stephen J. Stein. New York: Continuum Press. 2000. For a detailed look at apocalypticism in America, see Paul Boyer's *When Time Shall Be No More: Prophecy Belief in Modern American Culture.* Cambridge, MA: Harvard University Press, 1992.

43 Each of the Apocalyptic AI authors asserts his conviction in science's cultural preeminence but their rhetorical strategies belie such claims.

44 Ben-David, Joseph and Collins, Randall. Social Factors in the Origins of a New Science: The Case of Psychology. *Scientific Growth,* 49–70, 50.

45 Ibid., 61.

cultural priorities are established. To do this, they must be more than just scientists and engineers.

Scientists turn to religion to boost the prestige of science. It would be a useless effort at bootstrapping to use science as a tool for science's social gain; scientists must look outwards. That is, if science does not have the final say in culture, scientists cannot appeal to it to establish themselves as social authorities.

Apocalyptic AI advocates have two strategies intended to promote scientific over religious authority. First, several Apocalyptic AI thinkers assert that religion is foolish and without practical value. Marvin Minsky believes that "beliefs in spirits, souls, and essences" are "*insinuations that we're helpless to improve ourselves*."[46] His view has been largely accepted in Apocalyptic AI circles. By pointing toward the practical efficacy of science and the more elusive benefits of religion, Apocalyptic AI casts aspersion on religion.

But while they are unapologetically opposed to religion (in a mainstream sense of that word), the Apocalyptic AI crowd does more than just insult and deride. Rather, they use religion to beautify (beatify?) the technological claims of Apocalyptic AI. Ray Kurzweil, in fact, declares that religion will be aided by the mechanical salvation of humankind. Human beings will become *more* spiritual once they have the super-powered intellects enabled by downloading themselves into machines.[47] Kurzweil dangles spirituality as a carrot for supporting the technological apocalypse.



Ray Kurzweil is not the only Apocalyptic AI advocate to make explicitly religious promises. Moravec uses terms like "heavenly" and "transmigration" to refer to future technologies. Daniel Crevier, author of an influential history of AI, finds Moravec's predictions "convincing"[48] and wonders whether the invention of vastly intelligent computers will amount to "spiritual evolution."[49] He even asserts that the visions of Apocalyptic AI are not necessarily in conflict with the afterlife of traditional Christianity.[50] Hugo de Garis, an Australian-born U.S. researcher, believes that artificially intelligent machines with "godlike" intelligence should be an object of worship.[51] De Garis considers the building of such machines a realizable religious goal (presumably as opposed to other,

46 *Society of Mind*. New York: Simon and Schuster, 1985, 41, emphasis original.

47 *Age of Spiritual Machines*, 151–153. Naturally, the spirituality promised by Kurzweil is devoid of the usual content. It resembles Baby Boomer appropriation of Buddhism (without the Buddha, of course!) far more than any other recognizable religious expression. Kurzweil leaves no room for gods or any other supernatural phenomena.

48 *AI: The Tumultuous History of the Search for Artificial Intelligence*. New York: Basic Books, 1993, 339.

49 Ibid., 341.

50 Ibid., 278–280.

51 *The Artilect War*, 104.

less scientific approaches to transcendence). Although he believes a cataclysmic war over AI is inevitable, de Garis continues his work and justifies it through explicitely religious motives. De Garis, like Kurzweil, sees spiritual fulfillment in the AI apocalypse. His machines threaten humankind with disenfranchisement, possibly extinction. Whether we should build them, he argues, will likely divide human beings into violently opposing communities. He sugarcoats the future war he predicts by eliding the difference between religion and science. Birth pangs always accompany the arrival of new life. Divinity and artificial intelligence walk hand in hand toward the apocalypse.

Role hybridization in pop science does not explain paradigm change or the progress of science but it does show the social presence of technoscientific practice. It is one strategy utilized by scientists to gain cultural authority. But the blurring of religion and science in popular books does more than glorify scientists; it also aspires to bring about the predictions it makes. Popular science books are written as catalysts; their authors hope that the apocalyptic world will arise out of the printed word.

In pop science, a religious science replaces the ostensibly separate worlds of religion and science. Apocalyptic AI authors build up a new kind of religion, one grounded in the past successes and future hopes of technological progress. Faith in technological evolution replaces faith in the divine. Computational value replaces moral value. Virtual salvation replaces God's kingdom. Apocalyptic AI reconfigures the apocalyptic categories of Christian faith, creating a new kind of religion and a new kind of science, a hybrid.



## 4. Medium

Strangely enough, popular science books have become a major venue for the dissemination of religious ideas.[52] While the authors may explicitly reject doctrinal theologies, they recapitulate many of those theologies' central tenets in their own views of the future. 'Popular science' is a true medium – not just a means of mass communication but a breeding ground for the Apocalyptic AI future. The hybridization of religion and science in Apocalyptic AI demonstrates the continued relevance of theological ideas in supposedly secular media.

Apocalyptic AI is techno-religion for the masses. Scientists hope to spread faith in their work and in themselves throughout culture by writing popular science. Apparently, Apocalyptic AI needs to use theological categories to boost the social status of scientists. One year after the publication of Weinberg's *Dreams*

52 In addition to the sources above, see Mary Midgley discussion of soteriological promises among a wide array of scientists (e.g. physicist Freeman Dyson) in *Science as Salvation*.

*of a Final Theory*, a new version was updated with the disappointing news that the Superconducting Super Collider was dying in Congress. Weinberg's refusal to engage religion on any ground must be seen in this context. While Weinberg blithely devoted a chapter to the uselessness of religious faith, Apocalyptic AI authors cleverly repackage religious faith in salvation, immortality, and cosmic meaning in their work. Kurzweil, Moravec, de Garis, and Warwick all advocate AI and robotic technology on religious grounds. Their books may not be better for it and they may ultimately fail to convince the public, but clearly the Apocalyptic AI authors seek a shift in pop science paradigms. The old style could not save Weinberg's cherished Supercolliding Super Conductor ... what will be required to safeguard AI and robotics projects?

Apocalyptic AI advances a sanctified vision of technological progress. Popular science books are an important avenue for cultural critique because their authors envision how human beings should relate to technologies. Pop science articulates worldviews that carry weight in many circles; to understand and critique pop science, then, is to understand and critique how people connect human beings, science, technology, and religion. As all technologies are culturally embedded,[53] to study technologies is to study culture. Apocalyptic AI advocates, in particular, place their work at the pinnacle of culture; they create a hierarchy where machines take the place of gods and humanity aspires to become one with them.



Media are means of communication, means of expression, and even means of life. A medium is the breeding ground for ideas, styles, and bacteria (not to say ideas are the bacteria of human life!). This last – thanks to medical uses – becomes even the ferment for human life. Something lives in all media: something potential, something real. From media, life is born. In a virtual future, electronic media would be the only media and the only life would be electric life.

Apocalyptic AI envisions a radically new form of life, a new world and new bodies for the beings who are to inhabit it. That life will be full of meaning: computational meaning. The future of ubiquitous computation incubates in Apocalyptic AI pop science. At the same time, pop science is the host for a peculiar kind of marriage between religion and science. Though God has lost his officiating role, the marriage is very real. Theology and science form a hybrid in Apocalyptic AI.

Role hybridization of theology and science in Apocalyptic AI provides – or attempts to provide – cultural authority. It shores up the technoscientific argument, makes the scientist a powerful figure. Whether techno-

53 This has been a major element of Science and Technology Studies. For a clear example, see Phoebe Sengers, et al., Culturally Embedded Computing. *Pervasive Computing IEEE* 3:1 (Jan–Mar 2004).

scientific advocates continue this hybrid enterprise will depend upon its efficacy. Whether popular science can swing public opinion in favor of greater funding and more scientific prestige will determine the fate of Apocalyptic AI.

Sofia Sjö

# Are Female Messiahs Changing the Myth?

## Women, Religion, and Power in Popular Culture and Society

## 1. Introduction

Since Ellen Ripley saved the world in the ALIEN series, a number of female saviour characters have appeared in cinema and TV provoking the question of what this 'sex change' might mean with respect to both the stories told in the films and the audiences who watch them.

The following article looks more closely at the myth of the messiah in recent films and TV-series from a gender perspective. Using approaches from both the fields of religion and film and feminist film theory, the question of what happens to our understanding of myth, femininity and religion when a woman is allowed to save the world is explored. With the help of textual and narrative analyses, two science fiction films and two TV-series with female saviours are examined, and their recurring themes, strategies and solutions are brought to the surface. Both challenges to the myth of the messiah, and traditional ways of representing the relationship between women and religion are examined. Finally the article will ask what these representations can possibly tell us about religion, power and gender constructions today. Are female messiahs truly allowed to challenge the myth of the male messiah, or can these characters be shown to harbour a more complicated attitude towards the question of women and religious leadership in our society? The answer is both yes and no.



## 2. Saviours in Popular Culture

Religion and popular culture is still a relatively young field of research. A subject in this field that has, from the very beginning, interested a large number of scholars is different saviour characters and themes in the medium of film. From a religion and film perspective, just about every film that alludes to the life of Jesus, or more allegorically presenting us with a Christ-like character, has been analysed, discussed and compared to different religious and theological traditions.[1] That this is so is not particularly surprising. Of all the myths in our

1 See e.g. Lloyd Baugh, *Imaging the Divine: Jesus and Christ-Figures in Film*. Kansas City: Sheed & Ward, 1997.

culture, and I use the word 'myth' here as meaning simply a form of religious story,[2] the myth of a messiah is probably the most widely disseminated topos in at least the western world. For this reason, it is only natural that the way saviour and messiah characters and themes are represented in popular culture is of interest to scholars of theology and religion. This is especially so if one, as most scholars of religion and popular culture do, sees popular culture as playing an important role in shaping attitudes and ideas among us. This does not, of course, happen in a direct way. However, as Adam Possamai has commented on popular cultural representations, "there will always be an element of truth in them."[3] Naturally, this holds true for religion in popular culture as well. In the words of Conrad Ostwalt, "films can exert influence on attitudes, beliefs, and behaviors."[4] Film and popular culture is in other words "a viable and fertile repository of religious significance in contemporary, western culture."[5] This does not, however, mean that all representations of religion and in this case saviour characters and themes in popular culture, have been judged in the same way or even in a positive way.

For an easier overview of studies treating saviour characters in film, I have chosen to follow Peter Malone in his differentiation between Jesus figures and Christ figures, or, as I have chosen to call them, characters. The first character type refers to different representations of Jesus as a historical character, and the second, to characters that have been allegorically compared to, or understood from, the perspective of the Christian Messiah, e.g. characters that can be seen to live through a form of Passion.[6] To this list, I also add messiah characters, a character type that has especially interested me, and that I define as being a character who takes upon him- or herself to save the world, earth or humankind and is surrounded with religious themes, characters and symbols. That is to say, a character that can, like a Christ character, be expected and be ready to give his or her life for another, but who can also in a more general way be part of, or surrounded by, a religious structure.



2 For more on myth and the difficulty of defining it, see Lauri Honko, The Problem of Defining Myth, in: *Sacred Narrative Readings in the Theory of Myth*, ed. Alan Dundes. London: University of California Press, 1984, 41–52.

3 Adam Possamai, *Religion and Popular Culture A Hyper-Real Testament.* Brussels: P.I.E.-Pete Lang, 2005, 23.

4 Conrad E. Ostwalt Jr., Conclusion: Religion, Film, and Cultural Analysis, in: *Screening the Sacred: Religion Myth and Ideology in Popular American Film.* Boulder: Westview Press, 1995, 157.

5 Christopher Deacy, *Faith in Film: Religious Themes in Contemporary Cinema*. Hampshire: Ashgate, 2005, 4.

6 Peter Malone, Jesus on Our Screens, in: *New Image of Religious Film*, ed. John R. May. Kansas City: Sheed & Ward, 1997, 59–60.

The attitude towards Jesus characters and Jesus films from a theological perspective has often been quite negative. As Christopher Deacy has pointed out, these films will always say more about the ideas of the filmmakers and the time when the films were made than about Jesus himself.[7] For this reason, they will always be problematic for some. In comparison, the attitude towards Christ characters has generally been more positive and these characters have been seen to both borrow from and add to theological ideas about Christ in interesting ways.[8] Messiah characters and the study of these characters cannot always be clearly separated from the study of Jesus and Christ characters, and the messiah-characters have also been read and understood in different ways. For some, these characters and the films we meet them in are nothing but "escapist fantasies grounded in patterns of the past instead of the possibilities of the future."[9] For others, they offer fascinating ways of presenting mythological themes to a contemporary audience.[10] These characters and the films they are in can be seen to introduce us to important mythological themes, themes that are borrowed from well-known religious traditions, but themes that are also challenged and reworked for a modern audience. Even though we do, in other words, encounter traditional myths in these films, the myths are also adapted in various ways, and through an analysis of these adaptations, one can make important observations about the culture in which the films originated.



If we look at popular culture in general, the myth of the messiah is alive and kicking. We meet this type of character in some of the biggest and most famous films ever made, not the least in the genre of science fiction, a genre I have come to direct my studies towards. For most cinema goers today, the reading of Neo in THE MATRIX[11] and Anakin Skywalker in the STAR WARS films[12] as both Christ-characters and messiah-characters is unquestionable. However, both these film-series and other films dealing with apocalyptic themes have also been shown to rework and challenge the myth. As Conrad Ostwalt has pointed out, the recent surge of apocalyptical themes in films can be compared to the biblical apocalyptical tradition, but the relations within the narrative and the constructions of motives and roles are also different in various respects. While a religious language is kept intact, God is usually taken out of the picture. Instead,

7 Cf. Deacy, 107.

8 Cf. Baugh, 109–237.

9 Hugh Ruppersberg, The Alien Messiah, in: *Alien Zone: Cultural Theory and Contemporary Science Fiction Cinema*, ed. Annette Kuhn. London: Verso, 1990, 37.

10 Cf. James L. Ford, Buddhism, Christianity and THE MATRIX: The Dialectic of Myth-Making in Contemporary Cinema, *The Journal of Religion and Film Vol. 4, No. 2*, 2000, http://cid.unomaha.edu/~wwwjrf/thematrix.htm.

11 Andy and Larry Wachowski, USA 1999.

12 George Lucas, USA 1977–2005.

salvation is the task of a human character, a messiah, but not necessarily a God-sent one.[13] In a film like TWELVE MONKEYS[14] for example, humans themselves, as Francis Flannery Dailey has shown, choose their saviour.[15] Nowhere, it can be argued, is the myth more challenged, however, than in stories where women are allowed to save the world. Here, an essential change takes place.

## 3. Gender and the Myth

Questions of gender have not interested scholars of religion and popular culture to a very large extent. Though there are some important works that broach the subject,[16] it is in general an angle that has been left unexplored. However, in relation to the myth of the messiah, it is a question of great importance. As has been pointed out from a feminist perspective, this myth involves the gender aspect in a very immediate way: through it, we learn whose role it is to be the saviour and whose role it is to be saved. The gender structure of this myth is almost always the same, as Gaye Ortiz and Maggie Roux have pointed out:

> In many myths and legends the world over, the child born to save humanity is almost always identified as male, the child born to conceive the savior is always female. There is wholeness in this picture which is often distorted in the emphasis on the male-only redeemer role.[17]



While women, in other words, always have a part to play in this myth – that of the saviour's mother – it is a part that has seldom been given the same interest or considered as important as the usually male role of saving the world. Speaking from a feminist perspective, E. Jane Via points out the central problem of this mythic structure: "In it, woman is subordinate to her male child, who provides salvation of allegedly universal significance. Implicit in this role is the suggestion

13 Cf. Conrad Ostwalt, Armageddon at the Millennial Dawn, *The Journal of Religion and Film Vol. 4, No.1*, 2000, http://cid.unomaha.edu/~wwwjrf/armagedd.htm.

14 Terry Gilliam, USA 1995.

15 Cf. Francis Flannery Dailey, Bruce Willis as the Messiah: Human Effort, Salvation and Apocalypticism in TWELVE MONKEYS, *The Journal of Religion and Film Vol. 4, No. 1*, 2000, http://cid.unomaha.edu/~wwwjrf/Messiah.htm.

16 See e.g. Diane Apostolos-Cappadona, From Eve to the Virgin and Back Again: The Image of Woman in Contemporary (Religious) Film, in: *New Image of Religious Film*, ed. John R. May; and Joel W. Martin, Anti-Feminism in Recent Apocalyptic Film, *The Journal of Religion and Film Vol. 4, No. 1*, http://cid.unomaha.edu/~wwwjrf/antifem.htm, 2000.

17 Gaye Ortiz and Maggie Roux, The *Terminator* Movies: Hi-Tech Holiness and the Human Condition, in: *Explorations in Theology and Film: Movies and Meaning*, eds. Clive Marsh and Gaye Ortiz. Oxford: Blackwell Publishers, 1997, 153.

that man saves woman who cannot save herself."[18] In the myth of the messiah, the idea of man as active and woman as passive is central. But as Rose Horman Arthur has suggested, the idea of a male saviour and of this saviour as a symbol for divinity is also inadequate, in particular from the perspective of women's liberation.[19] That today we meet strong female characters who are allowed to save the world could potentially be important to the relation between women, myth, religion and society. This is important even if it 'only' takes place in popular culture and in the genre of science fiction, since it is not just when it comes to religion that popular culture is worthy of notice today.

Feminists and scholars in women studies have long shown a great interest in representations of women in film. Films and other forms of popular culture are considered to have an important effect on how we perceive femininity and masculinity. There is no room here to go into the area of feminist film theory in any great length. To give a short summary, however, the interest in feminist film theory has changed from a criticism of films for not representing 'real' women to an interest in the elements of film that lead to a degradation of women, and to an interest in psychoanalytical models of spectatorship. Thus, feminist film studies have moved from a concentration on the film text to a psychoanalytical view of the spectator.[20] Today, a growing awareness of the difference among women is characteristic for feminist film studies as for women studies in general. Lately, the question of representation is making its way back into scholarship. There are probably many reasons for this. But one is no doubt the fact that women in popular culture are no longer quite what they used to be.



## 4. The Female Hero

Strong women in popular culture are not a completely new phenomenon. Sherrie A. Inness has drawn attention to the dime novels of the 1800s and their female heroines,[21] while Jenny Bavidge has shown how the recent trend of stories with young female heroes can be traced back to the 19th century.[22] At least when

18 E. Jane Via, Women in the Gospel of Luke, in: *Women in the World's Religions Past and Present*, ed. Ursula King. New York: Paragon House,1987, 39.

19 Cf. Rose Horman Arthur, The Wisdom Goddess and the Masculinization of Western Religions, in: *Women in the World's Religions Past and Present*, ed. Ursula King. New York: Paragon House, 1987, 35

20 For more on feminist film theory see e.g. *Feminist Film Theory A Reader*, ed. Sue Thornham. Edinburgh: Edinburgh University Press, 1999.

21 Cf. Sherrie A. Inness, Boxing Gloves and Bustiers: New Images of Tough Women, in: *Action Chicks: New Images of Tough Women in Popular Culture*, ed. Sherrie A. Inness. New York: Palgrave Macmillan, 2004, 2.

22 Cf. Jenny Bavidge, Chosen Ones: Reading the Contemporary Teen Heroine, in: *Teen TV: Genre, Consumption, Identity*, eds. Glyn Davis and Kay Dickinson. London: BFI Publishing, 2004, 41–46.

it comes to their numbers the female heroes of today are, however, no match to previous eras. Nowadays, women are 'kicking ass' and saving themselves in every genre from Saturday morning children shows to blockbuster movies. It is more and more likely that we will encounter a woman in the role of the hero. Naturally, the interest for these new strong female characters has been great. The question in the mind of most scholars is, however, as Jeffrey A. Brown has put it, "when women are portrayed as tough in contemporary film, are they being allowed access to a position of empowerment, or are they merely being further fetishized as dangerous sex objects?"[23] Are these characters challenging our ideas about femininity and masculinity or are they reaffirming traditional ideas about gender? The answer is both yes and no.

As several scholars have demonstrated the tough and young female heroes that we meet in popular culture today usually adhere to a traditional concept of beauty[24] and usually work for a patriarchal organisation, rather than for a group of independent women.[25] Strong female characters are also often defined as exceptional;[26] they are usually the only women around, and only allowed to be strong if they are at the same time sexually attractive and available.[27] In relation to representations of female heroines, we can, in other words, find clear structures and strategies by which the characters are made less threatening and more easily acceptable. However, at the same time, these characters can also be seen to challenge ideas about gender, e.g. by bringing both traditional femininity and masculinity to its extremes and thereby uncovering how these concepts are constructed.[28] Even though the characters are far from 'perfect' from a feminist perspective, they have also been seen to have positive effects on women's views of themselves and their bodies.[29] For some, the fact that these strong women usually come to us via fantastic genres, such as science fiction and fantasy, has been problematic. We are, as it seems, only allowed to meet these strong women in fantasy worlds. For others, the potential of genres such as science fiction to



23 Jeffrey A. Brown, Gender, Sexuality, and Toughness: The Bad Girls of Action Film and Comic Books, in: *Action Chicks*, ed. Sherrie A. Inness, 47.

24 Cf. Deneka C. MacDonald, Iconic Eye Candy: BUFFY THE VAMPIRE SLAYER and Designer Peer Pressure for Teens, in: *Femme Fatalities: Representations of Strong Women in the Media*, eds. Rikke Schubart & Anne Gjelsvik. Göteborg: Nordicom, 2004, 111–126.

25 Cf. David Greven, Throwing Down the Gauntlet: Defiant Women, Decadent Men, Objects of Power, and WITCHBLADE, in: *Action Chicks*, ed. Sherrie A. Inness, 123–152.

26 Cf. Yvonne Tasker, *Working Girls: Gender and Sexuality in Popular Cinema.* London: Routledge, 1998, 69.

27 Cf. Sherrie A. Inness, *Tough Girls: Women Warriors and Wonder Women in Popular Culture.* Philadelphia: University of Pennsylvania Press, 1999.

28 Brown, 47–74.

29 For more on this see e.g. Mary Spicuzza, Bad Heroines, http://www.metroactive.com/papers/metro/ 03.15.01/cover/womanfilm–0111.html, 2001.

challenge our ideas about gender (and other social issues) has been important. As Sherrie A. Inness has pointed out, science fiction is

> [...] concerned with sorting out the problems and concerns of the present world, interpreting gender concerns, race relationships, class conflicts, and other issues of our daily lives. Yet it is able to transcend the limitations of our everyday world. This is one of the primary reasons science fiction is crucial to study when analyzing women's changing roles.[30]

The fact that we often meet strong women in fantasy worlds is not a reason not to take the representation of these female characters seriously. If ideas and structures are not challenged in this genre, it points to how deeply rooted they are, something that has been shown to be especially true about gender. While just about everything else has been rethought in many science fiction stories, gender roles have very often remained the same.[31] But as Brian Attebery has argued, the genre is also in a very direct way about viability: "Any group that cannot negotiate a place for itself in the imagined future is already obsolete."[32] The fact that women have been able to make their way into this genre, and very actively and affirmatively at that, is therefore an important fact that should not be ignored.



## 5. Women Saving the World

What I would now like to add to the discussion of strong female characters and feminist film theory is religion. Popular culture plays an important role in forming our ideas about both religion and gender and consequently our ideas about gender in relation to religion. This is something I find to be both an important fact and an interesting point to take into consideration. For what happens to our understanding of the religious aspects of the myth of the messiah when it is a woman who is allowed to save the world? And what happens to questions of religious power when the main religious character in the story is no longer a man? To explore these questions, I turn to two science fiction films and two TV-series where we can identify female messiah characters: ALIEN³,[33] THE FIFTH ELEMENT,[34] DARK ANGEL[35] and BUFFY THE VAMPIRE SLAYER.[36] For a better un-

30 Inness, 104.

31 Cf. Veronica Hollinger, Feminist Theory and Science Fiction, in: *The Cambridge Companion to Science Fiction*, eds. Edward James and Farah Mendlesohn. Cambridge: Cambridge University Press, 2003.

32 Brian Attebery, *Decoding Gender in Science Fiction.* London: Routledge, 2002, 191.

33 David Fincher, USA 1992.

34 Luc Besson, France 1997.

35 James Cameron et al., USA 2000–2002.

36 USA 1997–2003.

derstanding of potential modifications made to the myth, I will also compare these to some films in which we meet male messiah characters: STAR WARS, THE MATRIX, DUNE[37] and WING COMMANDER.[38]

Admittedly, at first glance, not that much seems to happen to the myth when we are dealing with a female rather than a male saviour. The women we meet in these stories are mostly active, white, heterosexual, with usually some form of supernatural power. Apart from their gender, these female messiahs do not seem to alter the mould of the traditional messiah in any way. But the fact that they are female is of course a change to the myth that should not be neglected. Just by being women these characters challenge the myth head on. This is also something the films and TV-series for the most part are very aware of and it is a challenge that they, at least in the beginning, do not seem to want to steer away from. On the contrary, the fact that these are *women* and even women *messiahs* is something that is clearly pointed out. Our expectations and understanding of who should be the hero are undermined and new ideas about gender and gender roles are immediately brought to the fore. Even though the stories usually in some way come to undermine this first challenge by e.g. always also giving men an important role to play in saving the world or pointing out the fact that though the female messiah, like Leeloo in THE FIFTH ELEMENT, is a superhuman, she is still weak, part of the challenge still remains. What is transferred onto the female characters here is what I would call a narrative power in relation to the story, a narrative power that becomes a religious power since the characters can be seen to play a religious role: they are saviours with clear religious references. But does this mean that the religious power in these stories is, if not transferred to the female sphere, at least divided more equally between women and men? I would argue that this is not the case.



My first point here has to do with religiosity or to what extent characters are presented as religious and given a religious voice, i.e. a defining religious power in relation to the audience: through these religious characters, we are introduced to another side of the world of the films and the TV-series. While the male messiah characters in the films mentioned above are all to some extent religious, in that they deal with questions of belief and religion, the female messiah characters are not. This can be explained and understood in several ways. One important fact is that, for the female and the male messiah characters, the stories are to a certain degree about different things. To put it simply, the female messiahs in all of these stories are more or less already messiahs when we first make their acquaintance. They have among other things already been given the special powers and the knowledge that will help them save the world. For the

37 David Lynch, USA 1984.
38 Chris Roberts, USA/Luxembourg 1999.

male messiah characters, in contrast, the stories are about them finding these powers. They are usually relatively 'normal' people when we first meet them. As the film progresses, they do, however, develop into something else and this journey is, in contrast to that of the female messiah characters, a journey with definitive religious references.[39]

The most obvious example is Neo in THE MATRIX films. The films are about Neo finding his way and saving humankind. Although at the beginning of the first film he is already special, he does not yet have what it takes to meet the agents and begin changing things. This is, instead, a position he slowly, throughout the films, acquires. If, however, we look at Ripley in ALIEN³, where her role as a saviour of the world becomes most obvious, she is, from the very beginning, the active, creative and tough person that we have already got to know in the previous ALIEN films. For her, the film is also about finding the courage to do what she has to do, but this is to a lesser degree portrayed as a form of evolution of her character.

Even though all the films and TV-series have a clear messiah theme, the issues and problems facing the male messiahs are in a more direct way connected to the myth. For the female messiahs, their destiny to become messiahs, i.e. their position in relation to the structure of the myth, is also essential, but the problems they face are in some sense more personal. For the male messiahs, their development can be described as a rite of passage, they become something they haven't been before. For the female messiahs, the road leads them down a somewhat different path. The change taking place has more in common with the transformation Maria LaPlace has described in relation to female characters in women's fiction: here, the female hero comes to a greater knowledge about herself and the world in the course of the narrative.[40] In comparison to the male messiahs, the development in the female messiahs is a progression rather than a clear change. As Yvonne Tasker has shown, this is true for Ripley, but can also be recognized in the other female messiahs in the material of this study.[41]



Perhaps because they come to us more ready-made, religious issues and questions are not brought up in relation to female messiahs. But this leaves them without a clear religious voice. Instead, we find doubt in them, as in Ripleys comment that she has not got a lot of faith, or a slight but uninterested bewilderment, as in Buffy's comment "Note to self, religion freaky."[42] Alternatively, the

39 For a discussion of the initation of a character into his/her role as a hero, cf. Florian Kröppel's article in this volume.

40 Cf. Maria LaPlace, Producing and Consuming the Woman's Film: Discursive Struggle in NOW, VOYAGER, in: *Home is Where the Heart is: Studies in Melodrama and the Woman's Film*, ed. Christine Gledhill. London: BFI Publishing, 1987, 138–166.

41 Cf. Yvonne Tasker, Spectacular Bodies , 137–139.

42 Season 2, WHAT'S MY LINE PT 1.

question of religious faith is not raised at all, as in Leelo's case, or the only choice presented to the female messiah is a patriarchal religion, as with Max in DARK ANGEL, whose only religious alternative is Roman Catholicism.[43] The important point here, however, is that these films and TV-series with female messiahs are not void of religious voices just because the female messiahs are silent on the matter. These voices are instead given to other characters: characters who are almost always male.

It is, however, not just the power of a religious voice that is lost for the female messiahs. The more traditional religious power that being a religious leader implies is also taken away from them. This is, as such, not that surprising. It is rather unlikely that a non-religious character will be seen as a religious leader. But the important point here is that once again this role is transferred to mostly male characters. It can, of course, be argued that not all the male messiah characters can be seen as religious leaders either. However, in all the stories, we meet religious leaders and in most of them they are male. These male religious leaders may not always threaten the power of the female messiahs, but they are clearly given an area of expertise that the female messiahs are left without. Even with a female protagonist, traditional ideas about the relationship between women and religious power prevail in these stories. What does this say about the relationship between the messiah myth, religion, femininity and women in our society?



## 6. Challenges and Limitations

Here, we are dealing with popular cultural texts, not 'real' religions or traditional religious myths, and must therefore naturally refrain from drawing any final conclusions about our own society. But, as has been pointed out above, popular culture, to some extent, always mirrors society at the same time that it affects it. It is therefore not impossible to point out certain trends and structures of ideas in our society that our analysis of the material has brought to the surface.

I would suggest that what we see in these films and TV-series with female messiahs is a clear development of, and challenge to, both our traditional ideas about acceptable and conventional expressions of femininity, and about how the myth of the messiah has traditionally been conceived. As we have seen above, several scholars have pointed out that the strong and active female characters we encounter in popular culture – even though they are not a completely new phenomenon –, of which most of the female messiahs in the material of this

43 Season 1, POLLO LOCO. This does not imply, however, that Roman Catholicism cannot provide women with a religious voice. But this does not happen in the series where the Catholic nuns we encounter all remain silent while the male priests are the ones given a voice.

study are a part, reflect a new attitude towards women and their bodies. These make-belief characters have in turn been shown to have real effects on how women see themselves.[44] At the same time, they can also be considered to represent traditional attitudes towards beauty or sexuality. Even so, they offer new and refreshing ideas about the possibility of female activity and authority. Since the female characters in the material for this study can clearly be defined as messiahs, they also invert the almost global agreement that it is the role of a woman to give birth to a male messiah whose role in turn is to save the world. In this sense, women can be said to be given a certain religious authority. They are allowed to step into the centre of the myth and be our saviours. However, there appears to be a clear limitation to this authority because the religious voice and religious leadership inevitably remains the sphere of men. Because this is noticeable even here in science fiction films and TV-series that otherwise can be seen to challenge ideas of femininity and that are not, in the same way as other genre-films and TV-series, bound to ideas of reality, the unwillingeness to give women power in religious issues can be considered to be deeply rooted in our society.

Yvonne Tasker and Sherrie A. Inness have drawn attention to the different strategies by which strong female characters can be seen to be made less threatening and more acceptable.[45] Some of these strategies, such as letting women be strong as long as they are also sexy, have already been mentioned above. In relation to female messiahs, I would like to add the question of a religious voice and religious leadership to the list. As I see it, the fact that religious voice and religious leadership in the stories with female messiahs are given to male characters is a way of making a strong female character, and a strong female character with a religious potential at that, less threatening. It is, in other words, allright for a woman to save the world as long as religious ideas and religious power structures as such are not challenged. Just as the strategies by which strong women are controlled in general can be seen as a mirror of the problem to really accept strong and tough women in society, I would suggest that the need to make the religious sphere mostly a sphere for men reflects a definitive problem our society has with the question of female religious leadership.

But is this really the end? Have the myth of a messiah and the question of religious leadership truly not been challenged on any deeper level than this in popular culture, and in science fiction at that? I would like to think that there is still some hope: let us return once more to a certain blond slayer, Buffy.



44 Cf. Sharon Ross, "Tough Enough": Female Friendship and Heroism in XENA and BUFFY, in: *Action Chicks,* ed. Sherrie A. Inness, 251–252; Spicuzza.

45 Cf. Inness 1999, Tasker 1998.

## 7. A Tiny Blond with Potentials

In BUFFY THE VAMPIRE SLAYER, as well as in the other films and TV-series with female messiah-characters that we have looked at, the religious voice and religious authority are to a large part connected to men or groups of men. Buffy, the first slayer, is created by a group of men and watched over by a Watcher, who is a representative of the (mostly male) Watcher's Council. As Sara Crosby has pointed out, Buffy, too, as well as Max in DARK ANGEL, and I would suggest Ripley in ALIEN[3], becomes a sacrificial heroine who, in a sense, undermines the idea of female power. This development occurs over three stages. Firstly, sacrificial heroines are made to feel guilty of their positions as heroines. Secondly, they are made to want to give back their power. Finally, the only possible community for them is a patriarchal one. For Buffy, this happens particularly in the fifth season when, after a long struggle and many questions of guilt, she gives her life for her sister. In contrast to Max, however, who also after being killed comes back, Buffy is allowed to evolve beyond this problematic position and also beyond patriarchy.[46] In BUFFY, the religious patriarchal power structures are, as we shall see, not only broken, but there is even a clear female religious voice introduced.



This becomes most clear in the last season of the series, but is something that can be observed from the start. From the very first episode, Buffy is portrayed as being her own boss. She might love and respect her Watcher, but in the end she is the one who makes the important decisions. When the Watcher's Council refuses to help her she breaks with them. In the fifth season, Buffy also comes to understand that in relation to the council, she is the one in power. Finally, in season seven she is allowed to meet her creators and by breaking their staff she clearly breaks with them and their ideas. What is, however, also important is that the story does not end here. Instead, the question of who is in power continues. And when it comes to religious power, it ends up in the hands of a woman.

Buffy is not, as was pointed out earlier, a religious character. But by putting women in the centre, which the series does not only do by having a woman in the lead role but also by introducing us to other strong women, a female religious power is allowed to develop. Moreover, and most importantly, it is to this power, or character, that Buffy in the end puts, if not her belief, then at least her trust: I am thinking of Buffy's friend Willow, who, in the series, develops into a powerful witch. An uncertain bookworm in the beginning, she becomes, across the span of seven seasons, the most powerful force in the story. One can, of course, with Christie Golden, ask where the religious element in the Wicca that Willow is said to represent really lies. As Golden has pointed out, it is not

46 Cf. Sara Crosby, The Cruelest Season: Female Heroes Snapped into Sacrificial Heroines, in: *Action Chicks*, ed. Sherrie A. Inness, 153–178.

'really' Wicca that Willow practices.[47] But since this is a TV-series we are talking about, this is not that surprising. What is important is that the clearly woman-centred religious power Willow represents is ultimately given centre stage and is even said to be stronger than the male powers that created the first slayer. In the last episode, it is Willow who is able to, according to Buffy's wish, transfer Buffy's power to all the potential slayers in the world. In this moment she also, for an instant, becomes a goddess of light. As Zoe-Jane Playdon has posited, BUFFY introduces us thus to something new also in relation to the divine: "Unlike other pop-culture heroes [...] the character of Buffy the Vampire Slayer is highly suggestive of alternative spiritual values and political relationships."[48]

This is not to say that BUFFY completely turns everything on its head. In some ways, Buffy is a quite traditional hero and messiah for that matter: she is white, young and beautiful. But the series BUFFY with its hero still clearly challenges the myth and gives female characters access to power, and even religious power, on more levels than the other stories with female messiahs that we have looked at. And it is a religious power that is furthermore disconnected from patriarchy and clearly defined as female.

## 8. Conclusion



BUFFY gives hope that a more open-minded attitude towards women and religious power is possible, and the series might to some degree also be said to show a more accepting attitude in our society towards female religious leadership. But BUFFY is only *one* TV-series and also, some would say, *only* a TV-series. Its worldwide success does, however, speak to the fact that a story with a clearly feminist vein – even when it comes to how religion and the myth of a messiah are portrayed – can find an audience and therefore obviously answers some social needs. The question for the future is to what extent other series or films will dare to follow in BUFFY's footsteps. The number of TV-series with strong female characters is still great, but, as should be clear by now, a female hero or a female messiah in the centre of a story is not always a guarantee that traditional ways of representing women and femininity, or religion and women for that matter, are challenged. The growing interest in religious issues in films and TV-series does suggest that the question of women and religious power will continue to be treated in popular culture and treated in ways that will be of interest for real

47 Cf. Christie Golden, Where's the Religion in Willow's Wicca? in: *Seven Seasons of* BUFFY, ed. Glenn Yeffeth. Dallas: Benbella Books 2003, 159–166.

48 Zoe-Jane Playdon, What You Are, What's to Come: Feminisms, Citizenship and the Divine in BUFFY, in: *Reading the Vampire Slayer*, 2nd ed., ed Roz Kaveney. New York: Tauris Parke Paperback, 2004, 165.

women. Recent films such as SUPERMAN RETURNS[49] also reflect that the saviour myth is still very much alive. I would, however, suggest that the importance of this myth and its viability for the future is connected with whether or not protagonists other than white men are allowed to step in and save the world. For those who are saved in a story, it does not perhaps matter who does the saving, but, as this study has hopefully shown, who gets to save the world is still important to the *audience*.



49 Bryan Singer, Australia/USA 2006.

Wolfgang J. Schöffmann

# Jesus, Luhmann, Marilyn

## Iconoclasm Meets Media Society

What have superstars got to do with theology – apart from the title of a well-known musical? Sometimes, the admiration they receive seems to reach the point of religious devotion.[1] The distinction between veneration and worship was one of the main arguments in 8th century iconoclasm, which ended with the final permission of the veneration of icons in 843. Iconoclasm is the cue. It was the war against the 'apotheosis' of things that were definitely not divine. Superstars seem to have become a functional equivalent to God in various respects, and this is one of the points of contact between the iconoclastic debates of the 8th and 9th century and today's age of mass media.

This article attempts to trace the parallels between iconoclasm and modern media theories. My thesis is that as the arguments used in the classical iconoclasm and modern media theories share some similarities, iconoclasm can be used as a tool to critically review and evaluate the use of images in mass media. Thus, the church can contribute its experiences to the modern discourses over mass media.



In a short overview of the iconoclastic debates and the arguments put forth in them, two functions of icons (the epistemological and the pedagogic function) will become visible, which will then be compared to the media theories developed by Niklas Luhman and Marshall McLuhan. The underlying thesis is that if the above-mentioned functions can be traced in such diverse theories as Luhmann's and McLuhan's, they can be regarded as constitutive for the function of images in modern mass media. The use of images, in particular in relation to the phenomenon of superstars in modern mass media, provides an interesting example for applying the results and for examinig some of the conditions that religion encounters in a media society.

1 Cf. Belting, Hans: *Das echte Bild. Bildfragen als Glaubensfragen*, München: Beck 2005, 20.

## 1. The Iconoclastic Debates of the 8th and 9th Century

In the first centuries, the church opposed the veneration of images, since such worship was considered as paganism and idolatry. Eusebius of Caesarea (c. 260–340), for example, expressed his objection to such customs in a letter to the emperor's sister.[2]

A few centuries later, however, images had become an important asset for both private and official piety. Icons, especially in the form of ἀχειροποίητα (pictures not made by man), were considered as a pledge for the divine support of cities or as advocates for private concerns.[3]

Iconoclasm was an issue mainly in the Byzantine Empire. In most studies of Iconoclasm, the removal of a mosaic depicting Christ from the Chalke-Gate in the year 726 is cited as the cause for the iconoclastic unrest. The crowd that gathered to prevent the mosaic's removal killed a soldier. In the year 730, the emperor Leon III (717–741) issued an edict that ordered the removal of all pictures which were accessible to the pious. The reasons of those orders are disputed. One motivation could have been political in nature: during the 6th and early 7th century, the times when icons were not venerated, the Byzantine



Empire was of great influence. In the late 7th and early 8th century, when icons became more popular, the Bulgars and the Arabs achieved considerable military successes. Therefore, at least a part of the population saw a connection between the strength of the Empire and the orthodoxy of its leaders.[4] In their opinion, the veneration of images (idolatry) provoked the wrath of God, manifesting itself in military and other catastrophes. Another reason could be the *Zeitgeist*: Joan Mervyn Hussey points out that during the same time period, similar trends can be observed in Islam and Judaism.[5]

The successor of Leon III, his son Constantine V (741–775), further pursued the path his father had taken. In preparation for a council held at his initiative

2 Cf. PG 20, 1545–1560.

3 The uses and abuses of the veneration of icons are numerous. For example, icons were chosen as godparents, they healed diseases and raised the deceased. Léonide Ouspensky reports an even more astonishing occurrence: "Certains prêtres enlevaient en grattant les couleurs des icônes, les mélangeaient avec les saints Dons et distribuaient ce mélange aux fidèles, comme si le Corps et le Sang divins devaient encore être complétés par quelque chose de sacré." Ouspensky, Léonide: *La Théologie de l'icône dans l'Église orthodoxe*, Paris: Les Éditions du Cerf 1980, 85.

4 Cf. Beck, Hans-Georg: *Geschichte der orthodoxen Kirche im byzantinischen Reich*, Göttingen: Vandenhoeck & Ruprecht 1980 (= Die Kirche in ihrer Geschichte Band 1, Lieferung D 1), 69–70; as well as Gero, Stephen: *Byzantine Iconoclasm during the reign of Leo III. With particular attention to the oriental sources*, Louvain: Secrétariat du Corpus SCO 1973, 94.

5 Cf. Hussey, Joan Mervyn: *The Orthodox Church in the Byzantine Empire*, Oxford: University Press 1986 (= Oxford history of the Christian Church 2.1), 34.

which condemned the veneration of icons in the year 754, he developed the argument that a picture had to be identical in nature (ὁμοούσιον) with the one who is depicted.[6] Obviously, an earthly image could not be of the same nature as the divine Jesus Christ. In consequence, the worship of such an icon is deemed to be worship of an idol and therefore to be condemned.

When empress Eirene (780–802) reigned in substitution for her minor son Constantine VI, she held a new council – the Second Council of Nicaea in the year 787 (today considered the Seventh Ecumenical Council). The council came to two important conclusions. The first is a thought taken from Basilios (c. 330–379): the veneration that is given to the image passes over to its prototype.[7] The connection between the prototype and the picture is based on the identity of *person* (ὑπόστασις), not on the identity of *nature* (οὐσία – nature as the very essence of something).[8] The second conclusion is the above-mentioned distinction between veneration (προσκύνησις) and worship (λατρεία), which is an argument taken from John of Damaskos (c. 650–749) and Theodoros Studites (759–826).

After the council, there was a short period of ecclesiastical peace before Leon V (813–820) reinstated the iconoclast edicts in 815. But before long, in the year 843, a synod finally decided in favour of the icons.

The main problem behind the debates concerning icons was the difference in the parties' understanding of what an image is in relation to its prototype.



The iconoclasts waged their war against the icons because in their opinion the veneration of icons was a veneration of idols because a picture should be/is ὁμοούσιον – of the same nature – with the portrayed person. A material icon of Jesus Christ can obviously never portray both the material and the immaterial nature of the second divine person. Either the portrait mixes the two natures or it claims an independence of the human nature, thus constituting a forth person in trinity. In this view, a true picture of Jesus Christ cannot exist, therefore the veneration of such a picture is always idolatrous. The main representative of this opinion was the emperor Constantine V.[9]

The iconophiles insisted on the difference between a picture and the person it portrays. It is not identity in nature that links the prototype with the image

6 The original text written by the Emperor has been reconstructed from various fragments by Georg Ostrogorsky. Cf. Ostrogorsky, Georg: *Studien zur Geschichte des byzantinischen Bilderstreites*, Amsterdam: Adolf M. Hackert 1964. Nachdruck der Ausgabe Breslau 1929 (= Historische Untersuchungen Heft 5), 8–12.

7 Cf. PG 32, 149 C.

8 Cf. Thümmel, Hans Georg: *Bilderlehre und Bilderstreit. Arbeiten zur Auseinandersetzung über die Ikone und ihre Begründung vornehmlich im 8. und 9. Jahrhundert*, Würzburg: Augustinus 1991 (=Das östliche Christentum, Neue Folge, vol. 40), 53. The argumentation of the council is best seen in its refutation of the synod of 754: Mansi XIII, 204–364.

9 Cf. Ostrogorsky, *Studien zur Geschichte des byzantinischen Bilderstreites*, 8–12.

but the identity of the figure (σχέσις) or person (ὑπόστασις) as Theodoros Studites puts it. "Ἄλλη μὲν γὰρ φύσις ὑλογραφίας, και ἑτέρα τοῦ Χριστοῦ· οὐκ ἄλλη δὲ ὑπόστασις, ἀλλὰ μία καὶ ἡ αὐτὴ τοῦ Χριστοῦ, κἀν τῇ εἰκόνι γεγραμμένη."[10] The problem he tried to solve was the following question: if not nature, what then is the link between the 'portrait' and the person portrayed? How is it possible to attribute a picture to a certain person? The solution was to understand their identity as one of figure. Furthermore, for Theodorus, the incarnation of God in Christ proves not the impossibility but the necessity of pictorial representation. If the mental notion sufficed then it would have been enough if Christ had appeared to us mentally.[11] For John of Damascus, the pictures are a means for illiterate believers to gain access to the history of salvation. By portraying Jesus Christ and the saints or illustrating events of their lives, they teach the faithful and inspire them to imitate their holy lives.

From these arguments, two functions of icons can be derived. Certainly, friends and foes of icons have divergent opinions on how images are linked to reality but both of them agree on icons having a particular relation to reality. This is what can be called the 'epistemological function' of icons. They are not neutral concerning reality but they constitute a particular way of 'seeing' reality. They render access to the reality of God and the saints by being an instrument of description and communication. By depicting Christ in a certain manner, they describe various aspects of his divinity, making them visible to the viewers. Icons shape what we perceive as reality, including the normally inaccessible reality of divinity.



The second function is elaborated by John of Damascus – the 'pedagogic function'[12] of icons. There is a reason why the saints have been portrayed and venerated as icons; they proved to be worthy of veneration in their lives. Those *vitae* are implicitly present in the portrait since they are the reason why it was painted in the first place. The pious, venerating the icons, are not only taught about the events of the history of salvation but also spurred to follow the example of the saints. In this case, it would be a permanent alteration of action as well. For the church of Rome, this pedagogic function was the main reason for using pictures in evangelisation. Even Luther concedes this function to images.[13]

10 "For the nature of a wooden painting is different from the nature of Christ; the person, though, is not different but the same that is to say the person of Christ himself and the one on the painted picture." Theodoros Studites, *Letter to Abbot Plato*, PG 99, 501 (translation WJS).

11 Cf. Thümmel, *Bilderlehre*, 47.

12 The term 'pedagogic function' was chosen to indicate that the use of icons leads to a permanent alteration – the remembrance of information in most cases.

13 Cf. Belting, *Das echte Bild*, 164.

There is a third function being referred to in iconoclasm as well, which can be described as 'affective'. The icons evoke or inspire religious feelings by depicting Christ or the saints in their glory. In the course of this article, however, I will not refer to this last function, since it is not important to my argument. Rather, I will concentrate on the epistemological and pedagogic function of images as found in contemporary media theory.

## 2. Epistemological and Pedagogic Functions of Media?

Niklas Luhmann uses a very broad definition of media, but he still distinguishes a particular system of mass media from other systems in society. Media are means which help transform the improbabilities of communication to probabilities. What does this mean? According to Luhmann, communication faces three different difficulties or improbabilities: the difficulty of 1. understanding, 2. reaching the addressee, if not personally present, and 3. the problem of success, i.e. that the other person will act according to the content of the communication. The understanding of the message is facilitated by the media of language, signs, etc.; writing makes it easier to reach an addressee, and successful communication is established by "symbolic generalized communication media", terms that provoke an action that the speaker had intended, such as 'truth', 'love', 'money', 'power', and so on.[14] This definition also applies to mass media, since they especially provide the opportunity to reach a large number of addressees, but they have other characteristics as well, such as the use of technology for distributing information or the lack of immediate, face-to-face interaction between transmitter and receiver.[15]



"Was wir über unsere Gesellschaft, ja über die Welt, in der wir leben, wissen, wissen wir durch die Massenmedien."[16] This is the first sentence of Luhmann's *Die Realität der Massenmedien*. Like every other system, the system of mass media depends on the construction of reality because the environment, i.e. the reality outside of the system, is beyond the limits of the system and therefore inaccessible from a position inside the system. The difference between the system of mass media and other systems lies in the fact that constructing reality is the *only* purpose of mass media. Their special task is to present a reality that we can observe. In this scenario, the observer of media is an observer of second order: he or she observes how mass media observe. It is important to indicate

14 Cf. Luhmann, Niklas: *Soziale Systeme. Grundriss einer allgemeinen Theorie*, Frankfurt am Main: Suhrkamp [1]1987 (= Suhrkamp-Taschenbuch Wissenschaft 666), 220–222.

15 Cf. Luhmann, Niklas: *Die Realität der Massenmedien*. 2., erweiterte Auflage, Opladen: Westdeutscher Verlag 1996, 10f.

16 Luhmann, *Massenmedien*, 9.

that, according to Luhmann, there is not such a thing as 'real' reality as opposed to the constructed reality of mass media, because every system constructs its own reality. Therefore, it is only possible to compare one construction to the other, but 'real' reality is simply inaccessible. This is Luhmann's epistemological approach of an "operative constructivism."[17]

One of the characteristics of all systems is their "autopoiesis:"[18] Every system has basic operations with which it reproduces itself. For the system 'society', this basic operation is communication, meaning that society is constituted and maintained by communication. For the social subsystem 'mass media', this basic operation is the distinction between information and non-information.

Mass media select certain information from all the information gathered and present this as 'new' information to the audience. As a consequence, there is an "unmarked space"[19] of information that has not been selected for publication, leading to the suspicion of manipulation: why were these pieces of information published, and others not? To quote Luhmann: „Es mag sein, daß alles zutrifft, was sie schreiben oder senden, aber das beantwortet nicht die Frage: wozu? […] Die Massenmedien scheinen ihre eigene Glaubwürdigkeit zugleich zu pflegen und zu untergraben.“[20] In this case, television has an advantage over other types of mass media. The event that is broadcast could only have been recorded in the moment of action, not before or after it. Of course, it is possible to manipulate the recording either by choosing a certain angle or by faking the scene, but it is still necessary to fake something in order to record it. This is true as well for single photos. Due to this intimate connection to reality, the photo creates an 'alibi-reality': "Das Bild zeigt ganz offensichtlich eine Alibi-Realität. Aber die Photographie garantiert zugleich die Entsprechung von photographierter und im Bild erscheinender Realität […] Ein Film kann nur aufgenommen werden, wenn das, was gefilmt wird, tatsächlich geschieht – weder vorher noch nachher."[21]



Marshall McLuhan has a different view of media. In his theory, media are "extensions of man" like the subtitle of his book *Understanding Media*[22] suggests. This is a very wide definition of the term 'media'; according to McLuhan mass media are included in this definition as well.[23] For example, the wheel is an extension of the foot or the book, an extension of the eye. These extensions,

17 Luhmann, *Massenmedien*, 17.

18 Luhmann, *Soziale Systeme*, 60.

19 Luhmann, *Massenmedien*, 75.

20 Luhmann, *Massenmedien*, 78f.

21 Luhmann, Niklas: *Die Gesellschaft der Gesellschaft*. Erster und zweiter Teilband, Frankfurt am Main: Suhrkamp1997, 306.

22 McLuhan, Marshall: *Understanding Media. The Extensions of Man*, Cambridge, Massachusetts: MIT Press 1999.

23 In contrast to Luhmann, who distinguishes media and the system of mass media.

however, lead to a mental self-amputation, meaning that the extension is no longer perceived as an extension of one's own body. The reason for that is the tendency of the human brain to react to an overwhelming pressure of stimuli by ignoring the respective stimulus. The increasing pressure that new inventions bring is met by an extension and the following amputation (or "narkosis"[24] as McLuhan puts it in allusion to the myth of Narcissus) of other body parts: "Thus, the stimulus to new invention is the stress of acceleration of pace and increase of load. For example, in the case of the wheel as an extension of the foot, the pressure of new burdens resulting from the acceleration of exchange by written and monetary media was the immediate occasion of the extension or 'amputation' of this function from our bodies."[25]

According to McLuhan, it is not possible to avoid the consequences of media, although the consequences may differ according to the surrounding cultures: "In audile-tactile Europe TV has intensified the visual sense, spurring them toward American styles of packaging and dressing. In America, the intensely visual culture, TV has opened the doors of audile-tactile perception to the non-visual world of spoken languages and food and the plastic arts."[26] By using media as our own extensions, we confirm the self-amputation rendering it even more difficult to perceive it.

For this reason, McLuhan sees media as a constituent part of our environment.[27] They do not just shape the perception of it but they *are* our environment. It may be possible to perceive them as constituting our environment but it is difficult: "Their ground rules, pervasive structure, and overall patterns elude easy perception."[28] The arts in particular have the ability to sharpen our perception for such environments. But even if we may manage to see those media-created environments, we still cannot escape them: "The instantaneous world of electric informational media involves all of us, all at once. No detachment or frame is possible."[29]



Luhmann and McLuhan both adopt an epistemological mode of inquiry in their theories. They both agree that media give a particular access to reality. The media, Luhmann describes, *construct* a reality like all systems do and the observer may observe *how* they construct it. According to Luhmann, the use

24 McLuhan, *Understanding Media*, 41.

25 McLuhan, *Understanding Media*, 42.

26 McLuhan, *Understanding Media*, 45. The strict division of European and American culture seems to be questionable; nevertheless, the idea of different consequences of media in different cultures is plausible.

27 This seems to be the term that McLuhan uses when referring to 'reality'.

28 McLuhan, Marshall/Fiore, Quentin: *The medium is the Massage. An Inventory of Effects*, Corte Madera: Gingko Press 2001, 84f.

29 McLuhan, *Massage*, 53.

of images has a particular influence on our perception of reality by creating an alibi-reality. Luhmann's theory of operative constructivism already implies a certain epistemological option so it is not very surprising that it can be found in his media theory as well. Yet the same function of images in media can be found in McLuhan's theory, too.

In McLuhan's theory, media *are* the reality because they constitute our environment. Media are a part of this environment, and they give access to it, both at the same time. In this respect, they seem to be very similar to icons, which represent the portrayed person and give access to his or her reality.

Besides this epistemological function, media fulfil a pedagogic function just as icons do. They tell something *about* the reality they give access to. At this point, the distinction between the two functions is fuzzy. It seems that they are so closely linked to each other that it is only possible to make out two poles between which the functions of media oscillate.

Luhmann describes the basic action of media as the distinction between information and non-information. This code can be regarded as a „Zwei-Seiten-Form, eine Unterscheidung, deren Innenseite vorausgesetzt [sic!], daß es eine Außenseite gibt."[30] This code can be seen as a formal access to reality as well and therefore again as part of the epistemological function. Information is the fuel that makes the media system work; a constituent part of information is its novelty, which leads to the fact that 'old' information immediately turns to non-information, because it is no longer news.[31] This leads to the definition of pedagogic as permanent alteration. The loss of the importance of old information can be related to the concept of pedagogy as aiming at permanent alteration; once the new input has left its impression on the recipients, it is useless, just as old information has become useless.



McLuhan's theory illustrates a broader definition of this pedagogic function in his famous words: "The medium is the message." The alterations that media bring to our environment do not depend on the *way* a medium is used but on the *use* itself. "For the 'message' of any medium or technology is the change of scale or pace or pattern that it introduces into human affairs."[32] This change is permanent since the respective medium shapes the environment and therefore all further developments. So it ties in with the definition of 'pedagogic' as aiming at permanent alteration.

By showing that the epistemological and pedagogic functions of icons apply as well to modern mass media, I was able to show that it is possible to compare these two phenomena. The actual comparison renders it possible to use the

30 Luhmann, *Massenmedien*, 35f.

31 Cf. Luhmann, *Massenmedien*, 42.

32 McLuhan, *Understanding Media*, 8.

iconoclasm of the 8th and 9th century as a point of reference when observing the situation of religion in a media society. Iconoclasm meant a decision in favour of images in opposition to 'traditionalist' foes of icons. Nowadays, the use of images is being questioned once again, and this time, the church can contribute its experience with iconoclasm to the debate.

## 3. Modern Icons

I now want to proceed from the general theory of mass media to the use of images in media, because it is even more comparable to the theory of iconoclasm for two reasons:

- The use of images in modern mass media is more related to iconoclasm since it deals with images as well.
- There is a special type of image in modern mass media that provokes religion-like practices: the phenomenon of superstars.

Pictures play an important role in the system of mass media. They have the great advantage of being more trustworthy than sheer text, as posited by Luhmann. It is possible to write a text at any time, whereas the picture can only be taken at the moment of action. Consequently, the picture seems to be real. This might lead to a preference of visual media over reality: if everything we know is derived from media, as Luhmann suggests,[33] then secondary experiences have won pre-eminence over primary experiences,[34] because it is easier to turn on the television than to go outside. Such a development needs critical consideration.



According to the coherence theory of truth, the decision whether a sentence is true depends on the fact if the sentence is coherent with the set of all other sentences known as true. This theory has the advantage of being able to deal with sentences whose immediate link to reality is not obvious. Reality as accessible through empirical experience is of relevance as a point of reference at the edges of this system. If an empirical experience suggests that some sentences are false, the whole set has to be adjusted. The problem with this theory is the possibility of creating fictional worlds, where there is a perfect set of true sentences with the only flaw that the correspondent world does not exist. This is why the empirical experience of reality was introduced to the theory. It is to ensure the

33 Luhmann, *Massenmedien*, 19.

34 This is part of the definition of 'Medial turn' that Stefan Weber gives. Weber, Stefan: Die Welt als Medienpoiesis. Basistheorien für den „Medial Turn", in: *Medien Journal* 23/1 (1999) 3–8, here: 3f. The distinction between primary and secondary experiences is taken from: Meyer, Guido: *Bilder, Bildung und christlicher Glaube. Eine Auseinandersetzung mit den Grundlagen einer religionspädagogisch verantworteten Bildtheorie*, Münster: LIT 2002, 9.

relevance of the coherence theory of truth for reality. If media win the position of pre-eminence over reality, then the problem is that manipulation becomes easier, because the point of reference for the whole system of true sentences will then be the world the media create instead of reality. In other terms: media as the pre-eminent source of experience would define truth. Something is true not because it exists, but because it is broadcast. This is a question important to theology because 'truth' is one of the most important terms in Christian faith. But there is another issue theology has to tackle in connection with mass media: the icons of the era of mass media, or superstars.

The use of images in media reaches its peak with the phenomenon of superstars. The phenomenon that superstars present is closely linked to modern mass media. Without the media, no one would know that a particular person is a superstar and there would be no stardom. The essence of being a star is *being known* as being a star.[35] From November 2005 to February 2006, an exhibition in Vienna, "Superstars. From Warhol to Madonna," illustrated the fact that superstars seem to exist only as surfaces reflecting our own dreams and imaginations. There is no 'real person' behind a superstar; there is just the 'phenomenon'. Inez van Lamsweerde and Vinoodh Matadin illustrated this idea in their work, "Trash". Marilyn Monroe, the archetype of a superstar, covers the surface of a garbage can. "It is completely irrelevant what is in it as long as there is the right picture on it," seems to be the motto that makes the phenomenon 'superstars' work.



This fact can be observed in other instances as well. Lara Croft is the example *par excellence*:

> Die Hauptfigur der von 'Core Design' entwickelten und weltweit erfolgreichen Tomb Raider-Serie hat eine globale Gefühlsentladung provoziert, die im Bereich von Comic-Helden und virtuellen Stars einzigartig ist. Lara Croft, komplett ausgestattet mit aristokratischer Biografie und markantem Charakterprofil, hat, vermittelt über die interaktive Situation des Computerspiels, eine existenzielle Dichte erreicht, die sie zur Großfürstin im Reich der 'authentischen Inauthentizität' (Lawrence Grossberg) macht.[36]

The strength of Lara Croft's mask was so powerful that it was able to shape its bearer. The actress Rhona Mitra who was the 'platform' of the first incorporation (or better in*carn*ation) of Lara Croft had her breasts enlarged from size A to D and took special classes to better represent Lara's character. Sadly, the effort was

35 Cf. Franck, Georg: Prominenz und Populismus. Zu Pierre Bourdieus Ökonomie des immateriellen Reichtums, in: Brugger, Ingried u. a. (eds.): *Superstars. Das Prinzip Prominenz. Von Warhol bis Madonna*, Ostfildern-Ruit: Hatje Cantz 2005, 26–39, here: 38 f.

36 Miessgang, Thomas: Digital Kids im künstlichen Paradies. Wie und zu welchem Zweck der Superstar die Weltbühne betrat, in: Brugger, *Superstars*, 16–25, here: 17.

not rewarded because after a year Rhona Mitra was replaced by another actress. A series of 'platforms' followed until Angelina Jolie who is at the moment Lara Croft's in-world double. Angelina Jolie did not undergo surgery in order to act as Lara Croft (she already resembled her a lot), yet she too is no more than a temporary platform, which could be exchanged at any time. This does not mean Jolie could not play other roles as well, but as Lara Croft she does not just play a role but she *is* Lara Croft. Here, the surface won priority over the content.

The image of Lara Croft has the power to affect reality. That's what partly seemed to be the motivation for the veneration of icons as well, as the above-mentioned occasions on which icons were used indicate.

Television in particular produces this special form of images. It produces 'icons', this is to say, images that enjoy a ritual veneration. The family no longer gathers in the kitchen around the Bible but in the living room around the television set. Pictures of saints used to ornate the walls, now there are posters of actors or musicians in the children's rooms. American women of the first TV-generation made gloves for their favourite actors, and the television companies distributed them among the poor like in the ancient temples the sacrificial offerings were handed out to those in need. In contrast to ancient temple ritual or traditional Christian worship, the modern ritual of mass media has become a mostly private matter, even though it is followed by the masses. Although in ancient religions there were altars in the homes of the people as well, the public temple was an essential part of the cult. In Rome it was even required as an act of loyalty to publicly burn incense in front of the statue of the divinized emperor – a practice that caused a lot of problems for early Christianity. Today, the 'holy shrine' is found in every living room and nobody needs to join the cult in public. Of course, there are possibilities to do so, but they remain a marginal phenomenon compared to the hours spent in intimate meditation of the screen.

In former days, the saints were regarded as examples of how to lead a good life; they were the ones that people chose as their role models. This was their pedagogic function. Now the superstars are the relevant role models. The difference is that the saints were role models by referring beyond themselves to God and his grace as that power which enabled them to lead their lives in the way they did. This was their epistemological function. Superstars do not refer to any other reality but themselves. They have seized one of the important functions of religion, that is providing orientation in life and can therefore be considered to be idols: "Der TV-Star ist immer schon Bild, wenn man ihm in den Medien begegnet, und berechtigt uns damit zu dem alten Begriff des Idols [...] Man kann Phantome nur lieben, wenn man sie als reale Wesen missversteht."[37]



37 Belting, *Das echte Bild*, 20f.

If the superstar is an idol, and, as a consequence, its worship, idolatry, do we need a new iconoclasm?

## 4. Conclusion

The iconoclasts called the veneration of the icons idolatrous because icons had to be of the same nature as the person portrayed whereas the iconophiles insisted that icons referred to something or someone else: the image refers to something that stands behind it. This referring function seems to decrease in modern mass media. The picture is not only of the same nature as the thing behind it; it *is* the thing behind it, referring to nothing but itself. It is no longer reality that the picture is compared to, but the other way round; reality is measured by its similarity to images we know from media: "Wir messen die Welt an der Ähnlichkeit, die sie mit den Bildern hat, und nicht umgekehrt. Die Welt ist nicht, wie Günther Anders noch meinte, die Matrize für Bilder, sondern diese sind zu Matrizen für die Welt geworden."[38]

This is the difference between the phenomena of superstars and iconoclasm. In iconoclasm, it was never contested that there is another point of reference beyond the image. In the particular form of icons, images are associated with the whole Christian tradition. Superstars, on the other hand, are nothing but the surface. They display themselves as mirrors for our dreams and hopes, but as mirrors become blind, superstars are consumed. That is probably the reason for the frantic search for new superstars, even though there are some who seem to outlast the ravages of time like Marilyn Monroe. Maybe they succeed in reflecting a 'timeless' deeply-rooted desire, which is the reason for their long-lasting popularity.

Today, we do not need a new iconoclasm but the arguments used and how it was handled may serve as a critical potential for the use of media, and 'critical' in two ways: iconoclasm may warn us about too naïve a use of images. Still, it is necessary to remember the decision in favour of images and to think about the various reasons that were put forth to support this decision: images make accessible aspects of reality that are otherwise closed.

Christian theologians have come to the conclusion that the use of images is not inspired by the devil, but they drew a very clear line concerning their use: images are relative. They relate to a prototype that is depicted and they are to be understood in the context of the history of salvation. This is the great contrast to the use of images in media. As soon as those images are considered

38 Belting, *Das echte Bild*, 24.

the 'real' world and their most prominent representatives, the superstars, the supreme gods of new religions, theology has lost its relevance. Of course, this is a very pessimistic scenario that has not come true so far, but it is where the unquestioned use of media might lead to.

To regain the relative status of images or at least a more sceptic use of them, theology needs allies. One such ally is art, for artists often questioned the mainstream. One of the artists who tried to question the status of images is René Magritte. Artists may create "anti-environments" as McLuhan puts it, which makes them socially unloved. "The poet, the artist, the sleuth – whoever sharpens our perception tends to be antisocial; rarely 'well-adjusted,' he cannot go along with currents and trends. A strange bond often exists among antisocial types in their power to see environments as they really are."[39] Thus images themselves can acquire an 'iconoclastic' function and criticise the unreflected use of images.



39 McLuhan, *The Medium is the Massage*, 88.

# ./make world

Birgit Meyer

# Religious Remediations

## Pentecostal Views in Ghanaian Video-Movies[1]

## 1. Introduction

Since the beginning of cinema more than a hundred years ago, over and over again religious forms and elements have been made to feature on screen. Many films have set out to visualize religious texts so as to bring them to life, as in the case of the numerous Jesus films or, in the context of Indian film, the Mahabharata. Throughout the history of film, such representations of religion on screen have engendered debates and been subject to contest.[2] In the United States, for example, conservative Christians from Fundamentalist and Pentecostal camps have been keeping a close eye on how religion features on screen – dismissing certain representations of Jesus, for example Martin Scorcese's LAST TEMPTATION OF CHRIST (USA 1988), as blasphemous; authorizing others, such as Mel Gibson's PASSION OF THE CHRIST (USA 2004) as more or less authentic; or warning against the potentially dangerous impact of watching occult or even demonic forces depicted on screen, as in the case of HARRY POTTER. While in the context of film studies the medium of film itself has been recognized as driven by filmmakers' urge to re-enchant and offer new spiritual forms,[3] there has been remarkably little attention for empirical or theoretical explorations of the relationship between film and religion.



1 This article was first published in *Postscripts* 2005 1.2/1.3, 155–181, © 2006 Equinox Publishing Ltd. The editors thank the publisher for the permission to reprint it here.
The article has been written in the context of my research program *Modern Mass Media, Religion and the Imagination of Communities* (see www.pscw.uva.nl/media-religion), that is generously sponsored by the Netherlands Foundation for Scientific Research (NWO). Many thanks to Stephen Hughes, Brian Larkin, Mattijs van de Port, Rafael Sanchez and Jojada Verrips for their thoughtful and stimulating comments on an earlier draft of this article.

2 Roland Cosandey, André Gaudreault, Tom Gunning (eds.), *Une invention du diable? Cinéma des premiers temps et religion/ An Intervention of the Devil? Religion and Early Cinema*. Sainte-Foy: Les Presses de L'université Laval, 1992.

3 Cf. Rachel O. Moore, *Savage Theory: Cinema as Modern Magic*. Durham, NC and London: Duke University Press, 2000. For a useful discussion of phenomenological realism in the work of the French film theorists André Bazin and Edgar Morin see Martin Jay, *Downcast Eyes. The Denigration of Vision in Twentieth-Century French Thought*. Berkeley: University of California Press, 1994, 459–484 .

This at least partly may be due to the view of cinema, and for that matter film in a broader sense, as an, albeit partial, surrogate for religion in an increasingly secularized world. Reducing religion to little more than a symbol bank upon which the culture industry can freely draw, this view grants film, as the technology of optical illusion and make believe par excellence, the ability to temporarily stand in for the decline of true religious belief in the wake of modernization and secularization. Such a view is of little use in grasping the interface of film and religion in our contemporary post-secular era, in which religion, far from being confined to the private sphere, appears to be enmeshed with the world of entertainment of which film is part. Recently, Brent Plate has called for an approach to religion and film, that not only transcends the disciplinary limits of film studies and religious studies, but also the euro-centric perspectives and strong bias towards popular Hollywood cinema still dominant in both disciplines, and pays due attention to the broader political and cultural field in which film and religion are situated.[4] Focusing on the interface of Pentecostal-Charismatic Christianity and video-films in contemporary Ghana, this article seeks to contribute to developing such a new approach.



The popularity of Pentecostal-Charismatic Christianity, and the emergence of video marked the advent of a new era characterized by mass mediatization and Pentecostalism's increasing public presence. This occurred in the wake of Ghana's turn to a democratic constitution in 1992, which entailed the privatization of hitherto state-owned and state-controlled media -TV, radio and film – thereby restraining the state from assuming full control over the politics of representation and, conversely, creating new opportunities to establish a public presence for religious groups. The easy accessibility of video technology enabled not only Pentecostal-Charismatic churches, who embraced these new opportunities, to broadcast their message to a broad audience beyond the confines of the congregation,[5] but also initially untrained film lovers to produce and market their own feature films. Portraying problems of everyday life in a melodramatic mode, these 'Ghanaian films' feature such stereotype characters as staunch pastors, faithful Christian wives and innocent children facing womanizing husbands and fathers, irresponsible girls that are easily enchanted by a little glitter and glamour, and evil mothers-in-law. Furthermore, in the midst of this profanity, many successful movies visualize the spiritual war between the Christian God and Satan and his

4 Cf. S. Brent Plate, Introduction: Filmmaking, Mythmaking, Culture Making, in *Representing Religion in World Cinema*, ed. by S. Brent Plate, New York: Palgrave Macmillan, 2003, 1–15.

5 Cf. Marleen de Witte, Altar Media's *Living Word.* Televised Christianity in Ghana, *Journal of Religion in Africa* 33/2 (2003) 172–202; Rosalind I.J. Hackett, J., Charismatic/Pentecostal Appropriation of Media Technologies in Nigeria and Ghana, *Journal of Religion in Africa* 28/3 (1998) 1–19.

demons. Locating these demons, in line with popular Christian understandings, right at the heart of local religious traditions, video-films partake in diabolizing the latter. The popularity of this kind of movie signals, as I argued earlier, the emergence of a new 'pentecostalite' mass culture, in which Christian views are popularized, yet at the same time made subject to the technology of video, and the formats and styles of mass mediated entertainment.[6]

Given the entanglement of Ghanaian films with a broader popular culture that leans heavily towards Pentecostal Christianity, it would make little sense, as intimated above, to analyze them in the light of more conventional approaches developed in the sphere of film studies. Ghanaian films are certainly not *auteur* films, crafted carefully by an artistic genius demanding interpretation and critical reflection. Their production very much relies on the repetition of successful formulas and the recycling of well-known materials. Ghanaian films mirror – and at times excessively exaggerate – everyday life and common sense (somewhat similar to soap). Having to appeal to paying audiences,[7] they are woven out of and feed into the dreams and frustrations, pleasures and specters that make up the texture of everyday life in the city. Any analysis of the video phenomenon needs to take into account its transactions with popular culture, and with Pentecostal Christianity, and thus has to move beyond movies per se. Conversely, it would be equally inadequate to approach these movies from a narrow religious perspective, and to examine the extent to which these films reflect biblical stories and themes (as is often the case in theological analyses of, for example, Jesus films). Such a view reduces visualizations of the divine and the demonic, which form one of video-films' key attraction points, to predefined conventions of (textual) representation. In so doing, it fails to acknowledge both the specificity of video as an audiovisual medium and the fact that the perception of these visualizations as adequate depends on historically particular practices of authentication and authorization. The medium and these practices should not be taken for granted, but need to be explored.



In short, as these movies are part of an evolving Christian mass culture, it would be misconceived to approach film and religion from narrow disciplinary perspectives that fail to address the links between both. This article addresses exactly these links. Taking the entanglement of video-films and Pentecostal Christianity as a point of departure requires to acknowledge their circular relationship. Not only do these films mediate Christian views onto TV and cinema screens, building forth on televisual formats and styles they shape popular reli-

6 Cf. Birgit Meyer, "Praise the Lord....": Popular Cinema and Pentecostalite Style in Ghana's New Public Sphere, *American Ethnologist* 31/1 (2004) 92–110.

7 Until the late 1990s video-films were screened in the cinemas before being sold as tapes, nowadays films are immediately reproduced as cassettes and VCDs.

gious structures of feeling, which eventually inspire new films. They mobilize belief by making use of techniques of make believe.

In the confines of this article, it is impossible to pay equal attention to all aspects of this circularity.[8] My main concern here is to focus on mass mediated representations of the divine and the demonic in video-films so as to chart the interface of religious conventions or styles of conveying the invisible realm, on the one hand, and the possibilities and constraints inherent in audiovisual technologies bound to represent, if not render present, this realm, on the other. This examination is based on the assumption, explained in more detail in the first section of this article, that the notions of mediation and remediation offer suitable entry points into the interface of Pentecostalism and video-films. While it may be obvious to talk about mediation in relation to video as a particular medium, it makes as much sense to understand religion as offering practices of mediation between human beings and the supernatural or invisible. The notion of remediation, signaling the recycling of messages in a new medium and format, is useful so as to grasp processes of transmission from the sphere of religious mediation onto the screen.



After having sketched a theoretical framework on the basis of the notions of mediation and remediation, this article will zoom in on the appearance of the divine and the demonic on screen. Key questions are: to what extent are Ghanaian video-filmmakers inspired as well as constrained by Christian forms of mediating the divine and the demonic, and which thrive on diabolizing traditional religion? How are video mediations of the divine and the demonic authorized as authentic (or, conversely, dismissed as fake)? How do Pentecostal beliefs, and the make believe that is intrinsic to this kind of film, relate to each other? Answers to these questions, this article will show, cannot be found in analyzing film fragments as such, but only through a more mobile kind of analysis leading from video-film scenes to the world which is depicted and addressed and back. The main aim of this article is to contribute on the basis of a detailed empirical study to mapping out the interface of film and religion from a post-secularist perspective. It will be argued that video-films, far from standing apart from the realm of religious belief, engage in invoking what I would like to call a 'techno-religious realism'. Calling upon audio-visual technologies so as to produce representations of the invisible world around which Pentecostal-Charismatic Christianity evolves, this techno-religious realism transcends facile oppositions of technology and belief, media and authenticity, and entertainment and religion.

8 See Rafael Sanchez for a brilliant examination of the incorporation of televisual modes into the Venezualan Mario Lionza cult, where adepts are possessed by characters from the sphere of film and television. Rafael Sanchez, Channel-Surfing: Media, Mediumship, and State Authority in the María Lionza Possession Cult (Venezuela), in *Religion and Media,* ed. by Hent de Vries and Samuel Weber. Stanford: Stanford University Press, 2001, 388–434.

## 2. Mediation, Remediation and Immediacy

Several scholars have suggested that the notion of mediation is useful to overcome the unproductive opposition of religion and media, according to which the former belongs to the province of spirituality and transcendence, and the latter to the province of technology. In so far as religions posit the need to overcome a distance separating human beings and the divine, they offer mediation practices of which media – understood in the broadest sense – form an inalienable part.[9] Any attempt to access and render present the divine – and, in the case that stands central here, to invoke the demonic so as to fight it – and to communicate among religious practitioners ultimately depends on media. The use of particular media, in turn, appeals to specific senses and generates particular religious experiences. Once media are understood as intrinsic to religion, it is possible to ask intriguing questions about the implications of the adoption of new mass media by established religious traditions. But an understanding of religion as necessarily implying mediation also opens up new possibilities to explore the interface of religion and film that stands central here, and to examine how cinematic or video mediations of the divine and the demonic relate to mediation practices in the context of Pentecostal Christianity. What is at stake when the 'Gospel moves onto the screen', that is, when a new audiovisual medium is made to express already existing religious forms hitherto tied to specific media, such as the biblical text, sermons and services? In other words, the question arises in how far Pentecostal representations, conveyed through a number of interrelated media, are transformed in the course of their transfer into the new medium of video-film. This transfer is not simply an act through which an existing message is stripped from its old medium and inserted into a new one, but a question of remediation. Remediation, in others words, refers to the ways in which different media relate to, and indeed, quote each other. What media remediate is other media, not content as such.



The notion of remediation, as it has been launched by Jay David Bolter and Richard Grusin, is a useful point of departure to grasp this transfer.[10] As reality

9 E.g. Hent de Vries and Samuel Weber (eds.), *Religion and Media.* Stanford: Stanford University Press, 2001; Jeremy Stolow, Religion and/as Media, *Theory, Culture & Society* 22/2 (2005) 137–163; S. Brent Plate, Introduction; Birgit Meyer, Praise the Lord.

10 Jay David Bolter and Richard Grusin, *Remediation. Understanding New Media.* Cambridge, MA: MIT Press, 1999. Although this notion makes immediate sense in relation to our contemporary media-saturated environment, in which the entertainment industries make ample use of 'repurposing' (e.g. borrowing elements from a textual medium and reusing it in cinema) and new supermedia absorb a range of previous media technologies (the latest being the mobile phone annex TV, pc, and camera), the authors insist that it would be mistaken to understand remediation as an entirely new process. On the contrary, it is a useful notion to demystify celebrations of new media, such as ICT, for achieving a complete break with the past, and urges us to conceptualize the relationships between new and old media in terms of media genealogies.

is always mediated, any mediation refers to and absorbs earlier mediations, and hence can aptly be described as remediation.[11] Bolter and Grusin use the notion of remediation in a quite generalizing manner and tend to represent it as driven by a fixed logic. However, notwithstanding their lack of attention to historically specific remediation processes, their ideas about the nexus of media and immediacy (or authenticity) are important to understand the recycling of Pentecostal materials in video-movies that stands central in this article. Remediation, the authors point out, thrives on a 'double logic': that of 'transparent immediacy' and of 'hypermediacy'. The 'logic of transparent immediacy' implies that media technologies are erased from the representations which they produce, making it seem as if these representations offer immediate access to reality in a raw and unmediated sense. In other words, the medium itself is rendered entirely transparent and invisible, like a window, and creates the illusion of the representation as an authentic presence. The distance on which mediation depends is paradoxically transcended by the promise of immediacy that denies mediation though depending on it. According to Bolter and Grusin, this somewhat naïve view of immediacy speaks to and expresses a „historical desire for unmediated experience", that is mobilized explicitly in shifts from one medium to another (in that new media are claimed to offer better access to reality). This promise is well captured by the Latin etymology of remediation: *remedere*, which means 'to heal, to restore to health'.[12] In this sense, remediation entails the possibility of reform. Photography and film, for example, were celebrated as able to document unmediated presence through visual representation. Such promises have been unmasked by poststructuralist critique as illusions or 'reality effects'. Hypermediacy, on the other hand, asserts multiple acts of representation – as in the case of Microsoft's Windows – and acknowledges that technology itself is real, in that it is gradually becoming our second nature and claims to offer pure, authentic experience.[13] In this postmodern logic, reality is not supposed to lie beyond representation, but to be constituted by it. Reminiscent of Baudrillard's simulacrum appearing as hyperreal, hypermediacy claims immediacy and authenticity not beyond, but through media.



This perspective on (re)mediation is intriguing because it highlights the paradox that immediacy and authenticity, though by definition opposed to media and allegedly unmediated, are produced by media. Nevertheless, as intimated already,

11 "...just as there is nothing prior to the act of mediation, there is also a sense in which all mediation remediates the real. Mediation is the remediation of reality because media themselves are real and because the experience of media is the subject of remediation" (Bolter & Grusin, *Remediations*, 59). See also William Mazzarella, Culture, Globalization, Mediation, *Annual Review of Anthropology* 33 (2004) 345–367.

12 Cf. Bolter & Grusin, 59.

13 Cf. Bolter & Grusin, 42.

Bolter's and Grusin's work has a somewhat dazzling effect. This derives from the authors' strong focus on media without actually situating them in particular social fields. As a consequence, the accent lies more on media as technologies than on historically situated mediation practices which shape communication among people. It is important to stress that remediation is not an arbitrary, unbounded process of absorption, but shaped and governed by established mediation practices, and hence subject to power relations. This is how remediation is understood in this article. Bolter's and Grusin's lack of attention for practices of (re)mediation at the expense of media *per se* also implies that the assumed 'historical desire' for transparent immediacy which new remediations promise to satisfy, yet – unavoidably – feed, gets little relief in their work. Striving for immediacy and authenticity should not be reduced to a dynamics of media, but be viewed as being part and parcel of broader processes of generating desire and authorizing immediacy in particular mediation practices. It cannot simply be assumed that immediate access to reality is always what new media promise, nor that this promise would always be effective. Instead its needs to be investigated how new media are made to speak to questions of immediacy and authenticity in particular social fields.

This is certainly the case regarding religious traditions, such as Protestant Christianity, which have developed and authorized particular modes of accessing and representing the invisible (see below). Rendering transparent the medium for the sake of invoking immediacy seems pertinent in relation to Pentecostal, and for that matter Protestant, attempts of rendering accessible the divine, without making God, whose presence depends on mediation (and hence on media), appear as a mere human construction. Representing God, and invoking his presence, in other words, is governed by more or less fixed conventions that have been authorized as adequate. Digression from such conventions may entail severe conflict (as in the Protestant struggle against the Catholic icon)[14], or entail charges of sacrilege and blasphemy. Not just any remediation, though possible in principle, is acceptable in practice.



Obviously, both the introduction of new media as TV and video into established mediation practices and the transmission of religious representations into the medium of video impinge on religious experience and raise critical questions among religious leaders and followers, in particular concerning the maintenance of religious authority and the authentication of media representations as truthful.[15] In fact, much literature on religious films in the sphere of theology – in particular on 'Jesus' films – is situated on this very same level, partaking in

14 Cf. Wolfgang J. Schöffmann's article in this volume.

15 See Charles Keil, From the Manger to the Cross: The New Testament Narrative and the Question of Stylistic Retardation, in Roland Cosandey et.al. 112–120.

discussions about the truthfulness of mediated representations and authorizing certain films as authentic.[16] Written from a standpoint located outside of such discussions, this article all the more seeks to grasp the dynamics on which they thrive. Below it will be shown that questions of authorization and authentication of religious remediations in the context of making, watching and interpreting video-movies are a matter of eminent concern for both the filmmakers and the audiences, and thus lead us right into the heart of the interface of Pentecostalism and video-movies.

## 3. Remediating the Divine and Demonic in Video-Films

### 3.1 Video-Movies and the Liaison with Pentecostal Christianity

Video-filmmakers' relationship with Pentecostal Christianity is complicated. While some of them attend Pentecostal-Charismatic churches, others are more reserved or even opposed to "all this Pentecostal crap", as one filmmaker put it. Nevertheless, most of them asserted in my interviews with them that in order to make a financially successful movie, it is pertinent to link up with Pentecostal perspectives, that have become increasingly popular in the course of the last twenty years and shape Ghanaian popular culture and the public sphere at large after the liberalization of the media. Pentecostalism, as I argued elsewhere, is characterized by a remarkable ability to encapsulate, and by the same token encroach upon, everyday life, while at the same time promoting the desirability to reach beyond the constraints of the local and become part of a global network of born again believers.[17]



The increasing relevance of Pentecostalism to video-filmmaking can easily be discerned by a brief retrospective. When filmmakers took up the medium of video in the late 1980s, the main concern was to make 'local films' that were not only an affordable substitute for celluloid, but would also be closer to people's everyday life than earlier productions by the state-owned Ghana Films Industry Corporation (GFIC) that had been devoted to the project of educating the nation through the medium of film. While 'Ghanaian films' pictured the local environ-

16 E.g. Adele Reinhartz, *Scripture on the Silver-Screen*. Louisville/London: Westminster John Knox Press, 2003; Eric S. Christianson, Peter Francis and William R. Telford (eds.), *Cinéma Divinité. Religion, Theology and the Bible in Film*. London: SCM Press, 2005; Richard C. Stern, Clayton N. Jefford & Guerric Debona, *Saviour on the Silver Screen*. New York: Paulist Press, 1999.

17 Birgit Meyer, *Translating the Devil. Religion and Modernity Among the Ewe in Ghana*. Edinburgh: Edinburgh University Press, 1999; Commodities and the Power of Prayer. Pentecostalist Attitudes Towards Consumption in Contemporary Ghana, *Development and Change* 29/4 (1998) 751–777.

ment, their plots were nevertheless inspired by foreign films, in particular Indian movies which paid much attention to depicting spirits and gods, and the western genre of horror films. Both of these genres, of course, had been around in Ghana for some decades. For example, the film DIABOLO (Akuffo, Ghana 1991),[18] depicting a snake-man who lures unsuspecting prostitutes into his home where he enters their vagina in the shape of a snake and makes them vomit money before they die, was inspired by the horror film AN AMERICAN WEREWOLF IN LONDON (Lardis, USA/UK 1981) and an Indian movie about snakes. The producer and director William Akuffo, pioneer in the field of Ghanaian films, told me that he wanted to make a movie involving occult powers that was embedded in the local environment and would speak to local anxieties, hence the choice of the snake rather than a werewolf. While the name 'Diabolo' invokes the image of the devil, the first sequel of the film (eventually four parts appeared) is certainly not obviously framed as a Christian film. DIABOLO I ends with a scene involving car mechanics who catch the snake-man and burn him. Interestingly, Akuffo even changed the ending after the first show, as he noted that audiences were furious about the fact that Diabolo was able to sneak away without being duly punished (a device chosen by Akuffo so as to make possible the snake-man's miraculous reappearance in part two). This attitude is as exemplary for filmmakers' strong sense of having to appeal to audiences as for viewers' expectations towards film as offering a moral lesson, showing explicitly who is good or bad, and making the latter receive a punishment on screen.[19]



Next to DIABOLO, there was a series of popular movies featuring ghosts, i.e. returning dead who suffered a violent death, seek revenge and restore the moral order by punishing evildoers. These movies, too, did not foreground Christian views very explicitly, but rather affirmed popular ideas about ghosts and morals in a broader sense. Interestingly, ghost films fit in with a more general obsession with the spirits of the dead that gained much attention in popular papers and rumors. It seems that in the beginning, Ghanaian films derived much of their appeal from making visible, through simple though ingenious special effects, how ghostly forces operate according to the popular imagination. This earned them much public critique from established filmmakers trained at the National Film and Television Institute (NAFTI) or affiliated with the GFIC, and from state institutions, who found that local movies affirmed popular superstitions, and thus failed to employ film for the sake of education. Though striving for

18 Cf. Birgit Meyer, "Delivered from the Powers of Darkness." Confessions about Satanic Riches in Christian Ghana, *Africa* 65/2 (1995) 236–255; Tobias Wendl, Visions of Modernity in Ghana. Mami Wata Shrines, Photo Studios and Horror Films, *Visual Anthropology* 14/3 (2001) 269–292.

19 This is an expectation that has at least in part been sustained by the requirements of the censorship board, which stipulate that morality be visualized on screen.

recognition, independent video-filmmakers realized at the same time that the popular taste on which they depended was almost diametrically opposed to that of the established film circles. Interestingly, in the shadow of these criticisms, the ghost films were also opposed from a Pentecostal point of view, the point raised here being that it was wrong to attribute to ghosts the power to take revenge and restore morality. Only God, or Jesus, were supposed to act in this way. The crux of this critique does not concern the visualization of ghosts *per se*, but their celebration as moral custodians and the absence of an explicit Christian frame.

Since the beginning of the 1990s one can discern an increasing, explicit alignment of video-films and Pentecostal perspectives. As intimated above, democratization and the liberalization of mass media offered unprecedented possibilities for Pentecostal-Charismatic churches to appear in public.[20] By skillfully making use of newly available media technologies – often in hi-tech church-run media studios –, these churches (in contrast to more orthodox Protestant churches and the Catholic church) seek to address new followers. Pentecostalism's deliberate use of audio-visual technologies indicates an almost seamless articulation of the religious quest for being able to look beyond the level of mere appearance (see below) to the possibilities of new media. At the same time, the adoption of these media into practices of religious mediation marks a significant rearticulation of Christianity in the era of technological reproducibility, instigating new modes of belief that rely on mass membership, spectacle, and a voyeuristic concern with the demonic.[21]



The obsession to stage spectacular struggles against demonic forces for a mass audience is a central point of convergence between video-films and Pentecostal-Charismatic churches. Pentecostalism has successfully absorbed popular forms of grassroots Christianity that place a strong emphasis on Satan and the demons that serve him. These demons, as I explained elsewhere,[22] are held to be behind the gods worshipped in the context of local religious traditions and the power of witchcraft, but also encompass new spirits, such a Mami Water, the erotic goddess at the bottom of the ocean who seduces people with sex and commodities. In

20 The striking popularity of this type of churches in Ghana stand central in Paul Gifford, *Ghana's New Christianity. Pentecostalism in a Globalising African Economy.* London: Hurst, 2004. For an overview on the popularity of such churches in Africa see Birgit Meyer, Christianity in Africa. From African Independent to Pentecostal-Charismatic Churches, *Annual Review of Anthropology* 33 (2004) 447–474.

21 See also Patricia Birman, Future in the Mirror. Media, Evangelicals and Politics in Rio de Janeiro, in *Religion, Media and the Public Sphere*, ed. by Birgit Meyer & Annelies Moors, Bloomington: Indiana University Press, 2006, 52–72; Marleen de Witte, The Spectacular and the Spirits. Charismatics and Neo-Traditionalists on Ghanaian Television, *Material Religion* 1/3(2005) 314–335.

22 Cf. Meyer, *Translating the Devil.*

the Pentecostal perspective, such demons are responsible for the hardships and problems in everyday life, and thus to be fought by the power of the Christian God. In other words, the obsession with demonic forces is positioned in a dualistic frame of God and Devil. As their struggle, though shaping the material world, by and large takes place in the 'realm of the spiritual', Pentecostals feel compelled to make visible what happens in that realm and to fight a spiritual war. In Pentecostal-Charismatic practice, much emphasis is placed on the need to reveal the operations of the powers of darkness. Making demonic forces visible is a necessary device in the fight against them.[23]

To my knowledge, the first movie that explicitly took up Pentecostal views is DELIVERANCE FROM THE POWERS OF DARKNESS, which spectacularly visualizes how a witch, in the course of becoming a born again Christian, is exorcized from her links with demonic forces, many of which she has embodied spiritually and is made to vomit out. This movie not only offers a visual supplement to Pentecostal-Charismatic exorcism practices, but also to the Nigerian preacher Emmanuel Eni's famous, widely circulating tract "Delivered from the Powers of Darkness", that raised the popularity of Pentecostalism throughout Africa, including Ghana. The filmmaker, director and producer Sam Bea told me that he had first seen this film appear on a white wall and that pastors had assured him that this had been a God-sent vision. Offering spectacular scenes featuring demonic forces and at the same time asserting the superiority of the Christian God over traditional powers, this movie signaled a shift from spectacular depictions of occult forces towards the incorporation of this kind of spectacle into a Christian dualistic frame in Ghanaian films. Although this film met the protest of established filmmakers and intellectuals, who were not only worried about the endorsement of popular 'superstitions' but also about the celebration of Christianity and demonization of local religious traditions, the remediation of Pentecostal views became a characteristic feature of Ghanaian films. The link with Pentecostalism was more or less outspoken, ranging from an explicit focus on the spiritual war of God and Satan to showing divine power at work in the midst of the profanity of everyday life. The bottom line was filmmakers' realization that a film critiquing Christianity and celebrating local cultural heritage might do well in international festivals as FESPACO, but would surely flop in the local market and hence destroy one's business. They found at least some positive reference to Christianity to be unavoidable. Conversely, the dualism of God and Satan allowed for spectacular representations of occult forces and stunning special effects, provided they were marked as demonic and hence inferior to the Christian God.



23 Cf. Birgit Meyer, Mediating Tradition: Pentecostal Pastors, African Priests, and Chiefs in Ghanaian Popular Films, in *Christianity and Social Change in Africa. Essays in Honor of J.D.Y. Peel*. ed. Toyin Falola. Durham, NC: Carolina Academic Press, 2005, 275–306.

This trend has been very much enhanced with the arrival of Nigerian video-films in the Ghanaian market in the late 1990s, which thrive on similar plots, but put remarkably more emphasis on demonic forces, involving computer-made special effects, violence, and the smashing power of God, and which, as Ghanaian actors working on Nigerian film sets and Ghanaian viewers assert, look "terribly real". A great number of Nigerian films are produced by Pentecostal churches, which use the medium to attract believers.[24] Having to live up to the new standards set by these Nigerian movies (which are usually made with more money and hence superior in terms of acting, set design and camera work, in addition to being able to circumvent the strict standards of the film censorship board to which Ghanaian video-movies are to be submitted), Ghanaian filmmakers realized even more the need to satisfy audience expectations, rather than bother about intellectuals' critique of misrepresenting local religious traditions. And hence video-filmmakers, irrespective of their personal conviction, developed modes of depicting the spiritual realm in film that mimicked pastors' oral accounts about this realm. Substituting the eye of God with the camera, many movies were (and still are) framed as Christian revelations and made to remediate Pentecostal concerns in the medium of video. Invoking a Christian frame – articulated through Bible quotes or statements as "Thank you Jesus!" or "Glory to God" – video-filmmakers strive to make their movies exceed mere fiction and make believe. In order to appear as genuine revelations of divine power, however audio-visual representations of divine and demonic power need to be authorized as authentic by the audiences. By explicitly addressing them as Christian viewers in search of revelation, calling upon the Bible to give credence to the film (and by the same token actualizing the Bible), and remediating familiar Pentecostal views, video-filmmakers try to assure that audiences are tuned in such a way that this authorization actually occurs.



An apt example is the film, STOLEN BIBLE (Ghana 2001), by Augustine Abbey. Having experimented with different genres (in particular melodrama and comedy) for some time and being in dire need of success, in 2002 Abbey decided to make a movie closely aligned with Pentecostal concerns. STOLEN BIBLE is about a group of selfish wealthy men worshiping an indigenous spirit, who offer money in exchange for a beloved person (in particular the wife), yet are finally destroyed by divine power. The theme of the sacrifice of the beloved wife has been endlessly recycled in paintings, written narratives, rumors and a host of Ghanaian and Nigerian films. Remediating these already circulating materials, STOLEN BIBLE does not claim to tell a completely new story, but rather to visualize an exist-

24 Cf. Obododimma Oha, The Rhetoric of Nigerian Christian Videos. The War Paradigm of The Great Mistake, in *Nigerian Video Films*, ed. Jonathan Haynes. Athens: Ohio University Press, 2000, 192–199.

ing one in such a way that it appears as ultimately authentic. In order to make STOLEN BIBLE look as truthful as possible, Abbey even decided to invite a real pastor to stage the harsh fight against the bloodthirsty spirit and his followers in his own church. In Abbey's experience, many actors, even though they might be staunch Pentecostal believers, were not able to embody the role of a pastor in a truly convincing manner. Therefore audiences might find certain scenes 'too artificial', and hence were unable to forget that they were just watching a movie. Shooting in a real church and collapsing the identity of the pastor with the film character of the pastor, STOLEN BIBLE seeks to convey authenticity. Successfully so – as Abbey assured me, tapes of the film sold like "hot cake" in the streets, and some churches even organized screenings for their members.

Despite these deliberate attempts to transfer Pentecostal views and practices onto the screen, it would be mistaken to assume that video-films fully converge with Pentecostalism. It is important to keep in mind that video-filmmakers, in order to keep the business going, need to attract large audiences. Writing off filmmakers' appeal to popular belief as 'mere' business, however, would be too simple. Such a view suggests an irreconcilable distinction between business as profit-oriented and belief as sincere. It is important to realize that Pentecostal-Charismatic churches are run deliberately in a business-like fashion. As the attraction of a mass-membership is key to their survival in the highly competitive religious market, these churches, in their own way, also have to make sure to appeal to a broader public. As is the case with video-films, Pentecostal-Charismatic media ministries also appeal to audio-visual mass media so as to secure popular support. Certainly in regard to the spectacular representation of miracles in the context of televised church services and prayer sessions, a striking elective affinity can be discerned between video-filmmakers' and pastors' attempts to use audio-visual technologies so as to make people believe.[25] Both the video-film phenomenon and Pentecostal-Charismatic churches are part and parcel of a broader process in which belief and spectatorship, religion and mass entertainment, being born again and making money, are becoming inextricably entangled.



Video-filmmakers' main targeted audience are women, who are supposed to make their boyfriends and husbands watch those movies that satisfy women's expectations in relation to standards of piety and morals, especially in relation to marriage. Many women feel attracted to Pentecostal churches, though they are involved to a stronger or lesser degree. Video-films adopt Pentecostal modes so as to achieve popularity. This implies that the Pentecostal remediations that characterize many movies need not be authorized as truthful by pastors per se,

25 On the elective affinity of miracles and special effects see Hent de Vries, In Media Res. Global Religion, Public Spheres, and the Task of Contemporary Religious Studies, in *Religion and Media*, 23–29.

but rather by popular opinion. Interestingly, when I questioned Pentecostal pastors about video-movies, I received quite diverse answers. Some, among them the pastor participating in STOLEN BIBLE, asserted the relevance of such Nigerian and Ghanaian films for creating a Christian mass culture, and stressed that many visualizations of occult forces did indeed capture adequately the operations of demonic powers. If only films would make clear that the power of God was superior, films were suitable devices for proselytization, certainly among youth and female audiences. A number of itinerant Pentecostal pastors, who moved through the coastal region so as to preach, also stressed that they would preach about films and at times show them to Christian audiences (the point not being that the films are good, but that the process of watching and the interpretation needs to be controlled.) On the other hand, some of the pastors I spoke to about this matter were rather dismissive of this type of movies, lamenting the low technical quality and being suspicious of entertainment per se, which they perceived as distractive and potentially a-moral. Still, these pastors also acknowledged that many members, in particular women, actually did watch such movies with much interest and often even questioned pastors about certain features.



In this sense, video-movies, remediating popular views that are heavily leaning towards Pentecostalism, though not entirely controlled by Pentecostal leaders, are an unavoidable reality to which pastors, too, have to relate. Here we get a glimpse of a paradox: in the course of the popularization of Pentecostal views that goes along with its spread into a Christian mass culture, it is increasingly difficult for Pentecostal pastors to control and streamline popular Pentecostal religiosity. In contrast to more orthodox churches which are organized around the model of congregations that are localized in particular areas and supervised by a pastor or priest, Pentecostal-Charismatic Christianity is much more mass oriented. Though omnipresent in public space, this brand of Christianity faces the problem of how to effectively claim religious authority over an ever expanding, dispersed mass audience.

### 3.2 Screening the Divine and Demonic

The representation of God, Satan and demons on screen by and large resonates with, and in turn informs, how these forces are envisioned in Pentecostal circles. Here the Pentecostal, and for that matter Protestant, stance towards religious images comes in.[26] Let us start with images in relation to God. Referring to the Second Commandment, Protestants claim that it is wrong to make an image

26 See also David Morgan, *Visual Piety. A History and Theory of Popular Religious Images.* Berkeley and Los Angeles: University of California Press, 1998.

of God, and this is the central argument raised against Catholic icons as well as against statues of local gods which are both dismissed as idol worship. Nevertheless many Protestants do have mass reproduced print images of Jesus on the wall insisting that they do not worship the image as such, but the power behind it. This somewhat inconsistent attitude towards the image also comes back in movies. In THE BEAST WITHIN (King, Ghana 1993), for example, there is a set of scenes in which a desperate Christian housewife prays in front of a picture of Jesus in the living room not knowing that a *juju* (an object embodying magical power) is hidden behind it. In the end, it is only the *juju*-man from the village who is able to control this power, whereas the prayer to Jesus does not help solve the problem and possibly even increases it, because it renders the *juju* hidden behind the picture more powerful. This movie, though well made, was not very successful because of these very scenes. The young people with whom I watched the movie (in 1996) did not at all like the suggestion that prayer to Jesus would be less efficient than an indigenous priest. This clearly went against the common idea, endorsed by many movies, that Christianity was far more powerful than local religious traditions, which were dismissed as diabolic. Therefore, these spectators were not prepared to authorize the film as a truthful representation.

However, against the background of later discussions about religious images I understood that the appropriateness of depictions of Jesus is considered problematic in Pentecostal circles. This became very clear to me through a conversation with an actress on the set of the movie TURNING POINT (Ghana 2002). This woman, a member of the Winner's Church (a popular Pentecostal-Charismatic church originating from Nigeria), told me that upon the advice of her sister she did away with the image of Jesus in her room. Her sister had told her that "there is a spirit in that image, not the spirit of God, but a devilish thing. The problem is that the spirits can look at you through images and masks, and the like. They use the eyes." When I did not get her point, she immediately brought a photograph. Pointing at the eyes, she said: "Wherever you are in the room, the image will look at you, so you are seen." This blurring of the distinction between a picture that is subject to a person's gaze and the picture looking back is attributed to the power of the Devil, who is even considered able to appropriate the eyes of Jesus in a picture so as to observe and confuse a Christian. This is why it would be dangerous to have pictures – even those depicting Jesus – in one's house. Against the background of this understanding, it could even be argued that THE BEAST WITHIN is less scandalous, for it points out exactly the danger imbued in a religious image and might also be interpreted as a warning against the use of religious pictures.

Pictures of Jesus feature in a number of films. Particularly interesting is the way his image is represented in WOMEN IN LOVE. This movie is about the disastrous implications of a pact between Mami Water, her adept and a young woman called Sabina, who has been lured into a lesbian relationship with the former. There is a scene in which Sabina, after having been reprimanded by a born again taxi driver that she should follow Jesus, has a dream in which she sees the evil plans of the Mami Water adept, who strives to offer Sabina as a blood sacrifice. When she wakes up in despair, she looks at the picture of Jesus in her room and starts praying to him. Western classical-religious music underlies a close up of the picture, focusing on the clouds behind Jesus, zooming in on lightness and a kind of smoke. In this way the picture of Jesus is rendered increasingly ephemeral, making it seem as if the camera were to offer a glimpse of an absent presence. This particular use of the picture of Jesus is significantly different from its use in the BEAST WITHIN, where the prayers were directed at the picture itself. The use of the picture of Jesus in WOMEN IN LOVE suggests the ultimate impossibility of depicting Jesus, the camera here being introduced as a device able to transcend the materiality of the picture as such and to invoke his presence irrespective of a medium.



It is also important to recall that this scene comes after Sabina's dream. The true power of Jesus, the movie suggests, lies in the fact that he is able to provide a kind of revelatory vision, that will protect a person from danger. In so doing, the movie links up with the popular understanding, much stressed in Pentecostal circles, that Jesus is able to offer believers what is also called the Spirit of Discernment or – in more traditional parlance – a second pair of eyes. Many movies have scenes with God-sent dreams, in which believers are made to see what is ahead of them. But also films as a whole, by offering spectators the privileged perspective of the eye of God, can be understood as offering to audiences a superior vision – or 'super-vision' – that makes it possible to peep behind the surface of mere appearance, beyond the mere 'physical' right into 'the spiritual'. Interestingly, in popular understanding the power to look into the realm that is invisible to the naked eye is likened to the medium of film. I was often told that both God and Satan would observe human beings with cameras that could look into people's deepest and darkest secrets and that would produce films of people's lives. To invoke the actress who told me about the danger of pictures once again: "The Devil and his demons are very smart, they have pictures of all of us and see us, because they have still the power they had as angels. And they can see, they will always try to get those who are born again and not too strong, they work on them, not on nominal Christians [i.e. people who have once been baptized but never attend church], because they belong to them already." While being observed by the Devil, as the fear of the picture looking back suggests, is to be avoided because objects of his gaze are supposed to be under his power, being observed by God is regarded as desirable. For in this way God can keep an eye on his followers, and protect them in time of need.

Being observed by God is not simply a matter of divine control, but also empowers believers by offering them a kind of super-vision, through which they are able to transcend the limitations of the eye, and achieve a religious way of seeing.[27] This, of course, comes at the cost of the awareness of being always observed and totally transparent – reminiscent of Foucault's panoptical view –, and hence obliged to confirm to Christian discipline. At the same time, as intimated above, the mass orientation of Pentecostal-Charismatic Christianity makes individual believers' control by pastors virtually impossible. The point is that Pentecostal believers have more or less internalized the idea of being watched by both God and Satan. They know that divine protection against demonic attacks ultimately depends not only on being seen by God, but also on attempting to lead a Christian way of life that would please him. In this sense, the mass approach instigated by Pentecostal-Charismatic Christianity heavily appeals to individual conscience and self-discipline.

By and large, Ghanaian – and as far as I can see Nigerian – movies, place much more emphasis on showing divine power at work than on depicting divinity *per se*. The most remarkable action kicking off the operation of divine power is the magical outcry "Jesus!" in times of utmost despair. In the language of video-films, as well as in popular Christianity, this is a sure device for divine intervention. The power attributed to this outcry is backed by the conviction, popularized in churches and popular newspapers, that demonic powers cannot stand to hear the name of Jesus, on the one hand, and that Jesus when called in sincerity will not let down a faithful person and chase demonic forces away instantly, on the other. The most spectacular scene I ever saw is the last scene of the Nigerian-Ghanaian movie TIME (2000), where a young, born-again woman who is bound to be sacrificed in a shrine in the bush, calls out Jesus' name, quietly first, and increasingly loud and desperate. From nowhere a string of fire appears, freeing the girl who has been tied to a pole, and making the whole shrine and its priest perish in flames. The fire here is a hot, violent and cleansing force that, in Pentecostal circles, is associated with the Holy Spirit. Watching this scene and similar ones, spectators would rejoice and stress the power of God to make this spectacular event happen. Remediating popular Christian ideas about the power of the name of Jesus and the Holy Spirit fire, movies visualize these ideas in the framework of spectacle.



27 See Birgit Meyer, Impossible Representations. Pentecostalism, Vision and Video Technology in Ghana, in *Religion, Media and the Public Sphere*, 290–312, where I explore Morgan's suggestion to understand 'looking' as a religious practice (David Morgan, *Visual Piety*, 8).

If the divine does hardly appear as such, movies deliberately picture demonic forces, including bloodthirsty witches, erotic Mami Waters, and mean African bush spirits who involve their followers in dangerous pacts that ultimately destroy them, but only after having harmed more or less innocent people. On the one hand, the inspiration to depict such demonic forces comes right out of the practice of Pentecostal deliverance services and prayer camps, where demonic forces are expelled in a spectacular manner.[28] Common understanding has it that the Holy Spirit forces the demonic forces that possess a person – at times without him or her being aware of this – to manifest themselves. Having been present at many such occasions, I often noted that persons, once the Holy Spirit had been invoked, started to move in a strange manner, as if they were embodying another kind of being (for example, wriggling like a snake on the ground – taken to be a sign of possession by Mami Water). I was told that this performance also had a dimension that was hidden to the naked eye and only visible to those who had the Spirit of Discernment. Only those could see, 'spiritually' as it were, frogs being vomited, snakes leaving vaginas, and other unsettling manifestations. Being compelled to showing up in this way is considered the first and necessary step in the procedure of exorcising an evil spirit.  In other words, the power of the Holy Spirit, invoked by the Pentecostal pastor and his prayer warriors (i.e. staunch Christians assisting the pastor in the spiritual war), forces demonic spirits to reveal themselves, albeit spiritually. This, of course, enhances the power of those blessed with the Spirit of Discernment which enables them to look into 'the spiritual'. While the Holy Spirit forces demonic spirits to make themselves visible, it also offers the faculty of divine vision to staunch born-again Christians.

Video-films partake in the endeavor of rendering demonic forces visible. What I find particularly interesting here is the role of the image in depicting demonic forces. Whereas, by and large, it is considered ultimately impossible to capture the divine in a picture or moving image – the point rather being to mimic divine vision power with the help of the camera – demonic forces are supposed to be fought through the very act of depiction. Rendering these forces visible is regarded as a necessary step in the spiritual war against them. In contrast to the Pentecostal prayer sessions, in which the power to witness what happens in 'the spiritual' is not available to everybody, movies put film technology in the service of the faculty of divine vision, the spirit of discernment. Making demonic forces appear and showing their capacity to change shapes and perform magic,

28 Therefore filmmakers, certainly in Nigeria, visit such deliverance session so as to get ideas for films. A Nigerian scholar studying a Christian church told me that at his first visit to the church he was asked whether he was a filmmaker. This exemplifies the extent to which at least Nigerian pastors are aware of the fact that their practice of fighting demons is a key resource for video-films.

movies remediate Pentecostal modes of fighting the demonic in such a way that they become accessible to all viewers. Certainly in the beginning of the video era, this was one of the main selling points.

As intimated already, the depiction of local religious traditions has been a point of considerable debate between state representatives, intellectuals and GFIC people on the one hand, and independent video-filmmakers on the other. Far from striving for adequate depictions of local gods,[29] the latter from the outset decided to visualize popular imaginations of traditional religion. Following up on the diabolization of local religious traditions that characterizes popular Christianity – successfully incorporated by Pentecostalism – video-filmmakers inscribe their movies into a Christian perspective on the world. They listen well to the spectacular stories of conversion that come out of Pentecostal-Charismatic churches and produce imaged supplements. What is at stake here is not a truthful representation of traditional religion, but the authorization, in the name of Pentecostalism, of the visualized demonic forces as truthful. As some sales women whom I interviewed in the street, and who stressed the importance of films showing that 'God always wins', put it: "Films have to teach, also about *juju*. They teach us about the evil forces that try to bring us down. In this country, when you want to progress and grow, some people will not like it, so they do something against you. Films show how this all works, so you can do something about it." With this statement they did not only recognize the usefulness of films to enlighten viewers about evil forces, but by implication authorized these depictions as true.



## 3.3 Blurred Boundaries

The closeness of the video scene and popular Pentecostal Christianity that I sought to highlight through the notion of remediation also figures in the perceived blurring of boundaries between film and everyday life. This is a central topos in the world of video-filmmaking. I heard numerous accounts, proudly told over and over again, of lead actors being addressed by viewers in town in terms of the role they played – the actor playing the snake man (Bob Smith) invoking fear and frenzy wherever he went in the heydays of the film, the recurrent film pastor (Eddie Coffee) being approached by people in the street for offering moral support, and the actress playing a witch (Edinam Atatsi) being scolded by children in her own church for being evil. Similarly, video-filmmakers recounted with much pleasure how people took for real their computer-produced special effects, which took a substantial part of the budget and were the film's

29 Whether it is possible at all to produce adequate film images of local religious practices is a matter of debate. Elsewhere I discuss traditional representatives' assertion that such forces refuse to be photographed or filmed, Birgit Meyer, Mediating Tradition, 291–195.

key attraction points. Filmmaker Socrate Safo told me how he listened to a radio program about witchcraft, in which people phoning in referred to Ghanaian films so as to prove that Satan truly exists and to explain how witchcraft works. Although filmmakers tend to be bemused about ordinary people's inclination to believe what is deliberately construed as make believe, there is more at stake than the assertion of a neat distinction between false beliefs about occult forces and true knowledge about film technology, or of the idea that the latter will eventually replace the former. Actually, as I experienced over and over again, video-filmmaking is situated betwixt and between the technologically facilitated representation of demonic forces and the fear that these representations become real – a kind of reality effect not confined to the film as a finished product, but also at work in making films.

The point is not simply that spectators would unmask the appearance of occult images as false once they were enlightened about the computer technology that made it possible to depict occult forces and magical powers. Filmmaker Michael Akwetey Kanyi recounted how an old acquaintance who had seen some of his films asserted: "you have occult powers!"How otherwise could he be able to show a person transform into somebody else, imprison miniature doubles of a bewitched person in a pot in the wardrobe, or let witches fly through the air on a carpet? While in this perspective a filmmaker is attributed with occult powers, a competing perspective views filmmakers as similar to pastors, in that they are found to have the power to look into the invisible – a capacity, as we saw, that is a prerequisite for claiming spiritual power (and in fact, power *tout court*). Rather than standing in opposition to spiritual power, technology is here called upon so as to affirm this power and make it materialize.



All in all, as in so many other settings, the explanation that extraordinary powers can be depicted thanks to computer-produced effects fails to disenchant these images and turn them into mere representations. Echoing Jacques Derrida's observation that "[t]he critique of televisual mystifications does not prevent them from operating, and from doing so in the form of the spectral noema of 'making present',"[30] here too spectators' knowledge that video-images of demonic forces are produced with the help of audio-visual technologies and special effects does not disenchant them. Instead, spectators are inclined – certainly if they identify as Christians – to authenticate these images as revelations of the invisible powers which hold such a central place in the popular imagination, and as a consequence, in Pentecostal Christianity. Knowledge about technological devices producing special effects and belief in the existence of demonic forces easily go hand in hand, or even appear to enforce each other. "Technology shows

30 Jacques Derrida, "Above All, No Journalists!", in *Religion and Media*, 87. See also Stolow, Religion and/as Media, 144.

what is there," would be a common remark. This reality effect occurs because video-films quite successfully appeal to audiences so as to authorize video-images as authentic. In short, film technology itself is considered not to stand in contrast to, but to be fully consonant with supernatural power. This pertains not only to video-films, but to the use of audiovisual technologies at large. Certainly in Pentecostal circles, as indicated above, one may notice a skilled and effective use of modern mass media, which are called upon so as to assert – and indeed produce – the pastor's charisma, or even his power to perform public miracles. TV and video are called upon so as to provide evidence for the truthfulness of spiritual power.[31]

Interestingly, the mediated images of demonic forces do not only have a kind of reality effect for spectators who are outside the context of film making and only see the finished product. Also on the set the visualizations of occult forces and the forces themselves were perceived to come uneasily close. The camera, and other devices, were viewed as technologies operating in accordance with an inbuilt logic, yet at the same time there was the belief that spirits or demonic forces are able to work on the camera, so as to stop it, or make it impossible to make certain shots. Actors, certainly if they were staunch Christians, were convinced of the necessity to depict the operations of demonic powers, and yet they felt incredibly vulnerable when doing so, and sought to protect themselves through prayers. Likewise, set designers felt insecure about setting up artificial shrines, since, according to the popular imagination, numerous spirits roam about in the sky, seeking suitable abodes to inhabit.[32] As Nina Nwabueze, a set designer from Nigeria working in Ghana put it: "Here the belief is still there that there are spirits in the sky. When you create an idol, they can get into the idol." This is reminiscent of the suspicion of the image pointed out above. Film-making, though defined by producing images, seems not beyond this suspicion. Paradoxically, movies are made to mimic Pentecostal vision as a power to make demonic forces appear, yet in the very process of mimicking, these powers may actually come true. Therefore, every day on set begins and ends with prayer.



## 4. Conclusion

As outlined in the introduction, this article has been devoted to exploring the interface of film and religion through an empirical study of the entanglement of video-films and Pentecostal Christianity in Ghana. Such a study, I claimed, requires a mobile kind of analysis that travels along the trajectories through which Pentecostal beliefs and practices are made subject to intense remediation in

31 Cf. Marleen de Witte, Mediating Charisma.

32 Cf. Birgit Meyer, Mediating Tradition.

video-films. While it is impossible to undertake a more detailed analysis of these trajectories in the confines of this article, at least the contours of the interface of Pentecostalism and video-films, and the dynamics of the transfer of Pentecostal mediation practices onto the screen, have become visible. For the sake of staying in the business, video-filmmakers mimic Pentecostal modes in such a way that audiences are inclined to authorize these visualizations as authentic. I have shown that in this setting, film is not confined to mere representation and the sphere of fake and illusion, but involves an unstable relationship between representing demonic forces and their actual presence. While practices of representation are understood to be separate from the actual presence of divine or demonic power, in the sense that video-films consciously create illusionary effects, audiences are by the same token addressed in such a way that they authorize these effects as technologically mediated revelations. Even though viewers often are aware of the technological processes through which special effects are made, this knowledge does not necessarily lead them to unmask video-films as unfounded illusions. And even actors, who know the ins and outs of film production, are prone to assume that initially empty technologies and props may easily be overtaken by the forces they seek to represent. Rather than merely representing the visible and invisible dimensions of reality, video-films embody reality, thereby breaking open the distinction between representation and presence, as well as that between media and immediacy or authenticity.



Video-movies' remediations of Pentecostal beliefs and practices give rise to what I propose to call a 'techno-religious realism'. This techno-religious realism, I would like to stress, does not merely derive from the power of films to "spontaneously appeal to his [the spectator's] sense of belief", their intrinsic capacity to "speak to us with the accents of true evidence, using the argument that 'It is so'," but above all from combining films' capacity to appear 'believable' with an appropriation of Pentecostal belief resources.[33] In video-films technologies of make believe and spectators' desire to believe in, and receive visual evidence for, the power of God easily go together. Pentecostal beliefs and technology act so much in support of each other that they become more or less indistinguishable. This being so, it is impossible to maintain a stable distinction between film and religion.

One of the most striking features of this techno-religious realism concerns the fact that video-movies' remediations of Pentecostal views do not so much claim to erase the medium and offer immediate access to the spiritual world out there in the dark. These remediations rather produce, to invoke Bolter and Grusin again, a kind of 'hypermediacy' that is generated by merging the me-

33 Cf. Christian Metz, *Film Language. A Semiotics of the Cinema*, New York: Oxford University Press, 1974, 4.

dium of video with practices of religious mediation. Audiovisual technologies are mingled ingeniously with the Pentecostal quest for divine vision and fear of being seen by the Devil (and the concomitant awareness of the tension between the need to depict the demonic so as to fight it and the potential danger of the image). This mingling suggests not only that these technologies are inalienable parts of Pentecostal mediation, but also that they are highly suited to be vested with spiritual power. Ultimately, this mingling breaks down the distinction between techniques of representation, on the one hand, and the presence of the powers depicted, on the other. This distinction is called upon, yet at the same time perceived to be transcended in the practice of video-filmmaking. By the same token video-filmmaking implodes the distinction between media and authenticity that characterizes, according to Bolter and Grusin, a naïve stance towards transcendent immediacy that views authenticity as a privileged origin situated beyond the sphere of media and remediation. By contrast, in the world of video-movies the authorization of film images as immediate and authentic depends on audiovisual technologies.

Obviously, this use of media for the sake of making appear a supposedly dark, invisible realm, and the concomitant transcendence of the rift between religion and technology implied by it, is not specific to the Ghanaian context. The techno-religious realism outlined here should therefore not be mistaken as an indication for the failure to understand the true nature of media technology as a neutral device. Instead, the particular use of media in the service of religious vision reveals an understanding that has much in common with postmodern practice and analysis. Far from more or less truthfully reflecting a world still held to exist out there, media are able to articulate a reality that features as convincingly true. Here immediacy is achieved not by virtue of the alleged absence of media, but instead is made to depend on them. The fact that media technologies are called upon to visualize the very religious views in the name of which these technologies are to be authorized as authentic, challenges all too simple views of religion and film, and urges us to devote far more attention to their interface than has been the case so far.

Charlotte Haines Lyon and Clive Marsh

# Film's Role in Contemporary Meaning-Making

## A Theological Challenge to Cultural Studies

### I

Stewart M. Hoover's *Religion in the Media Age* offers a major contribution to understanding the processes by which people in the contemporary west come to believe and behave as they do.[1] He studies the way in which use of a variety of media informs, shapes and expresses the values that people live by. 'Media' means a whole package of technologies and practices: TV, Internet, film, radio, CDs, DVDs. The reception-orientated 'culturalist' approach which Hoover adopts, however, puts the emphasis on the *use* of these technologies rather than the products they offer, i.e. upon the various practices within which the media 'texts', in the widest sense of the word, are consumed. 'Consumption' may or may not imply control of what people consume. Consumers/users certainly like to think that they are not being duped or manipulated (though inevitably they sometimes will be). Reception studies indicate, however, that no matter how much producers and texts appear to control or determine meaning, what receivers (readers, hearers, or viewers) do with texts matters more.[2] 

Hoover's collection and analysis of empirical data is inevitably limited. The data was gathered only from contemporary US citizens. Access to technology, local TV culture, and film-watching habits might differ across western nations.[3] Furthermore, his focus is largely on how consumers *think* they are making *religious* meaning.[4] Even if a main conclusion of his research is that the categories of 'religion' and 'media' are becoming rather fluid, he was not seeking to gather data from the anti-religious or explicitly non-religious. Nevertheless, his study provides ample evidence that the contemporary western form of 'the media age'

1 S.M. Hoover, *Religion in a Media Age*, London and New York: Routledge 2006.

2 Hoover, *Religion*, 41, 86, and 275–6, and esp. 175 and 203.

3 Not to mention the diversity which would result if the net were cast wider, to include non-western films, as received in and beyond western nations.

4 He does, however, develop his thesis around the concept of 'plausible narratives of the self', which is not in itself necessarily tied to a religious framework of thought.

highlights the broad, but nuanced – and often hidden – complexity of the way that people, religious or not, make meaning with respect to the diversity of media technologies available to them. The evidence of the use of media, and the fluidity of the categories of religion and media which results, therefore means that the form of meaning-making is not different in kind for the so-called 'religious' in western society in comparison with those who profess not to be religious. The way in which explicitly theological resources or reflection feature within common patterns of meaning-making thus needs to be explored within these general patterns. As a *practice*, contemporary theology – undertaken within, or with respect to, any religious tradition – will not, then, be able to see itself simply as the acquisition of a tradition (body of knowledge), or as an ideology /philosophy/worldview teased out from a relatively detached set of religious practices. If theology could ever have viewed its work in this way, those days are now long gone. Theology has to find and work with its subject-matter in the midst of a complex and ever-changing range of media and cultural practices, in which meaning is sought and found, or found and reflected upon, and in the knowledge that religions are, and always will be, part of human culture.[5]

What, though, is 'meaning-making'? Is the very phrase, when used by a scholar of religion or a theologian or philosopher, so loaded from the outset that more of a pattern is assumed in human life than may be possible for people to see or construct in everyday life? Full exploration of the term lies beyond the scope of this essay. For practical purposes, we are side-stepping the important question whether meaning is 'discovered' or 'constructed'. Elements of both are likely to be involved in all meaning-making. People use 'givens', and inherit (and perpetuate) assumptions about what to believe, think and do, as well as making choices. But where the emphasis lies, and what ontological implications result from where the emphasis is put, cannot be gone into here. It is nevertheless clear that 'meaning-making' is both a hidden, implicit and an explicit, purposeful activity, and that cultural consumption is part of the way in which people participate in the task. Hoover attaches great significance to the construction of the narrative self as a primary act of meaning-making. This is certainly a crucial part of the contemporary form which meaning-making takes in the west. How people narrate who they are and the values they live by, and the extent to which they do this in interaction with forms of media and popular culture, invite scrutiny not merely for the sake of sheer interest. People's structuring of their lives, and the shaping of their life-practices (e.g. how they earn and spend money, how they use natural resources, how they conduct their personal relationships,



5 See, for example, the beginnings of such study in the work of G. Lynch, *Understanding Theology and Popular Culture*, Oxford: Blackwell 2004, and K. Cobb, *The Blackwell Guide to Theology and Popular Culture*, Oxford: Blackwell 2005.

how they spend their leisure time, whether and how they value family ties) are all informed, and worked out, in conversation with the texts and practices of popular culture. This is what, for the purposes of this essay, is meant by 'meaning-making'. Meaning-making is thus best understood as a set of practices in and through which, consciously and unconsciously, human beings 'make sense' of themselves and their world. In the context of the consumption of multiple forms of media, it thus becomes clear that the use of popular culture takes on an increasingly religion-like form.

This essay has a simple purpose: to provide further confirmation of the essential accuracy of Hoover's thesis, drawing on UK data, and to draw out the consequences for theology in the light of the definition of meaning-making just offered. The data to be explored in Part II were gathered by Charlotte Haines Lyon in the summer of 2004, with the co-operation of the Ster cinema chain, from a group of 47 cinema-goers who had agreed to log their film-watching over a three-month period. The participants came from a variety of ethnic backgrounds, included 20 men and 27 women and were almost all in the 20–40 age-range. Each participant provided, on a set of forms which they filled in, details of their personal circumstances and life-style, feedback on four to eight films watched at the cinema during the research period, and a final reflection on the record-keeping process (see the Appendix to this essay). In addition to supplying evidence to enable exploration of Hoover's thesis, the findings provide data contributing to the expanding field of 'reception studies' in film studies, and to the growing call in theology and religious studies that attention be given to empirical material when film is used.[6] As we shall go on to argue in Section III, when taken alongside the material gathered and conclusions drawn by Hoover, these findings issue a keen challenge to those working in the field of cultural and media studies. The place of religious traditions within the meaning-making occurring within the contemporary west, even for the so-called 'non-religious', is not to be ignored.



## II

During the research period the 47 participants engaged in a total of 280 film-viewings, watching 52 different films. The most popular films are detailed below:

6 In film studies, see especially the work of Martin Barker (*From Antz to Titanic: Reinventing Film Analysis*, Pluto Press 2000), who co-edits with Sue Turnbull *Participations*, an on-line journal "devoted to the strengthening and development of the fields of audience and reception studies". In the inter-disciplinary field of theology, religion and film studies, see especially Christopher Deacy's call that the responses of ordinary viewers (as, for example, recorded on Internet film web-sites) be taken more into account (*Faith in Film*, Aldershot and Burlington, VT: Ashgate 2005).

| *Film* | *Viewers* | *% of total* |
|---|---|---|
| HARRY POTTER 3 (Cuarón, UK/USA 2004) | 28 | 59.57 |
| SHREK 2 (Adamson/Ashbury, USA 2004) | 24 | 51.06 |
| THE DAY AFTER TOMORROW (Emmerich, USA 2004) | 23 | 48.94 |
| TROY (Petersen, USA/Malta/UK 2004) | 23 | 48.94 |
| KILL BILL 2 (Tarantino, USA 2004) | 22 | 46.81 |
| VAN HELSING (Sommers, USA/ Czech Republic 2004) | 19 | 40.43 |
| ETERNAL SUNSHINE OF THE SPOTLESS MIND (Gondry, USA 2004) | 15 | 31.39 |
| MONSTER (Jenkins, USA/D 2003) | 10 | 21.28 |
| SPIDERMAN 2 (Raimi, USA 2004) | 9 | 19.15 |



The UK Box Office Archives page on the UK Film Council web-site shows that all of the films in the chart above were in the top 10 viewed films for an average of five weeks each during the research period. [7]

For the purposes of this essay, we have focussed on the responses to THE DAY AFTER TOMORROW and one of the two 'children's films' at the top of the list, SHREK 2. THE DAY AFTER TOMORROW, a film about the possible effects of climate change, seemed an obvious candidate for exploring meaning-making as undertaken by viewers. Some of the responses contain apparent contradictions, however, and we have therefore chosen to explore them further. SHREK 2 could easily be dismissed as 'mere entertainment'. But some of the responses to this film show how even seemingly light stories are used and proved fruitful in what may be called 'everyday reflection'. In our analysis of the written responses, we have sought to draw out some common threads which indicate how the films' content and effects upon viewers are being 'processed'. Our argument is that whatever the stated purpose for viewing such films, the processing which occurs

7 http://www.ukfilmcouncil.org.uk/. HARRY POTTER 3 was in the top 10 for 9 weeks, DAY AFTER TOMORROW, TROY and KILL BILL 2 for 8 weeks, VAN HELSING for 7 weeks, ETERNAL SUNSHINE OF THE SPOTLESS MIND, SHREK 2 and SPIDERMAN 2, for 4 weeks, and MONSTER for 2 weeks. Whilst SHREK 2 was not in the top 10 for as long as other films it is in the all-time top 10 box office films according to the BFI http://www.bfi.org.uk/filmtvinfo/stats/boxoffice/10films.html.

for viewers (cognitive and affective) at the very least contributes to, and may for some be a main locus of, the meaning-making which occurs in viewers' lives.

We note, however, that despite the evidence of this 'processing', viewers were surprisingly reluctant or unable to recognise or 'own up' to the fact of its occurrence, when asked about the process in more abstract terms. The concluding question of the second questionnaire (completed for each viewing) read: "What ways if any, did this film connect with your life?" 61% of the total of 280 responses reported no connection and 39% reported some form of connection. In the case of the two films studied in more detail, it was just as stark: 19 out of 24 reported "no connection" in response to SHREK 2. In response to THE DAY AFTER TOMORROW, not surprisingly, the lack of connection was less than the average. But even here, 10 out of 24 reported "no connection" despite the fact that it "made people think" and other answers people gave contradicted the basic response given.

The question was deliberately left as open as possible, so that the term 'connection' could be interpreted in a wide variety of ways. Providing examples of types of connection was ruled out lest it distort the responses given. The aim of this question was to provide respondents with the broadest possible space in which to describe how they considered their film-viewing habits to inform (or not inform) the rest of their lives. Our pilot studies had shown that people could sometimes see (and articulate) how they had engaged with a film, but at other times had engaged (and been affected) without fully realizing it. We therefore had to tease out as much as possible from viewers as to what was happening to them.



It is admittedly possible that there was confusion with the word 'connection'. In the case of THE DAY AFTER TOMORROW, fourteen people reported that they thought the film's theme of global warming connected to their lives. A further five people said elsewhere in the questionnaire that the film had made them think about global warming but then said there was no connection between the film and their life. Did they really think that global warming had no connection with their life or did they have a different understanding of 'connection'? Without follow-up interviews with these respondents it is difficult to know. It is, however, clear that the film did not just entertain. In response to Question 13 ("What themes or issues, if any, did the film make you think about?"), for example, Respondent 1 reported no connection but said, "It made me think about the end of the world, ice caps melting – global warming. Frailty of humanity vs. power of nature."

If film-watching does prompt meaning-making, though, we must show from our small scale survey in what ways this occurs. For ease, we have grouped the types of meaning making evidence in viewer responses to THE DAY AFTER TO-

MORROW and SHREK 2 under four headings: education, inspiration, values and morality, and 'what if?' scenarios.

## Education

Ten respondents expressed concern that "this could happen" when watching THE DAY AFTER TOMORROW, although some questioned whether the cataclysm would occur with the speed shown in the film. Some seemed shocked by what they had seen. Respondent 23 wrote "We are just one melted block of ice away from oblivion." At root, however, the film proved if not informative in a direct way, then eye-opening in so far as it encouraged viewers to consider further something they may not have wanted to face head-on. At the same time, there was concern about the lack of realism in the film. Respondent 8 was struck by the fact "that Hollywood have [sic] the ability to alter people's perceptions quite drastically. Some friends of mine have subconsciously believed that a rapid ice age is possible without actually looking into the science." Such a film thus informs and stimulates learning. But the power of film as a medium can mislead by being accepted as 'true' in all respects.



One response to SHREK 2 was especially instructive with regard to the educational potential of film-watching. Having noted how the film enabled reflection on personal relationships, Respondent 37 commented: "this is only because I am thinking I have to think something, not that I would ordinarily think that if I had not been asked a question about it!" In other words, a dimension was added to the film-watching experience by the very act of being asked to respond.

Film's educational role is, then, not necessarily linked simply or directly to what a film contains. A reflective prompt may be needed, and this may take a viewer well beyond what a film has shown or how it has impacted upon the viewer. But a reflection process can begin, which exists in continuity or in contrast with a film's impact. Rather than being imposed, it can be seen simply as an aspect of the way that films work.

## Inspiration

THE DAY AFTER TOMORROW led to responses concerned with environmental action. Respondent 25 commented: "[…] it made me think how little things can make a difference." Another Respondent (32) had become "slightly more environmentally conscious." Respondent 26 remarked: "Made me think about being more environmentally friendly" whilst Respondent 1 found the film "kind of uplifting" due to the fact that there are survivors of the natural disaster.

Admittedly, the film is also hampered in its effects by its unreality. It "wasn't as sad as it should have been. Millions died, but there was little mourning"

(Respondent 1). Respondent 17 "couldn't take the film seriously," as it has "a ridiculous far-fetched plot combined with a weak script and far too many American flags."

Despite these shortcomings, and even beyond its environmental concerns, however, the film proved inspirational. Five people said the film made them think about human nature. In answer to the question "Is there anything about the film that has stuck with you?," Respondent 6 wrote not only "Environmental issues of our age" but also "Human nature – how it can bring the best out of people in tough situations. Bravery – of boys who went to retrieve penicillin for girl." Respondent 17 wrote: "One of the men who goes on the expedition and sacrifices his life for that of his companions. Although the film does not dwell on it much, it is one of the few poignant and genuine moments in the film [... I was] full of awe and respect for his noble action."

Respondents were less forthcoming about the extent to which SHREK 2 was informing or inspiring them or making them think. More precisely, they seemed reluctant to admit that a children's film could be much more than "mere entertainment." Many of those who said there was no connection between the film and their life, however, added a qualifying statement. For example, Respondent 21 added: "But it brought some sunshine to my day!" Respondent 9 commented: "I saw some friends I haven't seen for a while." The fact of watching a film in public rather than private thus enabled a different kind of response about (re)connectedness than the question about 'connection' with the viewer had expected.



## Values and Morality

Similar reservations about the extent to which a children's film stimulated thinking amongst adult viewers is evident with respect to the ethical reflection provoked by SHREK 2. Respondent 37 felt there was no connection with their life, yet had already stated: "[...] things can try and get in the way of your relationship, but if it is strong enough then you will get through it." Such a statement seems, at the very least, to show how films can confirm hard-won experience. Respondent 36, by contrast, concluded the following as the connecting point with their life: "Struggles of love-life – the eternal problem."

Several viewers said that SHREK 2 carried a message that looks can be deceiving and also that we should be happy with who we are. Some went further in saying that "Love wins always, you should never try to change a person or change yourself, true love is when you respect and care for the person for who and what they are not what they could be" (Respondent 4).

This is admittedly scarcely world-shattering stuff. If one is looking for fresh, mind-stretching philosophy, then it will not be found here. But that is not the point of our exercise. Nor was it presumably the purpose of either of the films being considered. We note simply, under this third heading, that in the context of a leisure practice simple insights about behaviour and the rationale for that behaviour are brought to light and are confirmed, or re-examined in the process. This occurs in a way that may not be happening elsewhere in people's lives.

Ethical reflection was also stimulated in a further way: through viewers saying that a film had made them think about how dreadful a lifestyle or type of behaviour was and that it had no place in their lives. Although most such examples were found in other films such as CAPTURING THE FRIEDMANS (Jarecki, USA 2003) and THE STEPFORD WIVES (Oz, USA 2004), THE DAY AFTER TOMORROW elicited three interesting responses of this kind. All three expressed frustration, even anger, that the film depicted the United States saving the world or being invincible. Whilst this could easily be tangled up with British anti-Americanism, it could also be interpreted as political reflection during a world climate where the United States were involved in some unpopular wars and under criticism for their refusal to sign the Kyoto agreement.[8] Respondent 23 wrote: "Global warming affects everyone (except the US government!)."



## 'What if?' Scenarios

Finally, it also appears that films provide a space for viewers to think in a safe environment about 'what if?' scenarios. After watching THE DAY AFTER TOMORROW Respondent 25 asked: "How would I cope in such a situation? How would I have helped my loved ones to survive?" We are dealing here, then, with the way in which the imagination is stimulated and used to enable viewers to reflect on life-situations which may or may not happen in order to prepare themselves for similar, if less drastic, life-situations. In the case of THE DAY AFTER TOMORROW, as with any disaster movie, the viewer is being encouraged to anticipate, cognitively and affectively, how they might deal with an extreme situation. Other films viewed within the research project, e.g. KILL BILL 2 and PIECES OF APRIL (Hedges, USA 2003) offer further examples of this type of meaning-making.

8 The Kyoto Treaty drawn up in Japan in 1997 commits industrialised countries to reduce their carbon emissions by 5.2% of their 1990 levels in the next decade. To succeed, the agreement had to be ratified by the countries responsible for 55% of the 1990 carbon emissions. This was rendered largely impossible by President George W. Bush's refusal to sign the agreement in 2001, despite the US producing 36% of carbon emissions in 1990. Nevertheless the Kyoto Protocol was finally ratified by 146 countries and came into effect on February 16, 2005.

## III

What is to be made of all of this? One possible response is that it tells us nothing new. This recent empirical data merely confirms what has been long known about art and popular culture: they help people live. 'Art' is commonly thought to stretch people more (and stimulate and educate more intelligently). 'Popular culture' is assumed to be less taxing, more time-filling and relaxing, even if it might serve a useful purpose. Here is not the place for any debate on this, nor even on whether films – at least those considered here – are always both art and popular culture. It is the observations about *how* such films actually help people live that demands most attention. Three comments are needed in conclusion.

First, despite the evidence that education, inspiration, ethical reflection and anticipation of new life-experiences may be occurring in the cinema, this is clearly not people's primary, stated purpose for going. As the responses to the third questionnaire in the research indicate, when asked in more abstract terms (i.e. detached from being asked to articulate what happens to them during and immediately after a film), viewers are much more likely to use words such as "escape" or "escapism" (25%),"entertainment" (25%), "enjoyment", "fantasy", or "fun" as their main reason for going. Viewers may have been prompted by seeing a trailer for going to particular films, and some viewers clearly are expecting to engage in a rich emotional and aesthetic experience. But enjoyment is prominent. There is even hostility to the thought that people might be going for anything else. The notion that anyone's thought might be being 'controlled', or that education would be a primary purpose, was strongly resisted both when the research was set up and in some of the responses.[9]



This is confirmed even within the feedback on the specific films studied, especially SHREK 2. Despite all the evidence of what was actually happening within, for and to the viewers whilst and after watching the films on which they commented, there remained a reluctance to declare that these did anything more than entertain. Respondent 30 stated clearly: "This was excellent escapist fare as it is highly funny and being computer generated, I think, as a viewer you do not particularly identify with the computer-animated characters. This was a film which I enjoyed as a film without dwelling much further on it." Respondent 17 commented: "It didn't [i.e. connect with life] – it was far too light hearted and fantasy based." And yet both respondents indicated very directly the extent of how good it had made them feel. Each, in fact, was able to reflect on the fact

9 See Clive Marsh's chapter, On dealing with what films actually do to people: The practice and theory of film-watching in theology/religion and film discussion, in R.K. Johnston (ed.), *Re-Framing Theology and Film*, Grand Rapids: Baker Academic 2007. It should also be stressed that 'enjoyment' and 'education' must not be polarized here!

that, as a feelgood movie, it had refreshed and relaxed them. Respondent 30, for example, experienced "no 'negative' emotions" during the film.

One possible conclusion from all of this, then, is that the mismatch between what are commonly the main intentions of the cinema-goer and the *de facto* function of film-watching deserve closer scrutiny. It is clear that claims of cinema's 'religion-like' role in society may be too simply made by a scholar of religion. But it is possible for cultural and media studies to overlook the religion-likeness of the film-watching experience, as evident from what actually happens in the cinema. It is also possible to overplay *assumptions* about the escapist element in film and the fact that, when pressed, many cinema-goers themselves state that escapism is all they go for. All one has to do, however, is ask what a specific film did *to* and *for* a person to disclose that much of great significance happens in the cinema, and that cinema-goers usually know that this is the case.

There may, however, not be many places where a space is created in which emotional exploration and ethical reflection occur in response to such aesthetic experience (and without it being too 'hard work' in the process). There are, in other words, few prompts or opportunities to 'think further' in the manner required by this research project. But these processes are the very substance of what religions, philosophy, spirituality and ethics address. The religion scholar must press the important question: even if people don't 'do' organized religion very much in the west (though that over-simple assumption must itself be increasingly challenged), it still has to be recognised that what religions 'do' surfaces in other forms throughout culture. The cinema is clearly one such form.



A second comment on the findings of Part II concerns the intriguing way in which respondents dealt with their responses to SHREK 2.[10] We suggest that the nervousness shown in admitting to be stimulated to reflect by a 'children's film' raises important questions about primary narratives within a culture with which children and adults can both engage. As recently as fifty years ago (and before that for most of the previous two millennia) it could probably be argued that biblical texts supplied a basic narrative currency which people could use to speak of beliefs and ideals in the west. With the passing of Christendom, the Christian currency has gone. But the need for some common texts remains. Furthermore, the need for texts which both children and adults might be able to access, if in different ways, remains. 'Noah's Ark' has always had the capacity to function on multiple levels, but children's picture-books have not usually handled the bit of the story which tells of the destruction of most of humanity. The popularity, then, amongst adults as well as children, of SHREK (Adamson/

10 E.g. Respondent 17 said: "[...] I felt the more 'serious' themes of the film were really meant for children." Similarly, Respondent 9 commented: "The issue of personality over beauty is there, but whether kids today take it on board is another thing."

Jenson, USA 2001), SHREK 2, of the Harry Potter books and films, or of Philip Pullman's novels may, then, be less a matter of the infantilism of culture than of the recognition that cultures need common narratives, accessible across ages. The void left by the Bible's increasing absence may not again be filled by the Bible, but will still need filling.

Third, a number of points should be made about the extent to which cinema-going is, or is not, a communal experience. Hoover makes the telling point that his research indicates that a shift is underway from institutions and social contexts to individual quests.[11] This is surely accurate. A cinema is a community in the weakest sense of the term. People share a common experience. But there is no commitment between those who are gathered beyond their brief time together. As an experience occurring within the 'media age' described by Hoover, individuals are choosing to participate in the practice of cinema-going as individuals. It is one more experience, one more accessing of part of the media package, amongst many.

But a further slant is needed on the cinema experience, suggested by the empirical data presented in Part II. That is the question of communities that cinemagoers *do* relate to, in the ways that they process their film-watching experiences. Though it may be true that there is a shift from institutions to individuals in the way that meaning-making happens, it is not true that institutions disappear off the scene altogether. Moral communities, and life-shaping narratives, still carry authority for individuals. How could it be otherwise? Individuals do not invent new philosophies on a daily basis. Every case of the confirmation of values or every prompt to re-assess a firmly-held conviction which occurs in the context of film-watching relates an individual to a value-system and to a moral community to which s/he attaches significance.



This is a point which religion scholars are especially able to perceive and explore. For the study of religion highlights the way that moral reasoning is not simply a matter of cognitive reflection. Beliefs, life in community and the cultivation of virtues and dispositions all play their part in the development of thought about action. Furthermore, through their ritual practices, religions show how narratives play a role within people's development. Whether or not people are religious, narratives are still 'lived within'. Religions simply make more explicit, through their linkage to a theological belief system, the narratives which devotees of a particular religion inhabit.

11 Hoover, *Religion in a Media Age*, 52.

12 See, for example, John Walsh's reflections on his early film-watching years in *Are You Talking to Me?: A Life Through the Movies*, London: HarperCollins 2003 (paperback; HarperPerennial 2004).

Film-watching merely confirms the importance of narrative for human development and the cultivation of moral reasoning. Films supply stories for people to live within, either very temporarily or, if particular films prove influential, over a lifetime.[12] But because the practice of regular cinema-going exposes a viewer to a disparate, wide range of narratives, cinema-going itself does not necessarily provide a single, coherent narrative. 'Narrative unity' or 'moral coherence', if they occur for the individual, would be related elsewhere (e.g. to a social class, to a family background, to a political stance, to an ethnic identity, or, of course, to a religious community). In practice, a narrative self, and a personal identity, draws on multiple communities. Our point is that despite the accuracy of Hoover's insight – individuals are calling the shots in a media age – it is mistaken to overlook how individuals relate to the communities of which they remain a part.

For religious (and by extension, theological) reflection on film, therefore, it is crucial for interpreters of cinema-going to show how theological narratives are accessed by individual film-watchers. Furthermore, in media and cultural studies analyses of film, it is vital that religious communities are recognised as part of the rich complexity of life-shaping, narrative-carrying moral communities within which, and with respect to which, film-watching happens. Without such recognition, full respect for what films *are actually doing* in society will simply not occur.



## Appendix

The three questionnaires used in the research undertaken by Charlotte Haines Lyon in the Summer of 2004 gathered data as follows:

*Questionnaire 1* was used to gather personal information about each respondent, using the following categories and questions.

| | |
|---|---|
| Age | Gender |
| Ethnic origin | Occupation |
| Relationship status | Whether a parent |
| Number of people in house | Annual income |
| Highest qualification | Place of work |
| Type of location of home (e.g. city, town, village) | Location of cinemas visited (e.g. vis-à-vis home, work) |
| Number of different cinemas visited regularly | Frequency of cinema-visits |

Whether going to the cinema alone or accompanied (and if latter, who with?)
Frequency of watching films at home on DVD and/or video
Whether a subscriber to film magazines
Whether a subscriber to film channels via cable or satellite
Whether a purchaser of film-viewings via cable or satellite
Types of films enjoyed
5 favourite films watched during 2003
Most important factors when choosing a film to watch

*Questionnaire 2* was completed for each film watched, and used these questions:

1) Date
2) Name of film watched
3) At which cinema did you watch the film?
4) Approximately how many screens does this cinema have?
5) Why did you go and see this particular film?
6) Please state whether you watched the film alone, or who you were with and the nature of your relationship with them, e.g. '5 friends and partner'.
7) What did you do after the film e.g., 'go for a meal', 'go home with friends', 'go shopping'.
8) Did you discuss the film with anybody afterwards? What was the nature of the discussion?
9) What are the first reactions, thoughts, words or pictures that come to mind when you think about this film?
10) Is there anything about the film that has stuck with you?
11) Were there any characters that particularly affected you? If so please say why.
12) Were you aware of any emotions or physical feelings during the film or immediately after it? If so please describe.
13) What themes or issues, if any, did the film make you think about?
14) What ways if any, did this film connect with your life?



*Questionnaire 3* enabled each respondent to reflect on the whole process, using the following questions:

1) How have you found this process of keeping film diaries?
2) Have you changed the way you think about films that you go and watch?
3) To what extent, and in what ways, did you think and/or reflect on films before you joined this project?
4) Do you consider that films affect your life? Please state why you think they do or don't.
5) Would the answer to the above question have been any different before you became involved with the project? If yes please state why.
6) Do you think that films ever help you think about life's big questions? If so please say what kind of questions.

Michael Hölzl

# "One God – One King"

## Political Theology in Sergej Eisenstein's ALEXANDER NEWSKI

Three years after Vladimir Illych Lenin died, Vladimir Mayakovsky wrote a poem for his friend and colleague Sergei Jessenin who committed suicide in 1926 by drinking himself almost to death and finally cutting his wrists. Mayakovsky wrote this poem in honour of Jessenin, paraphrasing one of Jessenin's own lines. The poem ends with:

> "Dying
> in this life
> is not so hard,
> building life
> is harder,
> I daresay."[1]



At this point, the *avant-garde*, to which Sergeij Eisenstein, his mentor Vsevolod Meyerhold, the Noble Laureate of literature Boris Pasternak, Kazimir Malevich and, to a certain extent, Anna Achmatowa, belonged, must have realised that under Stalin the dream of a better world following the revolution had definitively become an illusion. In 1939, Mayakovsky, promoter and then the foremost poetic defender of the new order, whose reputation like Eisenstein's, had even spread across the Atlantic, became its victim. In April of that year, like so many others, Vladimir Mayakovsky chose to put an end to his life. For the *intelligenzia* the situation seemed to be hopeless and their ambitions, betrayed.

Unsurprisingly, Eisenstein's film shot during this period, ALEXANDER NEWSKI, is therefore viewed by the majority of commentators as a way out of his personal misery, and as a guarantee to his future career – even his physical survival[2] – by abiding to the Stalinist rule of force. Clearly, ALEXANDER NEWSKI is a piece of propaganda, hailing Stalin and demonising the Germans on the eve of the Second World War. Eisenstein did not produce many films and among

1 Mayakovsky, V. *Selected Verses*. Vol. 1. Union of Soviet Socialist Republics: Raduga Publishers, 1985, 171. Jesenin's lines are: "Dying in this life is not so new, yet living, certainly, is not much newer." Ibid., 277.

2 Eisenstein, S. *Jenseits der Einstellung*. Lenz Felix and Diedrichs, Helmut, H. (eds.). Frankfurt: Suhrkamp 2006, 437.

those which he produced, ALEXANDER NEWSKI is usually glossed over by critics[3] as a step between BATTLESHIP POTEMKIN (1925) and his unfinished trilogy IVAN THE TERRIBLE (1944–46). The instability of the political system at that time is reflected in the fate of the film. Shot in 1937 in collaboration with the famous Sergej Prokofiev as its music composer, the film was banned in the Soviet Union following the Hitler-Stalin pact in August 1939, and then glorified and screened all over the Soviet Union after the war had entered its final phase, due to Adolf Hitler's attack on Russia in June 1941.

The plot of ALEXANDER NEWSKI follows a simple, straightforward, and very effective line of narration. Alexander, a 13th century prince, is asked by the nobility to defeat the threats of the German Order of the Temple. According to Felix Lenz, the editor of a recent collection of Eisenstein's theoretical writings in German, it is a cinematographic story, "to make the Russian people ready for war."[4] This interpretation already explains why the climax, musically and cinematographically, occurs at the end of the film: the battle on the ice-covered lake of Chudskoye when the Russian forces defeat the Germans. Eisenstein portrays the victory through a look behind the scenes at war planning.



It is Prince Alexander's genius to employ an old battle strategy, invented by Hannibal, as it is reported in Livy's *History of Rome from its Foundation*. The story reported in Livy – the battle at Cannae fought in 216 BCE at Lake Trasimene – is not only a milestone in Roman history but also an archetype of a battle where the inferior forces defeat the superior enemy by the wit, courage and prudence of their leader. The German Knights of the Temple, equipped with heavy armour and ferocious horses, outnumber the Russians just as the Romans outnumbered Hannibal's army at Cannae. Alexander Newski, i.e. 'Hannibal', leads the enemies into a trap. The outnumbered succeed because they count on the enemy's hubristic conviction of their physical strength. This turns out to be their fatal mistake. The stronger force underestimates the enemy. In the end the Germans are surrounded, trapped and defeated. In the film, Eisenstein portrays Prince Alexander as a second 'Hannibal' in his finest hour. In this battle, the commander Prince Alexander demonstrates his possession of the virtues of a true king. When Eisenstein translates this archetypical story of warfare into film, he composes an image, drawing on the formalism of the *Agit-Prop* art of that time.

The opening scene depicts the threat by the Germans and the decisive readiness of the Russians. The screen is white. At the bottom of the screen we see the ice-covered lake Chudskoye. The image shows two-thirds of a blue-grey, ice-cold sky complemented by one-third of the dark soil. The intersection between

3 *Time Out. Film Guide*. 10th ed. by John Pym. London: Penguin Books, 2007, 18.

4 Eisenstein, S. *Jenseits der Einstellung*, 437. (All translations are mine except stated otherwise M.H.)

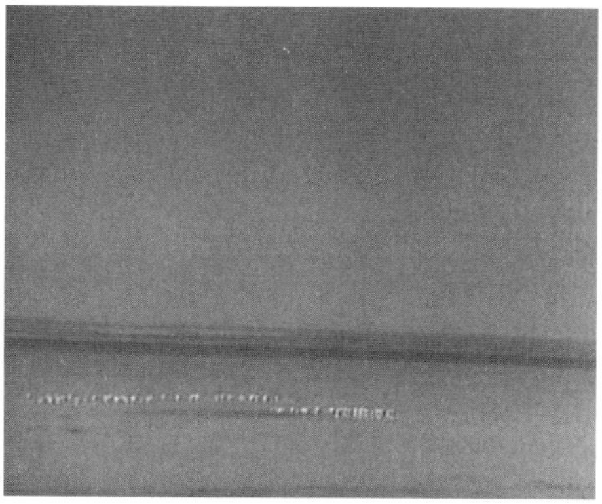

*Germans attack*

heaven and earth, a thin white line, shows the German invaders moving towards the spectator. Alexander Newski anticipates a merciless attack but orders his troops to stand still. The plan is to lead the German invaders onto the ice-covered lake where their horses will struggle to move. In the moment when the German Knights step onto the ice, he surprises them with an attack from the flanks to break their phalanx. Finally, the Germans are defeated as the ice breaks and the Germans, like the Egyptians in the story in Exodus, drown. In Ex 14:27–28 we are told:

> So Moses stretched out his hand over the sea, and at daybreak the water returned to its accustomed place; but the Egyptians were in flight as it advanced, and the Lord swept them out into the sea. The water flowed back and covered the entire pharaoh's army, the chariots and the cavalry, which had pressed the pursuit into the sea. Not one man was left alive.

*Germans are defeated*



Eisenstein builds the glorious victory of the Russians around the Exodus motif. Even the 'pharaoh' is shown. At the end of the film, the German Roman Catholic bishop is crawling on the ground mourning the loss of his men. The battle scene on the ice is perhaps the most famous scene of the entire film. It is famous not only because of Prokofiev's music but also because of the intriguing use of the Exodus motif. Eisenstein re-enacts the defeat of the 'Egyptian perpetrators' in a Russian-German context; the water is frozen, it is winter (Napoleon has already failed to conquer Russia in winter), and the German Knights of the Temple are portrayed as heretics. This resembles the enduring controversy between the Roman Catholic church and Russian Orthodoxy, between orthodoxy and heresy. Alexander Newski is the true leader. He is portrayed as a theologico-political Moses. Prince Alexander is a saint *and* a political leader. Eisenstein points this out when he explains why Alexander Newski was canonised by the Russian Orthodox church:

> Why was Alexander called a 'saint'? I don't mean by the Church but by people. [...] Let us be clear about the meaning of the word. In those days the title was the highest possible appreciation of merit [...] 'Saint!' It is not a matter of the ecclesiastical meaning of the epithet, which the clerics have exploited for ages. The gist of the matter lies in the true popular love and veneration which surrounds the name of Alexander Newski to this day. In this sense the epithet is highly revealing. It shows that that hero and man of genius saw far ahead what he was doing: he saw Russia great and unified.[5]

Eisenstein uses the historic episode to describe the current situation: "[...] the Battle on Ice was the genius of the Russian people, who, for the first time in history, become conscious of their strength as a nation, of their unity" and no force is capable of shattering it, "when it has become a socialist state."[6] Eisenstein's message is political by theological means. In the political theology in ALEXANDER NEWSKI, he combines both the theological image of the messiah and the political ideology of the socialist state and its leader.



## 1. Montage

Before we discuss Eisenstein's political theology in detail, we have to examine his method. The example of the Exodus motif already demonstrates Eisenstein's groundbreaking technique in film-making. He parallels two 'images' to produce an intended effect in the mind of the spectator. The understanding of 'image' must not be narrowed down to a single picture. Eisenstein's writings, drawings and even thinking is iconographic. To illustrate this, I want to cite his own reflection on the making of ALEXANDER NEWSKI:

> Bones. Skulls. Scorched fields. Charred ruins of human dwellings. People enslaved and driven far from home. Plundered towns. Human dignity trampled underfoot. Such is the awful picture rising before us as we think of the early thirteenth-century Russia.[7]

The parallelisation (i.e. juxtaposition or splicing) of images in ALEXANDER NEWSKI is particularly intriguing because Eisenstein *juxtaposes a theological imagination with a political vision*. As mentioned above, the saviour of Russia,

5 Eisenstein, S. *Notes of a Film Director*. New York: Dover, 1970, 40.
6 Eisenstein, S. *Notes of a Film Director*, 35–36.
7 Eisenstein, S. *Notes of a Film Director*, 32.

Prince Alexander, is paralleled with Moses, the rout of the Germans with the defeat of the Egyptians, and the pharaoh with the Roman bishop. These are just a few examples and we will examine some paradigmatic scenes where Eisenstein parallels the theological with the political.

What we have to ask first of all is: how is this 'parallelisation' organised? Are there rules or, in other words, is there a 'law' according to which the *montage* of two images, as Eisenstein calls it, has to be put together in order to achieve the intended effect? Eisenstein explains: "If any two images were put together, they form inevitably an idea, which results from this juxtaposition as a new quality."[8] An example of this technique is when Eisenstein describes the opening scene of Alexander Newski:

> Bones.
> Skulls.
> Scorched fields.
> Charred ruins of human dwellings.[9]

I have altered the layout of these lines to show both the similarity between Mayakovsky and Eisenstein and the dialectic principle of montage. The two images are "bones" and "skulls." The montage of the two images produces the third image of "scorched fields." In the fourth line, Eisenstein tells us what the dialectic of the montage aims to provoke in the eye of the spectator: "charred ruins of human dwellings." The question is whether *any* two images can be used for the intended combination to cause the wanted effect. According to Eisenstein, the 'material content' of the images must follow the rule of similarity, that is the images, which are combined must be *representamen* of the intended third image. To use the example given above, the image of both 'bones' as well as 'skulls' are *representamen* of the greater image of 'scorched fields'. In other words, the combination or montage of image A and B is a combination of two metonyms of the resulting third image.[10] Moreover, the opening scene of Alexander Newski works particularly well due to the intrinsic resemblance of the two images 'bones' and 'skulls.' It is important to bear in mind that the synthesised third image through the montage of two metonymical images transcends the meaning of each individual image. Therefore, the synthesised third image (C) is 'more' than the sum of the combined images (A | | B); which we can express in the formula: A | | B < C. Curiously, the name Eisenstein also allows an illustration



8 Eisenstein, S. *Jenseits der Einstellung,* 159.

9 Eisenstein, S. *Notes of a Film Director,* 158.

10 See: Yampolsky, M. The essential bone structure. Mimesis in Eisenstein. In: Richard Taylor and Ian Christie (eds.), *Eisenstein Rediscovered.* London: Routledge, 1993, 178–188, and Eisenstein's own reflections on metonomy in his essay, Pars pro toto. In: Eisenstein, S. *Jenseits der Einstellung,* 367–371.

of the method of montage. The name EISENSTEIN itself can be understood as a montage of the two German words *Eisen* (iron) and *Stein* (stone). According to the principle of montage, both iron as well as stone are *representamen* of the synthesised third image which results of their combination: iron-stone. Once again, not only does the combination of iron and stone create the image of 'hardness' as its third image, but also the resemblance of *Eisen* and *Stein* as its *representamen* appear to be a permutation of letters to each other. Only the letters 'e' and 't' distinguish the words *Stein* and *Eisen* from each other. With Eisenstein, we can summarise the principle of the method of montage:

> Juxtaposed, piece A and piece B, both taken from among the elements of an unfolding theme, produce an image embodying the content of the theme with utmost vividness. Expressed in the form of an imperative, with greater precision, the premise will read as follows: *Representation A* and *representation B* must be so selected from among all the possible features within the unfolding theme, they must be so chosen as to make their (*theirs*, and not any other elements') *juxtaposition* arouse in the spectator's perception and feelings the complete possible *image of the theme itself.*[11]



It is easiest to imagine the complexity of the montage of two 'images' by taking into account the acoustic possibilities (in fact, Eisenstein saw the possibility of sound-film as the fourth dimension of film), and the colour and variety of possible perspectives from which an image is shot, i.e. the total, half-total, and close-up etc. It is characteristic of Eisenstein's films to compose a series of corresponding *tableaux vivants*[12] which unfold *one* theme. It was Eisenstein's genius to discover that the logic of a film lies in the *repetition* of a specific motif that rehearses the general theme. Ideally, any piece of the film (that is, the montage of two images creating a third) represents the general theme or 'meaning' of the whole. It is like a fractal, as described by Benoit Mandelbrot.[13] Eisenstein imagined the film as a spherical book, where meaning can be approached from any position.

In this essay, I am concerned with the meaning of that 'third image' or general theme provoked in the 'eye of the spectator' as Eisenstein creates it in ALEXANDER NEWSKI. I have already mentioned that ALEXANDER NEWSKI was a wake-up call for the Russian people (and the entire Soviet Union); to prepare them for the war against the Germans. That is his intended effect: people should realise who the enemy is and, therefore, who the kin. The question remains, however, as to what the nature of the imagination used to provoke this perception is. It is sig-

11 Eisenstein, S. *Notes of a Film Director,* 65–66.

12 See: Khopkar, A. Graphic flourish. Aspects of the art of mise-en-scène. In: Richard Taylor and Ian Christie (eds.), *Eisenstein Rediscovered.* London: Routledge, 1993, 151–164.

13 See: Mandelbrot, B. *The Fractal Geometry of Nature.* New York: W.H. Freeman, 1982.

*Alexander Newski, fishing*

nificant that, at that time, when the communist party erased religion, Eisenstein returned to *religious memory and religious symbols* to give his film and, finally, Stalin's rule authority and credibility.

Let us examine the scene when Prince Alexander is summoned by the people. This summoning occurs in two stages. In the first stage, Alexander is portrayed as the Christic chosen one. Alexander is a fisherman pulling the net. He stands in the water; his shirt clings to his chest, and he is surrounded by other men. In the still, we can see the other men who are his bondmen standing as a white line at the horizon. This ensemble is framed by the cloudy sky above and the infinite horizon of the sea below Newski. In the beginning, only his back can be seen and he draws in the net. But, in the next image, a struggle emerges. Alexander turns around and raises his voice, saying, "Keep your peace."



Eisenstein employs a visual parallel to illustrate the spherical character of the film by juxtaposing the peaceful scene at the beginning of the film to the moment of the attack of the Germans towards the end. Both images are composed in the same way with similar elements: the wide sky and the thin line of fishing people versus the thin line of the Knights as they attack, dividing the sky from the frozen water. But he also introduces a parallelism between a theological and a political image. Alexander is seen as the lord of peace, he is the fisherman who becomes the fisher of men as portrayed in Mk 1:16–17:

> Jesus was walking by the sea of Galilee when he saw Simon and his brother Andrew on the lake at work with a casting-net; for they were fishermen. Jesus said to them, 'Come with me, and I will make you of fishers of men.' And at once they left their nets and followed him.[14]

At the second stage, Alexander is summoned by the people and confirmed as their leader. As the acclaimed leader, he leads the war in the name of a white Orthodox church identified by the Orthodox cross. The orthodoxy and legitimacy of Alexander as warrior lies in opposition to the illegitimate Christian (Roman Catholic) invaders. These are portrayed by helmets that fully cover their faces, allowing only an eyehole that takes the shape of a Roman cross.

14 Mk 1:17–19.

*„Rise up for Kiev!"*

*Germans are blessed for the battle*

Contrary to Eisenstein's other films, such as BATTLESHIP POTEMKIN for example, the montage of theological and political images in ALEXANDER NEWSKI is more self-conscious and visible. Despite the complexity of the montage as such and the vast richness of visual effects produced by the montage of the theological and the political, ALEXANDER NEWSKI seems to work on the basis of *one* message. In other words, the meaning of the film's 'third image' is created through the use of *political theology* in the strict sense of its meaning.



We will now have to continue our analysis by turning to the work of Carl Schmitt, who coined the phrase 'political theology' in 1922. Therefore, we move from the analysis of images to the examination of specific concepts.

## 2. Political Theology

Since the publication of Carl Schmitt's *Politische Theologie* in 1922 up to the present day, the phrase 'political theology' has seen wide circulation among a number of disciplines. It is used metaphorically and rhetorically or even as a warning against those who confuse two antagonistic domains: religion and politics. Among these different readings of political theology, the theological discussion appears to be the most prominent. After the Second World War, a specific school of theology emerged whose members call themselves 'new political theologians'. New political theology had a significant impact on both German-speaking and English-speaking theologians. Needless to say, the theological appropriation of Schmitt's famous phrase seeks to avoid any association with Schmitt's work, his biographical engagement with the Nazi regime and his anti-liberal political conviction.

What is then political theology according to Schmitt? And to what extent does the term 'political theology' help us to appreciate the message of ALEXAN-

DER NEWSKI? First of all, the term political theology, in the sense that Schmitt uses it, is ambiguous if we just refer to Carl Schmitt's book *Politische Theologie* (1922). But, if we also take into account Schmitt's final book, *Politische Theologie II* (1969), then 'political theology' has a much less ambivalent political and theological meaning. This helps us to analyse and appreciate Eisenstein's intention.

In the first elaboration of political theology, Schmitt wished to provide a substantial and convincing argument against Hans Kelsen's legal positivism. The heart of Kelsen's theory of law is the concept of sovereignty, and, in contradistinction to Kelsen's de-personalised view of the constitution as the sovereign from which the entire legal system and all its norms can and legitimately must be derived, Schmitt argues for the concentration of sovereign power in one single individual who finally has to make decisions. We do not either have to detail or evaluate Schmitt's critique of Kelsen here at length, nor do we have space to go into details of Kelsen's 'theory of pure law.'[15] It is sufficient within the context of this essay to emphasise the two meanings of political theology in Schmitt's book from 1922.

First, political theology attempts to develop a political theory according to which sovereign power is concentrated in one single person. This proposed form of government is directed against any form of distributive power and liberal democracy in particular. As far as the 1922 book *Politische Theologie* is concerned, the arguments are restricted to the theory of law. Nevertheless, the author makes clear what actual political form of government he prefers. This becomes evident when he refers to key-figures of the Catholic counterrevolution like Donoso Cortes, Joseph de Maistre and Louis Gabriel Ambroise de Bonald as benchmarks for political philosophy. Moreover, his understanding of law and political theory, which he calls 'decisionism' and is derived from Hobbes, is opposed to Kelsen's legal positivism and constitutionalism. The idea of decisionism can be summarised, as Schmitt often did, by a quotation taken from Hobbes' *Leviathan*: *Auctoritas, non veritas facit legem*.

Second, political theology is also linked to a specific theory of secularisation. Following Auguste Comte and his theory of the three stages (the theological, philosophical and sociological) Schmitt views the development of civilisation over the last four centuries as a process of secularisation. According to this theory of secularisation, there are four distinct stages, or as Michel Foucault would say, four different kinds of *episteme*. The first stage is the theological. The theological epoch is then followed by the metaphysical epoch, which is subsequently replaced by the moral humanist stage and finally comes to its

15 Kelsen, H. *Reine Rechtslehre*. Wien: Verlag Österreich, 2000.

conclusion with the economic 'order of things'.[16] According to this process of secularisation, the present is inevitably rooted in the theological. As far as law is concerned, Schmitt argues for a genealogy of legal concepts. "All significant concepts of the modern theory of the state" (as he introduces in the opening chapter in *Political Theology II)* "are secularised theological concepts".[17] Therefore, any analysis of either legal or political concepts must go back to their theological origins. Schmitt calls this genealogical method a 'sociology of juridical concepts'. It is evident that the sociology of juridical concepts is diametrically opposed to Kelsen's theory of *pure* law; i.e. an idea of law that is entirely free from politics, history and social context.[18] In other words, Schmitt (in contrast to Kelsen) denies the autonomy of secular, modern politics and its project of liberal democracy. Hans Blumenberg, one of the most acute critics of Schmitt's second book on political theology points out: "Secularisation is for the theorist of the state, Carl Schmitt, a category of legitimacy. [...] It provides historical identity and it does not really matter whether this is done by using 'other means'." Blumenberg concludes that the term 'political theology' masks Schmitt's true intention: which is, "theology as politics."[19]



This verdict might be too strong because Schmitt, at least in his writing, restricts himself to an understanding of political theology in purely academic, i.e. sociological, terms. Political theology, according to this second meaning proposed in *Politische Theologie* from 1922, is nothing more than the hidden bone-structure for juridical concepts which has to be excavated by a proper 'sociology'. Characterised by the example of sovereignty, Schmitt defines his 'sociology of juridical concepts' with respect to Max Weber:

> Altogether different is the sociology of concepts, which is advanced here and alone has the possibility of achieving a scientific result for a concept such as sovereignty. This sociology of concepts transcends juridical conceptualisation oriented to immediate practical interest. It aims to discover the basic, radically systematic structure and to compare this conceptual structure *[begriffliche Struktur]* with the conceptually represented social

16 Schmitt, C. *Politische Theologie. Vier Kapitel zur Lehre von der Souveränität.* Berlin: Duncker&Humblot, 1996, 7. In fact, there is a striking similarity between Schmitt and Michel Foucault with respect to their view of history as a process of decay. Jürgen Habermas was right in labelling Foucault as a 'young conservative' and to associate him with ' Martin Heidegger, Ernst Jünger, Carl Schmitt and Hans Freyer'. Habermas, J. *Der Diskurs der Moderne.* Frankfurt: Suhrkamp, 1996. All of them, together with Oswald Spengler are part of what is called *Kulturpessimismus* in German.

17 Schmitt, C. *Politische Theologie,* 43.

18 For Schmitt's critique of Kelsen's logic, which is borrowed from Immanuel Kant and his operation of the transcendental deduction, see: Schmitt, C. *Politische Theologie,* 28.

19 Blumenberg, H. *Legitimität der Neuzeit,* Frankfurt: Suhrkamp, 1999, 108.

> structure *[begriffliche Verarbeitung der sozialen Struktur]* of a certain epoch.[20]

Schmitt's proposed sociology is a historical investigation, an attempt to describe a certain social constellation, for which a specific discourse of political organisation was the most obvious, or the least problematic. According to Schmitt, certain forms of political organisation like absolutism, parliamentary democracy etc. are only possible in certain epochs. In other words, Schmitt is convinced that any form of political organisation, like democracy or absolute monarchy etc. corresponds to and is a product of a defined social constellation. He writes:

> The presupposition of this kind of sociology of juristic concepts is thus a radical conceptualisation, a consistent thinking that is pushed into metaphysics and theology. The metaphysical image that a definite epoch forges of the world has the same structure as what the world immediately understands to be appropriate as a form of its political organisation.[21]

Schmitt suggests, not unlike Michel Foucault, that only certain forms of political organisations are possible at certain times. Given a specific metaphysical and theological condition, the key question then becomes: What form of political organisation is the most appropriate? The answer to this question is given by Schmitt in *Politische Theologie II*. 

As I have said, the first book on political theology was an attack of Kelsen's theory of pure law; but the last one is an attack on the theologian Eric Peterson and his criticism of the earlier exposition of political theology. According to Peterson, a Christian political theology is impossible because of the dogma of the trinity. Consequently, any political theology is either heretical or pagan.[22] Contrary to Peterson's claim, Schmitt argues that political theology can be developed in two directions:

> The limitation from the political side seems to be clear: the subject of examination and the matter of our argumentation is only monarchy in terms of the power and government of one single person. This seems to be a self-evident limitation because of the concentration on monotheism. The limitation is expressed by the formula: one God – one King.[23]

The formula 'One God – One King' defines the concept of *divine monarchy*. This is also the title of Peterson's influential essay published in 1931.[24] Divine

20 Schmitt, C. *Political Theology*. Transl. by George Schwab. Chicago: University of Chicago Press, ²1988, 45.

21 Schmitt, C. *Political Theology*, 1988, 46

22 Schmitt, C. *Politische Theologie II*, 45.

23 Schmitt, C. *Politische Theologie II*, 45.

24 Peterson, E. Göttliche Monarchie. In: *ThQ* 112, 1931, 537–564

monarchy as the subject of political theology would not be contentious, especially in terms of the historical analysis of early Christianity. The political potential of divine monarchy becomes evident by Peterson's publication from 1935 called *Monotheism as political problem,*[25] in which he examines the concept of divine monarchy and parallels it with the rising Nazi regime and the emerging *Führerstaat*. Schmitt comments:

> When, in the year 1935, a treatise about the formula 'one God – one monarch' was published in Germany, it automatically entered the sphere of being dangerously relevant to the current situation, more so when the *monarch* is occasionally (p. 52) also called *Führer*. This was seen then as contemporary criticism and protest; as a well-disguised and intelligently masked allusion, to the cult of the *Führer*, the one-party-system and totalitarianism. Its motto[26] contributed to that; it was a sentence by St. Augustine who warns of the false striving for unity that originates in the worldly lust for power.[27]



Peterson's claim of the closure of any political theology was intended to expose the Nazi regime and the *Führerstaat* as illegitimate and, furthermore, as a Christian heresy. In his view, the theological and metaphysical structure of monotheism was used to prepare the people for the cult of the *Führer*. Political theology is not then simply a methodology in terms of the sociology of juridical concepts. Peterson emphasises the monocratic potential of political theology and argues that political theology was at the heart of a political religion of totalitarianism. I will elaborate this claim in the concluding section of this essay by returning to Eisenstein's ALEXANDER NEWSKI. However, for a fuller understanding, I want to briefly outline the *pluricratic* understanding of political theology, which is also possible.

Schmitt, who, in 1935, was the leading theorist of law in the Third Reich and whose fate was to be ostracised after 1945, also develops the idea of political theology in a democratic direction. He comments on Peterson:

> Thomas Hobbes in his *Leviathan* (1651) has systematically positioned the concept at stake: the Highest, the sovereign can be a single human being but also an assembly or a majority of people capable of action. If the formula is no longer 'One God – One King', but 'One God – One People', and if the political side of political theology is no longer orientated

25 Peterson, E. *Der Monotheismus als politisches Problem. Ein Beitrag zur Geschichte der politischen Theologie im Imperium Romanum.* Leipzig: Jakob Hegner, 1935.

26 "Habet ergo et superbia quendam appetitum unitatis et omnipotentiae, sed in rerum naturalium principatu, quae omnia transeunt sicut umbra." Sanctus Augustinus, *De vera religione* 45, 84 (Patrol. Latin. 34, 160).

27 Schmitt, C. *Politische Theologie II,* 15.

> towards the monarch but towards a people, then it becomes democratic. The plausible coincidence of monotheism and monarchism breaks down and is no longer valid.[28]

The democratic development of political theology can no longer operate on the equation of 'One God – One King'. It needs to be transposed onto a collective level: 'One God – One People'. Interestingly, Schmitt acknowledges the different political theology at work, when he cites Peterson: "This dissonance has not gone unnoticed by Peterson's sharp mind. '*One* people and *One* God – but this is the Jewish slogan'."[29]

## 3. From Political Theology to Political Religion

I want to introduce the term 'political religion' in order to distinguish political theology from totalitarianism. Both Eisenstein and Schmitt use the method of parallelisation. Schmitt's 'sociology of juridical concepts' draws a parallel between theological-metaphysical representation and its appropriate form of political organisation and Eisenstein's 'montage' is a dialectical arrangement of two images. In addition to their methodological similarity Eisenstein's ALEXANDER NEWSKI, as well as Schmitt's political theology, later became instruments for Nazism on the one hand and Stalinism on the other. It is not necessary in this context to join the debate[30] about Carl Schmitt's political engagement with Nazism[31] nor do I want to accuse Eisenstein of any form of collaboration with Stalinist tyranny. However, the fact is that both, in one way or another, contributed to the rise of their totalitarian systems.



Political religion is a term, as Emilio Gentile states, which "was employed to define the absolute exaltation of the party and of the state, the cult of the leader, mass fanaticism, rites and symbols of collective liturgies, which were fundamental aspects of the new totalitarian regimes. The tendency to attribute a religious character to totalitarian dictatorships started to spread at the beginning of the 1930s. In 1935 historian Karl Polyani wrote that National Socialism had the tendency to produce a political religion, whereas the same term was applied to Bolshevism by Reinhold Niebuhr."

28 Schmitt, C. *Politische Theologie II*, 47.

29 Schmitt, C. *Politische Theologie II*, 47.

30 Gentile, E. Political Religion: A Concept and its Critics – A Critical Survey. In: *Totalitarian Movements and Political Religions*, Vol. 6, No. 1, June 2005, 25

31 See the excellent biography of Schmitt: Koenen, A. *Der Fall Carl Schmitt. Sein Aufstieg zum "Kronjuristen des Dritten Reiches"*. Darmstadt: Wissenschaftliche Buchgesellschaft, 1995; and on Schmitt's changing political theory: Hofmann, H. *Legitimität gegen Legalität. Der Weg der politischen Philosophie Carl Schmitts.* Berlin: Duncker&Humblot, 2002.

Protestant and Catholic theologians first used the term 'political religion' to unmask the pseudo-religious nature of totalitarian systems. The term sought to be more accurate than ideology with its various positive, negative and neutral connotations. It is telling that the release of ALEXANDER NEWSKI as well as the publication of the second edition of *Politische Theologie* – with a new foreword adjusting the book to the new political condition – in 1933 coincide with the coinage of the term 'political religion'.

Gentile even gives an explanation of the rise of political religions claiming, "it was a consequence of modernity and of secularisation. It was connected to mass society, to the decline of traditional religions, to the spreading of irrationalism and activism, to the expansion of bureaucratic power of the state, to the 'new Machiavellianism' of totalitarian leaders and parties, who made use of fanaticism of the masses to impose their tyranny."[32]

Political Religion is not identical to political theology, but every political religion contains a political theology just as every religion contains, to a greater or lesser extent, a theology. In the case of ALEXANDER NEWSKI, the political theology at stake is exactly the monocratic metaphysical image of 'One God – One King', which is provoked in the spectator by the artistic use of images combining the theological with the political. Eisenstein's films are not simply propaganda.[33] They are artistic in the way they are composed and they work subtly. In line with Schmitt's understanding of political theology, Eisenstein creates a theological-metaphysical image which corresponds to a specific form of political organisation. The divine monarchy 'One God – One King' is the general theme in ALEXANDER NEWSKI. It is due to a *secularisation of the theme* that it became a blueprint for a Stalinist political religion.



I want to conclude with another striking example of montage in ALEXANDER NEWSKI, which reveals the thin line between the dictator and the just king. The German Grandmaster's cruelty and bestiality is demonstrated when he throws little children into a sea of fire. Roman crosses surround the Grandmaster and the spectator is inevitably reminded of Herod's slaughter of the innocents. The other image is taken from the end of the film when Prince Alexander enters the liberated city in a triumphal procession. Children are handed over to him and he carries them on his horse. The religious image invoked here is that of Jesus entering Jerusalem, hailed by the masses.

32 Gentile, E. Political Religion, 25.

33 For an analysis of symbolism used in totalitarian regimes see: Maier, H. Political Religions and their Images: Soviet communism, Italian Fascism and German National Socialism. In: *Totalitarian Movements and Political Religions*, Vol. 7, No. 3, September 2006, 267–281; Riegel, K.-G. Marxism-Leninism as a Political Religion. In: *Totalitarian Movements and Political Religions*, Vol. 6, No. 1, June 2005, 97–126.

*Murder of children*

*Alexander Newski enters the city*

The image of the child is a metonymy for the future of humankind. The montage of both images in the film sends out the message: the just king guarantees the future of the people whereas the false king, i.e. the dictator, seeks to perish the people. He must be resisted at any price. The Russian people may have to die for future generations, which have to re-build life – once again.

Sebastian Schlöglmann

# Japan. Manga! Religion?

## The New Myths of the Japanese Ninth Art

The dawn of the 21st century has brought a multitude of changes in society, community habits, media, work situation, politics, traditions, and all the more so in the fields of religion and religiosity. In this crucial phase of transition, young people in particular cannot identify with the answers to their existential questions that are provided by religious groups; rather, the code of religious practice seems to be – in their eyes – archaic and outmoded, and therefore irrelevant. Interreligious conflicts and scandals within religious groups reinforce their hostility towards religion in any institutional variety. Answers to those 'grand questions', therefore, are more and more sought after in alternative spheres, such as the world of media.

This article sets out to explore a medium which is gaining importance in western culture and which seems to be able to provide such answers to young people in particular: the Japanese art and entertainment form 'manga'. As "worldly wisdom in comic format,"[1] manga explores a variety of human concerns and takes a particularly close look at current changes in society. Because it deals with fundamental problems of human existence, manga has found a growing fandom in the west too. It is my thesis that it excels in its sense-making function for people in the east and west, because it provides a unique mix of motifs and traditions which have both an identificatory and alienating effect, which in turn makes its audience reflect on their own life. The analysis of manga is also an example of how the study of media products can be a way of better understanding a foreign culture (in this case, Japan) – an important issue in a globalised world.



## 1. Comics – an Underestimated Art Form

Through the work of the French scholar Francis Lacassin, the genre 'comics' has taken – as *le neuvième art* – its place in the canon of the arts, next to music, architecture, painting, graphics, sculpture, dance, literature and film and/or

1 Petra Polak, Lebensweisheit im Comicformat, *Der Standard*, 12 September 2006, 12 (translation Sebastian Schlöglmann).

television.[2] Since then, 'the ninth art' has been used as an academic term for the genre of comics, which is defined as painted stories with comical, amusing content. For too long, 'comics' have been regarded as pop trash and therefore an artistically inferior medium, produced for children or people with little intellectual interest. But this disregards the fact that there are plenty of genuinely artistic masterpieces among the supposedly trivial genre of comics. As 'the ninth art', comics are taken more seriously and are recognised as a medium for (often too) serious messages. Like every artistic genre, comics comprise a variety of topics and are of variable quality.

Rejecting comics entirely as an object of serious analysis is an underestimation of their significance: they form an important part of the life of a noticeable group of people, and they are a social phenomenon[3] which addresses both young people and adults in their form, contents and values. Recently, the western comic community has been looking towards the far east with growing interest: Japanese ninth art – manga – is becoming popular, trendy, hip. But what is it exactly?

## 2. Manga and Anime – What's That?



The term 'manga' derives from the two Sino-Japanese words *man* ('spontaneously' or 'funny') and *ga* ('picture' or 'design').[4] The manga business looks back at a long and prosperous tradition. Its origins lie in a religious context: the first examples of illustrated stories can be found in the works of the Buddhist monk Toba from the early 12th century BCE.[5] Over the centuries, a great variety of categories and subgenres has evolved; the most important and influential categories are: manga for infants *(yonen manga)*, manga for children *(kodomo manga)*, the largest and most significant categories of manga for boys *(shonen manga)* and girls *(shojo manga)*, manga for men *(seinen manga)* and for women *(josei manga* or *ladies' komikku*), and the recently developed category of silver manga which mainly aims at an older audience. Apart from this rough classification according to the age of its target group, there are plenty of subcategories according to style, narrative patterns, and – of course – quality.

What is characteristic about manga is its diversity of genres, which is in no way inferior to other art forms such as literature and film: manga can be children's entertainment, thrillers, science fiction novels, the pornographic *hentai*, patriotic epics, social criticism, horror, splatter and crime manga, romantic

2 Cf. Francis Lacassin, *Pour un neuvième art*, Genève: Slatkine, 1982, 13.

3 Cf. Frank Brinkmann, *Comics und Religion. Das Medium der "Neunten Kunst" in der gegenwärtigen Deutungskultur*, Stuttgart: Kohlhammer, 1999, 52.

4 Cf. ibid., 51.

5 Cf. Iris Frank, *Eine semiotische Analyse von französischen bandes dessinées und japanischen Manga*, Diplomarbeit Universität Wien, 1993, 31.

melodrams, sports, edutainment and many other genres, which all exhibit the same qualitative variety as western literature and film. Neither the term 'manga' nor 'comic' do justice to this multiplicity of forms and contents in their literal-etymological meaning ('funny', 'humorous'); manga is more than short comic strips: it includes monographs, comprehensive series whose stories extend over hundreds or thousands of pages, satire and caricature, serious entertainment and education. The term 'manga' also includes animated films and series. In order to be able to differentiate this genre from its printed form, animated Japanese comics are called 'japanime' or more commonly, 'anime'.

Manga and anime are part of Japanese mass media culture and take up an important place in Japanese culture and everyday life – they accompany the daily routines of students as well as adults, blue or white collar workers as they leave their suburban flats in the morning and go to school or work until they return in the evening. They are a formative influence on Japanese television; operating manuals are designed as manga to make them easier to understand. An analysis of manga and anime, therefore, helps to better understand Japanese culture and society. Because manga accompanies such a large proportion of the lives of its recipients, it is also important to have a close look at the functions it fulfils, the messages it transmits.



## 3. Sex and Crime – Stereotypical Forms of Manga?

At first glance, western observers are perplexed by the apparently excessive amount of sex and violence in manga. Consequently, many reject manga as a whole and condemn it as an aggressive and sexist media form. *Hentai*, whose representation of sexuality ranges from soft core to violent pornography, is considered to be the ultimate manifestation of an immoral pop culture. An unprejudiced evaluation, however, has to take into account that first of all, *hentai* and other violent manga are the exception rather than the rule of Japanese manga production. It is essential to keep in mind that these are not comics mainly aimed at children. In Japan, adults are the target audience of a large proportion of manga and anime production. They are considered to be able to deal with violence and sex in a reflective and mature way and to be able to differentiate between the story and their own lives. As Frederik L. Schodt argues, "[c]omics thus depict a fantasy world outside of the rigid conventions, where the truly impossible is possible. While comics can convey a message about reality, very few of them depict it realistically. And Japanese comic readers, who are very much at home in their medium, rarely confuse the two worlds."[6]

6 Frederik L. Schodt, *Manga! Manga! The World of Japanese Comics*, Tokyo: Kodansha International, 2001, 132.

Japanese theatre tradition might have contributed to this ability: while the western theatre in its classic form has tried to construct an illusion of reality on stage, in Japanese theatre, the fictional character of the play is even emphasised, e.g. by masks, the specific movements of the actors, props, etc. And both form and content of Japanese theatre have their impact on manga authors as well as their audience.[7]

In the particular context of Japanese culture, manga and anime can even be seen as a form of compensation for the restrictions posed by deeply felt obligations in everyday life, school, work or family situations.[8] Schodt also mentions that the Japanese crime rate ranges among the lowest in the world and has even noticeably been decreasing since the beginning of the manga and anime boom.[9] Thus, it seems that manga's violent content cannot be blamed for the real-life violent behaviour of some of its recipients.

## 4. Manga – Reception in the West



Interest in manga and anime is no longer limited to a small group of 'Japanophile' western insiders or students of Japanology[10] who see themselves as fanatic *otaku.*[11] Manga has found its way into western pop and high culture. Manga and anime authors are increasingly perceived as what they actually are: artists, who are received well by the western audience, and exhibited in museums in the west.[12]

The influence of manga has now reached the American and European film industry too, e.g. in Quentin Tarantino's KILL BILL I (USA 2003) which includes short subchapters in an animated 'manga style'. In a more subtle way, there is the significant impact of manga's aesthetical and narrative tradition on western science-fiction: filmmakers, such as Larry and Andy Wachowski (THE MATRIX [USA 1999]) or James Cameron (TERMINATOR [USA 1984]), have acknowledged the influence of Japanese animated films on their work. Finally, manga provides new impulses and inspiration for western comic artists, introducing a broader

7 Cf. Antonia Levi, *Samurai from Outer Space. Understanding Japanese Animation*, Chicago: Open Court, 1997, 22.

8 Cf. Jacqueline Berndt, *Phänomen Manga*, Berlin: edition q, 1995, 149.

9 Cf. Frederik L. Schodt, *Dreamland Japan. Writings on Modern Japan*, Berkeley: Stone Bridges Press, 1999, 50.

10 Cf. ibid., 31.

11 The term is a Japanese loanword and means 'freak' or 'geek'. It's commonly used to refer to a fan of manga and anime though it is sometimes used for any kind of intensive fandom.

12 E.g. Hayao Miyazaki, author of MONONOKE HIME (Princess Mononoke), SEN TO CHIHIRO NO KAMIKAKUSHI (Spirited Away), who was exhibited together with the European comic artist Moebius in the Musée de la Monnaie in Paris in 2004/2005.

spectrum of forms of expression and the interest to create new subgenres for a wider audience.

## 5. Stories out of Nowhere?

Western observers are often irritated by the storylines and narrative structures of Japanese manga literature. On the one hand, the incalculability and unpredictability that some manga and anime demonstrate are provocative to western viewers. Sometimes it is extremely difficult to follow the thread of the narrative. On the other hand, there is a vague feeling of familiarity with the plot, the story's structure or complete storylines. But what is the reason for this? Why is western reception of manga marked by such ambivalence?

Japanese manga artists do not create in isolation, but are surrounded by a culture and society with a long and rich artistic tradition providing a huge repository of stories and motifs for the artists. Elements of religion and history, myth and legend, reality and fiction of the artists' Japanese cultural background are revitalized in the plots of manga and anime and composed in new ways that generate new meaning.

Shinto religion also offers a great repository of stories and motifs: eight million deities or spiritual entities, the so-called 'kami', are the protagonists of an enormous treasury of legends which have largely remained inaccessible and only now find their way west through the medium of manga and anime.[13]



The insularity of Japanese geography and culture make it difficult for Europeans to gain access to and understand Japanese culture, history and myth. Western recipients might, therefore, well misunderstand traditional myths and sagas – easily recognised as such by Japanese readers – as original stories created by the author's imagination.

All this makes manga so strange to a western audience. What makes them familiar, on the other side, is the fact that the producers of manga and anime take the liberty of using pieces of any story pool they find and that are worth being used: European religious myths and literature, philosophy and symbolism become elements in their stories that create familiarity, but are combined with own fantastic ideas and elements of Japanese culture which result in the unique mix of traditions which characterises manga and anime.[14]

13 Cf. Levi, *Samurai*, 34.

14 Cf. http://xoomic.de/webneu/anime/themen.html, accessed 26.08.2006.

## 6. Secularisation and Manga

Given the enormous popularity of the narratives of manga in the east and west, the question arises as to what role they play in sense-making processes in contemporary societies after the end of the 'grand narratives' of Christianity, Enlightenment and rationality. How does the combination of secular and religious elements of various traditions in manga influence their function for people today? In particular, what does it say about Japanese culture, and its unique combination of technophilia and traditionalism?



As mentioned above, the boom of manga in the west coincides with a time of rapid social change. Former generations could choose – if at all – from just a small selection of concepts of life, all of which were legitimated by ideologies and institutions and seemed – at least initially – to work well. Young people today grow up in a postmodern context, which means: multiple concepts of life, an unpredictable global situation with wars, the threat of terrorism, and the spread of poverty in developing countries as well as in the west. Spiritual movements and religious concepts of life thrive and expand the range of possibilities to choose from: traditional and institutionalised religious communities find themselves often literally (in the topography of cities) next to sects, occult communities, pseudo-religious esoteric groups and a booming fitness and wellness sector with religious-like functions. To choose from these options – a choice between different options that are regarded as equal – becomes more and more difficult. This leads to a 'trial and error behaviour' in finding the religious model that best fits one's needs in particular situations or times in life.

*Kazuya Minekura, Stigma.*
*Stuttgart: Ehapa 2002*

The decrease of membership in the traditional, institutionalised religious communities cannot be understood as a loss of faith; instead, today, faith and religiosity can be expressed in a greater variety of forms.[15] Religion and religiosity have not disappeared from the reality of a post-modern society, but rather, been transformed. Thus, we can still say that "[r]eligion is a dimension of modern reality and a dimension in the lives of many modern people."[16] The quest for personal religious and spiritual experiences and meaningful answers to existential questions has not been abandoned. But while the answers to those questions used to be provided by religious communities, today, the search for an answer has moved to the world of media – and, in particular, to manga and anime: in dealing with topics such as the problems of everyday life, the eternal fight between good and evil (e.g. NEON GENESIS EVANGELION by Hideaki Anno et al. [Japan 1995], EL HAZARD – THE MAGNIFICENT WORLD 2 by Hayashi Hiroaki, Japan 1997), the value and immortality of the soul (e.g. *Blade of the Immortal*[17]), the forgiveness of sins, and finally, the search for God (*Stigma*[18]), they try to give answers and provide material for the individual's meaning-making process.

Manga also deal with the unique relationship between technology and society in Japan: it is a modern, techno-phile society, in many ways a cultural avant-garde, with all the fascination, but also problems, this entails. New technologies provide comfort in everyday life, extend the human life span, but they also pose a threat to nature (reflected e.g. in MONONOKE HIME by Hayao Miyazaki, Japan 1997), raise the question of free will (discussed e.g. in JIN-ROH by Mamoru Oshii, Japan 1998) and can be (ab)used as weapons of mass destruction (e.g. in AKIRA by Katsuhiro Otomo, Japan 1988). Manga and anime take up the challenges of a changing world and use them for their stories – sometimes naïvely and unreflectingly, but often in a new, inspiring way that can help to address problems and questions that arise for the individual in a western context, too.

In Japan, a country living between tradition and progress, manga and anime therefore help people to combine these aspects of culture in order to understand and integrate traditional goods and values in a rapidly changing society.

## 7. Japanese Ninth Art as Modern Myth

Western society's high regard of rationality, that has lead to the demythologisation and disenchantment of modern society, nature and religion, has been

15 Cf. Jutta Wermke, *Comics und Religion. Eine interdisziplinäre Diskussion*, München: Fink, 1976, 9.

16 Georg Hilger, *Religionsdidaktik. Ein Leitfaden für Studium, Ausbildung und Beruf*, München: Kösel, 2001, 107 (translation Sebastian Schlöglmann).

17 Samura, Hiroaki, *Blade of the Immortal*, published as short stories in the manga-magazine *Afternoon* (1993ff.).

18 Minekura, Kazuya, *Stigma*, Tokyo: Shinshokan, 2000.

replaced by the need for and creation of new 'myths'[19] and freer and more emotional forms of religiosity in postmodernity. Jan de Vries notes that humans have always and everywhere expressed the central aspects of their lives and concepts of the world in the form of myths.[20] Institutionalised mainstream Christianity, which has been 'cleansed' of its mythological aspects in the wake of Enlightenment rationality, provides less identificatory potential. Instead, this seems to be found (among other things) in the world of the ninth art – a world that is explicitly fictitious, mythical and fantastic – and in the new or transformed myths of this world.

Just like traditional myths, the myths of modern mass media convert existential questions and problems into narratives which both reflect the societies they are produced in, and provide reasons for why things are as they are, and a vision of a world as it should or could be.

The following study of GHOST IN THE SHELL II: INNOCENCE (Mamoru Oshii, Japan 2004) will show the relevance of these mythological elements and the transformation processes they undergo in the narrative of the film. It will show that religious and quasi-religious motifs are essential for the storyline as well as for the reception process.



## 8. GHOST IN THE SHELL II: INNOCENCE

The anime GHOST IN THE SHELL II, which has been extremely popular in the west, is set in a future world not far away from now, in which society and everyday life have changed dramatically. Democracy has cleared the way for international companies which direct the world out of free-trade zones in which no government, nation, or international organisation can control them; human memory is expanded by a universal matrix – a kind of enhanced internet everyone can access from anywhere given the necessary bodily adaptations; furthermore, cybernetics is part of everyday life and is widely used by almost everybody. The protagonist Batou, whose body almost entirely consists of mechanic parts, is part of the elite anti-terrorist unit 'Section 9'. Even though his biological make-up is reduced to a few brain cells, he still possesses a 'ghost' (i.e. human spirit) which makes him human but – due to the interconnected nature of cyborgs – also vulnerable to manipulation or so-called ghost-hacking. Accompanied by his colleague Togusa, whose body is still mostly human, they investigate a company called 'Locus Solus' which creates and sells androids in the shape of young women who are used as sex toys, but have malfunctioned and killed their owners. The gynoids are equipped with a 'ghost'/a soul. To accomplish this, Locus Solus has to copy a 'ghost' of a real human being resulting in the death of the 'original'.

19 Cf. Wermke, *Comics und Religion*, 9.

20 Cf. Jan de Vries, *Forschungsgeschichte der Mythologie*, München: Alber, 1961, 296.

*Innocence: Ghost in the Shell II (Mamoru Oshii, Japan 2004)*

The investigation leads Batou and Togusa to the Yakuza (the Japanese mafia), sinister hackers, and a well-known guardian angel, Major Motoko Kusanagi. Ghost in the Shell II combines several independent clusters of motifs into a stringent storyline: quotes from religious texts (Psalm 139 as well as Shinto, Confucian and Buddhist elements), legends (the story of Golem), world literature (such as Villiers de L'Isle-Adam's *L'Eve Future*, John Milton's *Paradise Lost* and Mary Shelley's *Frankenstein*) as well as allusions to philosophy (Plato, Descartes, and Max Weber) are interwoven with the output of the imagination of author Masamune Shirow and director Mamoru Oshii. The main theme of the anime is the human obsession to create something that is equal to themselves. It reflects the concept of the human spirit or human soul, the so-called 'ghost', and its value for a society ruled by economic interests and technology that try to transcend evolutionary boundaries. Following theories of radical constructivism, the protagonists reflect on the terms 'humanity' and 'reality' in a world that is increasingly created by technology.

Ghost in the Shell II is a very complex film due to the many symbolic allusions that are incorporated in a technical and artistic masterpiece of traditional manga painting and trend-setting 3D-computer-animation. But a simple interpretation of the film is not what Oshii, the director of the film, wanted to achieve: "I'm happier if 10.000 people see the film 10 times each than if 1 million people see it once. I'm not making it for the general public, but for a core group of fans – I hope it will make a big impression on them. If I can do that, I'm happy."[21] By confronting the audience with a story and a topic that seem to be far away from contemporary everyday life, the film provokes the audience to reflect upon the question of what it means to be human, upon the understanding of human beings as biological 'machines', and the ethical implications of advancements in technology, such as the accountability of scientists, as well as the responsibility of society for what is going on.

The simultaneous experience of familiarity and alienation provided by the anime's mix of well-known and unfamiliar elements serves as attraction and form of entertainment for the audience. The identificatory, emotional value provided by the inclusion of mythical elements is counterbalanced by a more distancing, reflective effect caused by the complexity of form and story. It is the interaction of these elements and effects that cause the anime's success not just as entertainment, but also as an important component in contemporary sense-making processes. Manga and anime offer, suggest, and produce religious, quasi-religious, and mythological ideas as markers or guideposts for those who engage in the quest for meaning.



## 9. Surplus ... Why Should We Bother With Manga and Anime?

The analysis of mythological and religious elements in Japanese manga and anime and of their answers to the 'grand questions' of humanity offers an insight into an unknown society very different from a western one. A thorough analysis can also help to better understand the questions that are important for today's people (technology, the essence of the human etc.) as well as the answers that are sketched in a unique combination of eastern and western, traditional and original ideas. This is particularly interesting because manga and anime emerge in a culture fascinated by technological developments.

Even though the majority of manga and anime are set in a future or past, fictional or exotic world, in any case, a strange environment, the problems that their characters face reflect the challenges the audience have to deal with in their own societies. Each culture, each society, and each religious community act and communicate on the basis of a multi-layered system of plots, concepts and symbols. As Frank T. Brinkmann argues, "in every culture and society, events

21 Interview with Mamoru Oshii, in: *The Japan Times*, 17.3.2004, quoted at http://en.wikipedia.org/wiki/Ghost_in_the_Shell_2:_Innocence, accessed 28.09.2006.

and interactions take place, are reflected and given shape within a dense network of culturally established patterns of meaning and perception and before the background of quasi-institutionalized meaning-making systems."[22]

Manga – which makes up a third of Japanese print media – and anime are extremely important in Japanese society and increasingly beyond, and therefore can be seen as a vital meaning making system and trendsetting factor. Frederik L. Schodt states in his book *Dreamland Japan* that manga and anime can be seen as a kind of 'metamedium' that reflects the multiplicity of subsystems and audiences the medium manga is aimed at – all social classes, ages and genders – and therefore the complexity of contemporary societies. In its combination of traditional myths and avant-garde forms, it is also a reflection of how media work as sense-making systems through a dialectic of familiarity and alienation. Manga – for a long time neglected like its western counterpart, comics – is increasingly regarded as an important aspect of society and as a suitable instrument to communicate pedagogic, didactic and social values.

Like other mass media, but in its own, unique way, manga is also a reflection of the society it has emerged in, and can therefore provide a glimpse into that society, thereby fulfilling an important function in a globalised world. Schodt states that it is not possible to understand modern Japan if the role of manga is neglected[23] or, in the words of Antonia Levi, "[a]nime can show you a side of Japan few outsiders ever even know exists."[24] So why don't we just pick up a few manga magazines and learn a little bit about a foreign culture while being entertained and – at the same time – provoked to focus on essential questions about our place in life? Entertainment and intellectual reflection do not have to be incompatible; indeed, manga is the proof that they can come in one and the same narrative. Manga is an essential part of our pop culture, and it would be a pity to disregard it and the questions it raises – you might be missing something ...!



22 Brinkmann, *Comics und Religion*, 17 (translation Sebastian Schlöglmann) .

23 Cf. Schodt, *Dreamland Japan*, 20f.

24 Levi, *Samurai*, 9.

Rafael D. Wiener and Markus R. Löhnert

# The Pleasure of Seduction

## The Role of Christian Symbols in Advertising[1]

Whenever you turn on your TV, it will not take long before the first commercial break comes on. Unless you confine yourself to public broadcasting, sooner or later, a commercial will try to convince you that, for instance, only one particular mobile network allows you to communicate (almost) anywhere and whenever you want at (almost) no cost while all the others are overpriced and inferior with regard to coverage and network. In this market competition, it seems as if there can be only one winner: the company that attracts the maximum of attention and succeeds in appealing to customers' needs and wants will likely be the one that can sell the product best. It is not always the quality of the product that is the decisive factor for the consumer to buy it. Even more important is the message that is delivered in the commercial. Besides emphasizing the quality of a product – and sometimes not even that – some commercials touch on more immaterial aspects in order to sell their material goods. In fact, advertisements often convey a lot more than one might realize at first sight, and they do this with the help of religious symbols.



Most people in the western world are probably familiar with Christian or religious symbols in general whether they are members of a religious community or not. This fact is used in advertisement, where those familiar religious symbols and references are employed to increase the interest of the potential consumer in the product by adding an extra level of meaning and association: an apple is no longer an apple, for it becomes Eve's juicy fruit of temptation in paradise; a low-fat yogurt is no longer merely a dairy product, but a savvy way to enjoy the full taste without having to worry about the guilt of eating more than one needs. Insurance companies do not only promise to cover accidents or misfortunes; they offer security as a value in itself. The language of advertisements uses religious expressions in order to make a 'divine' offer one cannot refuse.

Our thesis is that the use of religious symbols in advertisement is a reflection of society's need for an answer to existential questions in life; yet it also shows that the answers have changed more than the questions have. This will have an effect on their use in a religious context too.

1 The authors would like to thank Victoria Moser for her help with translating and revising the article.

In the following, we will firstly clarify the meaning and function of symbols in religious language, and then have a closer look at how advertising works, and which role religious symbols have in it. As the "Our Father" is probably the most common and best known prayer in Christianity, we will take our examples from this and analyze three symbols that are used both in the prayer, and, extensively, in advertisement: 'father', 'our daily bread', and 'sin/temptation'. For our conclusion, we will develop some thoughts on changes in meaning and reflect on the possible relevance of these to both society and theology.

## 1. Symbols in a Religious Context

In order to understand the use of religious symbols in advertisement better, a short definition of what a symbol is and how it functions is necessary.

A symbol[2] (Latin: *symbolum*, from Greek: *synballein*, 'to throw two or more things together') is a sort of picture, an item, or a word that expresses a meaning (connotation) beyond its literal meaning (denotation). It refers to a greater reality behind the symbol itself which is only visible to those who know about the religious or cultural context of the object. It is this surplus of meaning that distinguishes the symbol from a sign. Symbols have always played an important role in the arts, literature and religion, and whenever one tries to give answers to questions of faith, or the meaning of life, that are difficult to answer by using everyday language or simply refuse to be answered at all.



In order to understand a symbol *as* a symbol in the first place, and to understand its connotative meaning, the reader or viewer has to be aware both of the genre of a text or image and of its context. Even though sometimes the same words might be used, depending on their context and whether they are used symbolically or literally, they might evoke very different associations.

An obvious example is the word 'father'. In everyday life, it is used to refer to the male parent. In a Christian context, however, 'father' is often used to refer to God, the Creator, the Almighty. In the Christian prayer "Our Father", the word 'father' is used to express a special, very intimate relationship between the believer and God.

### 1.1 "Our Father who art in heaven"

The prayer starts with what will have been a small sensation for Jesus' contemporaries: never before had anyone addressed God in such an intimate way.[3] The

2 http://de.wikipedia.org/wiki/Symbol, 10.10.2006.

3 Philonenko, Marc: *Das Vaterunser. Vom Gebet Jesu zum Gebet der Jünger*. Tübingen: Mohr, 2002, 34f.

Aramaic word *abba* is a term of endearment like 'Daddy' which adds a new layer of associations to the word 'God' for those saying this prayer:[4] God is not only Jesus' father but everybody's father; he is a parent who lovingly cares for each and everyone.[5] God as *abba* is no longer a patriarchal authority associated with severity, discipline and obedience, but a father who wants to be close to his children, a father one can trust totally, a father who loves and is loved in return.

## 1.2 "Give us this day our daily bread"

The daily bread is not only a symbol for food in general which is necessary for human survival, but a symbol for all that is essential in our life. Yet, our concerns for our everyday life must not make us blind to other things, like our family, people that need our support, or ultimately our and everybody's salvation in the kingdom of God.[6] In this understanding, the term 'daily bread' becomes a symbol for all in our life that matters the most. Jesus himself pointed this out: "[k]eep falsehood and lies far from me, give me neither poverty nor riches, but give me only my daily bread. Otherwise, I may have too much and disown you and say, 'Who is the LORD?' Or I may become poor and steal, and so dishonor the name of my God." (Prov 30:8f)[7] It is easy to become distracted by commodities, gadgets, and tools that make life more comfortable, but make us forget about the needs and the suffering of our fellow human beings. It is easy to worry about the amount of calories in a food product, and forget that 852 million people worldwide suffer from malnutrition.[8] While it is, of course, not wrong to enjoy life, life being God's gift, it is important to find the right balance between our needs and the needs of other people. Most importantly, though, we should not enjoy our life at the expense of other people. This could be called the ethical imperative of the term 'daily bread'.



## 1.3 "And lead us not into temptation"

Most people will recall Gen 3, when they hear of temptation in a religious context: although they were warned by God not to eat the fruits of the tree that was in the middle of the garden of Eden, Adam and Eve could not resist the

4 Boff, Leonardo: Vater unser. *Das Gebet umfassender Befreiung.* Düsseldorf: Patmos, 1981, 53; Philonenko, 34ff.

5 Ratzmann, Wolfgang (ed.): Übersetzungsversuche – Predigten über das Vaterunser und das Apostolische Glaubensbekenntnis. Universität Leipzig, 2001, 12.

6 Mt 6:19-34.

7 All Bible quotes are from the New International Version.

8 http://www.bmz.de/de/themen/ernaehrung/hintergrund/Ernaehrungssituation/index.html, accessed 06.12.2006.

temptation to taste the apple and become like God. Temptation in this context is associated with turning from God, rejecting his commandments which had been imparted for the best of humanity.

Praying to God not to be led into temptation reminds us of the importance of re-thinking and re-evaluating both our moral standards and our behavior towards ourselves and others.

These symbols of the „Our Father“ refer to three important realities of human existence: our relationship to God, the concerns of our everyday life, and our relationship to other human beings.

## 2. Religious Symbols in Advertising

In order to understand the function of religious symbols in commercials, a short overview of strategies in advertising is necessary. Advertising can be seen as a link[9] between economy and society. It aims to promote either the product and its advantages, or a specific brand. Companies that produce similar products compete with each other and, therefore, one of the aims of advertising is to promote the advantages of a specific brand (often called 'branding'). Commercials try to attract the attention of consumers and associate products or a brand with a specific way of life and with a kind of extra value that makes a specific product or products sold under a specific brand more desirable. Often, commercials try to create that very desire that only the advertised product can then fulfill.



Norbert Bolz[10] argues that today, advertising companies ascribe immaterial values to material products that were formerly addressed by the arts or religion, and thus become providers of religious and quasi-religious values and contents. They use religious symbols to boost the product's attractiveness until it seems like heaven on earth.[11] It is precisely these quasi-religious qualities of a product that make it desirable for customers who already have everything that is needed for their material survival. The desire for a spiritual extra value is in itself a sign that religious needs are as urgent today in the so-called secular society as they have always been, even if they are no longer satisfied by traditional religions or in traditional ways.

Whenever a religious symbol is used in a commercial, it gives the product added value and helps to make a 'normal' product more interesting: one always buys more than just the product itself. For example, one does not simply buy

9 Cf. Schirner, Michael: Alle reden vom Wetter. In: Wippermann, Peter (ed.): *Der Spiegel. Anzeigentrends: Was bleibt, was geht, was kommt?* Mainz: Schmidt, 1997, 79.

10 Bolz, Norbert; Bosshart, David: *Kultmarketing – Die neuen Götter des Marktes*, Düsseldorf: Econ, 1995, 191.

11 Cöster, Oskar: *AD'AGE – Der Himmel auf Erden. Eine Theodizee der Werbung*. Hamburg: DOC's Communications, 1990.

Volvic mineral water because one needs liquid to drink. Instead, one buys it for the extra value of helping to create a better world: with the purchase of a liter of Volvic water, the consumer supports a project initiated by Volvic that aims at providing clean drinking water for people in Ethiopia. When patients buy medicine, they in fact want to buy health; consumers are not interested in purchasing an insurance itself; they want the security that is promised by the insurance companies. They don't buy a car just to drive from Smallville to Grandville; they want the style, elegance, and prestige that comes with it. The advertisements promise that the purchase of their product will provide similar salvation to that promised by religions. Commercials have come to replace religion[12] with their claim to guarantee security, make the world a better place and provide happiness to everybody (who buys their product). Often, these symbols also refer to questions that touch the very heart of human existence, no matter if you are a believer or not. It is that exact extra-value that is supposed to come with a product that will convince consumers to invest their money. The understanding of the symbols depends on the background information of the viewers: in a western context, Christian symbols will at least in a general sense be known. For advertisement strategies in the east, however, companies have to refer to other concepts, values and the symbols that express them.

The following examples from advertisement have been broadcast by the Austrian public broadcasting service (ORF) during prime time, i.e. just before the news.



## 2.1 Commercial for: Financial Services

A white man in his 40s and a young boy are on a roller coaster. For the boy, the whole thing seems to be a lot of fun, but the man looks uncomfortable. A banker suddenly appears on the scene saying: "Even if your life goes up and down, your financial life should be based on a steady ground." Then two text messages appear on a blue screen: first, the name of the bank's investment plan "Best of fonds – Erste Bank und Sparkassen" and then, the company's slogan: "In erster Linie zählen die Menschen" ("Humans come foremost").

In the commercial, two father figures can be found: the biological father – 'father' in its literal meaning – on the roller coaster, and the banker who represents fatherhood on a metaphorical and symbolic level: while a biological father cannot always protect his children from the ups and downs of life, the symbolic father represents security and reliability no matter what happens, and takes on qualities of almightiness that remind the viewer of the religious meaning of God as father.

12 Bolz, Norbert: Spiritueller Mehrwert, and: Wippermann, Peter: Die Sprache der Bilder. Both in: Wippermann (ed.), *Der Spiegel.* Also: Bolz, Norbert; Bosshart, David: *Kultmarketing*; and: Cöster, Oskar: *AD'AGE – Der Himmel auf Erden*. And further: Ex 31:12–33:6.

This image is transferred from the character to the product, the investment plan, which offers the same security. The immaterial value – support in all situations in life – of the very materialistic product is reinforced by the ethical guideline: "Humans come foremost," which is introduced at the end.

## 2.2 Commercial for: Low-fat Yogurt

In the cloisters of a monastery, a priest is passing by. Someone from behind the camera stops him, shows him a cup of yogurt and asks, "Excuse me, Reverend, do you think this counts as fasting?" After having a taste, the priest responds, "No, because fasting would mean renunciation. But this really tastes a little too much like a sin." His statement is commented by a male voice: "The new fasting. Works like fasting – tastes like sin." A picture of the yogurt is faded in with a purple tape measure moving around the 'waistline' of the cup like a serpent. Once again, we see the priest reading the list of ingredients of the yogurt. Frowning, he asks, "0.1 % fat?" and with his index finger lifted up, continues: "Thou shalt not lie!"



In the spot, fasting is associated with renunciation. This agrees with the religious concept of fasting, which means the temporary renunciation of food or something else one enjoys in order to achieve the cleansing of one's body and spirit. In the spot, fasting is represented as, in general, something unpleasant or negative (because it is associated with renunciation), whereas sin is connoted with pleasure and enjoyment. This yogurt, however, is so special, the advertisement tells us, because it combines the two: when eating it nobody has to give up worldly pleasures, but will still reap the benefits of fasting. The temptation of the sinful taste of the yogurt is therefore not really temptation, because it does not have the usual negative effects (weight gain in its secular context; turning away from God and thus a reduction of the humanness of humanity in a religious context). The original spiritual meaning of fasting is, therefore, reduced to the aspect of losing body weight which used to be only a side effect of the religious practice.

Another detail in the advertisement refers to the story of the first temptation, about Adam, Eve, and the serpent in the garden of Eden. We see a purple (the liturgical colour of Lent) tape measure entwine the middle of the yogurt cup like a serpent, shaping a waist. Instead of seducing Eve to take a bite from the apple, it seduces the viewers to taste this very special, tempting yet not sinful yogurt. Sin and temptation are harmless, associated with no more than the amount of calories in a yogurt, and without existential consequences.

At the end of the advertisement, there is another religious reference, this time to the Ten Commandments: "Thou shalt not lie!" The priest assumes that, given the 'sinful' taste of the yogurt, the low amount of fat can be but a lie. But given that he has eaten it, we, the consumers, can trust the advertisement and the priest's authority and can both enjoy the sinful taste and the benefits of fasting.

### 2.3 Commercial for: Casali's Rum Coconut Candies

A beautiful beach in the Caribbean, coconut palms, white sand. An attractive young woman with long dark hair, dressed in a bikini, runs across the beach into the water. She has a small bag of rum coconut candies in her hand. A moment later, she is in the water, with men swimming around her, snorkeling. They are moving closer and closer until she starts dropping the candies into their snorkels. Another beautiful blond woman appears on the scene doing the same thing. A male voice whispers: "Mmmm, rum cocos, rum cocos, Pina-Colada," 'Pina Colada' referring to a new version of the Casali candies. In the next scene, the dark-haired woman stands at a beach bar with a cocktail shaker in her hands. She opens the shaker and white rum candies fall out. This time, a female voice whispers: "Let me seduce you – Casali!"

The scenery of the advertisement looks just like paradise: everything is perfect, everybody is beautiful and free to do whatever he or she wants, the voices express joy, pleasure, and satisfaction. Each of the two women represents one of the two kinds of candies: white and dark chocolate. Both women can easily be seen as Eve seducing Adam in paradise. In the context of this advertisement, however, seduction is presented as something positive and desirable, which is in contrast to both the original story of the Fall, and the phrase in the "Our Father:" "And lead us not into temptation." The feeling of being in paradise is the main message of the advertisement which overshadows all negative associations with sin. The temptation to taste the candies is ultimately positive: it does not lead to evil, but to a paradisiacal experience of taste and pleasure – paradise without the Fall.



## 3. Some Reflections on the Theological Implications of Religious Symbols Used in Advertising

All these religious images and symbols as they are used in commercials promise 'heaven on earth'. For the directors of the commercials, this might be an appropriate way to attract attention for the advertised product. But the problem is that unlike religions, the products advertised cannot provide true and eternal salvation; at the most, they can offer a very temporary satisfaction of needs. Yet the advertisements do not even want to promise anything else – all they want to do is stimulate a longing for new and better products. Their aim is not to satisfy human needs, but to create new ones.[13]

Salvation becomes a term for momentary satisfaction and pleasure, and its meaning in the advertisements differs widely from its religious usage. This might have an effect on the religious teaching about salvation: if it is believed to be a momentary and inner-worldly concept, providing easy and pleasurable solutions to life's challenges, the more complex theological answers appear less attractive and desirable. On the other hand, the term 'salvation' acquires a new dimension of pleasure, of holistic well-being through its use in advertisements that has often been overlooked in traditional theology in favour of a more spiritual concept.

A similar difference in meaning can be observed in the use of the symbol of bread. Originally, a person who prayed for his or her daily bread asked for much more than just having enough to eat. 'Daily bread' was a symbol for everything that is necessary and essential in life but cannot be taken for granted and is given by God. Daily bread/food in the commercials, however, is no longer needed for survival but becomes a luxury item associated with the pleasurable tension of doing something forbidden or unnecessary. On a deeper level, for the advertising companies themselves, the term 'daily bread' becomes a symbol for their need to remain successful in selling products, in keeping the consumer on the edge between satisfaction and the desire for new things in order to survive in the market. Thus, any satisfaction promised by advertisements will be – and has to be – temporary: in a few months, a newer and improved version of the product will be brought on the market and the process starts all over again.



Similarly, in advertising, the terms 'temptation' and 'sin' are obviously being reinterpreted. It is no longer something to be wary of. Being seduced by a beautiful woman or by something very delicious is no longer a sin against God's commandments, it is more like a (not so) secret pleasure everybody deserves and should enjoy. Temptation in this context merely means to follow human curiosity and explore something new. The commercials encourage people to do so, no matter what the consequences might be. The new message in advertising is not "deliver us from evil"; it is, rather, "deliver us from our limitations."

This brings us to one last motif which is used quite frequently in advertisements: moral issues. For many, the Catholic church has lost its authority to define morally binding rules of how people should live together. In some cases, the church has undermined its own authority. For instance, the character of the priest in the yogurt advertisement talking about the sinfulness of taste both claims the authority of the church for the product and mocks it at the same time by the way he is represented. While the moral authority of the church is called upon on the one hand in order to testify to the quality of the product,

13 Bolz, *Spiritueller Mehrwert*, 210f.

on the other hand, it is also implied in this and many other advertisements, that its strict views on the sinfulness of bodily pleasures or worldly joys is outdated and being replaced by the 'gospel' of the market.

In conclusion, advertisements make extensive use of the language of religious symbols, their associations and connotations, in particular with respect to moral values. Yet, their use in a context so different from the original one changes their meaning in significant ways: sin is no longer detrimental to human existence; salvation has a material and temporary aspect; luxury, pleasure and enjoyment are a human right. It is an important task for theology to keep track of these changes as a benchmark for what society is longing for and where it looks for satisfaction of these needs. Where do people get their understanding of security from, what do they long for, what matters to them? The use of symbols such as fatherhood, bread/food or temptation implies a still existing link to Christian values, and the need for them, yet their widely different meaning in advertisements also demonstrates that instantaneous satisfaction has become more important than the life-long journey to salvation that is implied in its Christian meaning. On the other hand, the symbols' association with pleasure and joy as basic elements and needs in human life might provide material for theology to reconsider its own take on the essential qualities of being human.

Contrasting the symbols' meaning in the context of an advertisement with that of religion, theology can also help to uncover market strategies that promise false hopes and misuse the trust people place in those symbols.



With its understanding of the religious meaning of these symbols, theology can stimulate a discourse on today's values that could help people reflect on what really matters in their lives and where they can start to find answers to their existential questions. A comparison of, for example, advertising's meaning of salvation and its religious understanding, can show that in the long run, temporary and instantaneous satisfaction of desires will not be helpful in dealing with life's challenges, illness or death, nor with extreme, unexplainable joy or the gift of life itself.

# ./immersion

Graham Ward

# All You Need is Love

## Moulin Rouge or Christian's Tragedy

Moulin Rouge (USA/AUS 2001) is the third and final film in Baz Luhrmann's 'Red Curtain' trilogy. Each film is concerned with the complex interception of theatricality and staging with genuine human pathos, particularly the pathos of love. We find this in his depiction of the Australian dance competition scene in Strictly Ballroom (AUS 1992), Shakespearean drama in Romeo and Juliet (USA 1996) or the musical in Moulin Rouge. In each of these films, subtle portrayals of human emotions are caught up in hyped-cliché, the burlesque and the kitsch. Moulin Rouge takes a young British writer (Christian) who, sensing his art needs a greater range of experience, flees the conventional life and ends up in a garret in bohemian Paris. Here he falls in love with a courtesan (Satine) who works at the famous Parisian nightspot, the Moulin Rouge. This fantasy world is owned and run by an affectionate but mercenary man called Ziggler, who wants to convert the place into a true theatre rather than a dance-hall and brothel. To this end he brings together Satine and a man who will financially back the project of the conversion, the Duke. But cutting across Satine's business relationship with the Duke is a growing romantic relationship with Christian; Christian who is now writing what will be the first production in Ziggler's newly constructed theatre. To complicate matters further, Satine like Mimi in Puccini's La Boheme, is dying of consumption. After much prevarication, a night comes when Satine must sleep with the Duke and betray her genuine affection for Christian. On the point of giving in to him, she sees Christian beneath her window and refuses the Duke. The Duke's jealousy drives him to threaten Satine that if she does not give up Christian, he will kill him. At the opening night of Christian's musical play, *Spectacular, Spectacular*, Satine and Christian publicly declare their love for each other, the Duke rises from the audience to shoot Christian and Satine dramatically collapses and dies on stage. The film ends with Christian looking distraught, in a garret strewn with empty bottles, and bending over his typewriter.



What I wish to explore in this essay are the theological and metaphysical motifs employed by Luhrmann in his depiction of that interception between the theatrical and the pathetic. Most particularly, with Moulin Rouge, this is the tragic pathos of a true love lost, that opens and closes the film. But first, we need to put this film into the context of a particular genre – the musical – to appreciate Luhrmann's original treatment of this type of cinematic production. I do this because the theological and metaphysical motifs issue from this treatment which reaches back beyond Hollywood entertainment to levels more violent and primitive.

What strikes me about the musicals I most remember and found most aesthetically interesting is the way how through song, dance, characterisation and cinematography they negotiate the violent. Musicals in the tradition of Rogers and Hammerstein, come of age with *Cabaret, West Side Story* and MOULIN ROUGE. The escapism of colour, movement, rhythm, song that come together to celebrate life – summed up in the bicycle scene of *The Sound of Music* where the von Trapp family sing 'Doe a deer', or the fairground scene in *Showboat* – reveals its dark side in these later musicals. The musical as a genre begins to negotiate a certain politics of entertainment that is inseparable from a wider cultural politics. The fertility rituals for the rite of Spring suddenly confront the bacchanalian frenzy out of which the musical was born – in the theatres of ancient Greece. We need to examine these disclosive (and explosive) moments in the history of the musical for, and I will return to develop this further, it is here that the genre enters the mythical, and mimesis begins to engender that pity and fear which Aristotle saw was at the heart of the tragic pathos and the catharsis of dramatic action. It is also at this point that the musical engages the theological.



Nowhere in Baz Luhrmann's MOULIN ROUGE is this moment of disclosure better realised than in the magnificent tango scene to the song 'Roxanne'. And all I have to say about Luhrmann's film will issue from an exposition of this complex and highly charged sequence (see shot one).

The scene represents one of the great tonal shifts in the film. The comic and the burlesque turn to the violent and the raw. The violence is only more

*Shot 1: MOULIN ROUGE, DVD-Still*

intense because of the controlled and measured dance-steps. The Argentinean, who we first saw dropping through Christian's ceiling as a clowning giant, suffering from narcolepsy, now speaks and sings in an entirely different register. For the first time the film that has as its *mis-en-scéne* the nightclub/brothel infamous throughout *fin de siècle* Paris, is treating prostitution directly. It does this on several levels. Literally, this is the point where Satine has to sleep with the Duke if Ziggler is to have his 'real theatre' and Satine become a 'real actress'. Metaphorically, Satine's prostitution of herself is part of a much wider exploration of commodification. The commodification of sex is presented by Luhrmann through the commercialisation of pop music, and the rich array of fabrics, jewels, costumes and colours on display in the nightclub. The film is lavish in its attention to this commercialisation, these multiple economies of exchange and intercourse within which the marketability of the film itself is situated. Through the camera's lingering and lavish attention to the sumptuous, the film celebrates its own commodification and commercialisation. The filmmaker, too, prostitutes his talents, as Christian himself does, for a price. If, as Marx saw, capitalism fetishizes its own production; creating simulated desires and objects; celebrating itself as the most dazzling of all things, then this film self-consciously is turning itself into a fetishized production about a fetishized production by Christian called *Spectacular, Spectacular*. The Moulin Rouge was a decadent, sensual theme-park and the film not only replicates but heightens both its isolation from the mundane world and its total investment in fantasy. In the netherworld of a Parisian night, the real is obliterated so that the repeated pursuit of the real in the desire of Satine (to be 'a real actress') and Ziggler (to own 'a real theatre') is one more erotic desire that will find its surrogates and fetishized objects. Every object in the frame of Luhrmann's film is fetishized from Nicole Kidman's clothes, to jewellery, to curtains, and colours. The Moulin Rouge presents the world as a theatrical props store in which capitalism, the pursuit and economy of the dazzling God of gold (for Marx), diamonds (for the Moulin Rouge), dollars (for the film industry) makes whores and hookers of us all. The windmill turns like the spool-reel in a cine camera or a projection reel. No one, and nothing – and people and objects are interchangeable in this world, witness the way the woman is thrown around and dragged in the opening of that tango scene – no one and nothing is innocent. In the world of the fetish idolatry abounds, true divinity – the iconic – is absent. This, as we shall see is the tragic heart of Luhrmann's vision – which nowhere finds more poignant expression that in MOULIN ROUGE. In an interview, Ewan McGregor who plays Christian, observed that this was the first film he had made in which no one left the studio for weeks. Into this simulation of the real, this narcotic hyperreality are thrown four metaphysical transcendentals (truth, beauty, freedom, love) and a Christian.

The four transcendentals are not quite the classic transcendentals – beauty, truth, goodness and justice – found in Plato. These were all ideal forms, archetypes whose shadows were found among the things of this world. In the film, they express the ethical and political aspirations of the Bohemian group of *artistes* which Christian falls among when he arrives in Paris. They are aspirations given aesthetic form in the production of *Spectacular, Spectacular*. For Plato the transcendentals are profoundly associated with eros – for they draw us to desire them. But it is an eros that goes beyond the purely sexual – as Plato informs us in *The Symposium*. In the Christian tradition, from Augustine to Aquinas, the four transcendentals are all convertible one into another because they name the effects of the operation of God in the world. They become cardinal theological virtues worked out in the labouring of love. For both Plato and the Christian tradition love as such was not a transcendental, but the means whereby the transcendentals come to expression.

The changes the Bohemians make to these metaphysical and theological transcendentals betray modern emphases. Freedom is espoused, rather than justice. Freedom understood in liberal terms as the maximisation of an individual's freedom to chose was itself not a transcendental, classically or theologically. It has become a transcendental only in modernity. To sketch a genealogy of modern understandings of liberty would be too long a diversion. Suffice to say it has its cultural landmarks: Luther's stand at the Diet of Worms ("Here I stand I can do no other"), Descartes meditations on the cogito and, of course, the slogan of the French Revolution ("Liberty, Equality and Fraternity"). Equality plays no part in the vocabulary of the 'children of the Revolution', but freedom does bear upon the world of the Moulin Rouge, the world of simulation generated by rampant and unchecked capitalism. For, it is not only Satine who is imprisoned – "one day I'll fly away, leave all this to yesterday" – we are all imprisoned within the glitter, promise and fantasies of consumer-desire. Love and desire are closely associated in the film, and it is the heart of Christian and Satine's struggle to distinguish them. Metaphysically and theologically, as I pointed out, love is the condition for the manifestation and operation of the transcendentals. Acts performed in love always give expression to the good, the just, the true and the beautiful. The transcendentals as the fruits of love testify to acts that are not simply rooted in an individual's desire. In fact, such acts may demand the sacrifice of individual desire. The Bohemians, then, parading their modern transcendentals have turned them away from the metaphysical and theological frameworks, weaving them into a new framework that is governed by both aesthetics and the fulfilment of subjective desire. As the Argentinean states at the beginning of the dance – "First there is desire".

While Christian, Satine and to some extent Ziggler all maintain a hope in the transcendental values, the tango scene itself stages the betrayal of such values. The dance portrays relationships caught up in lies and deceptions (there is no truth); the violence of a desire that only wishes to consume and be satisfied (there is no love); an aestheticism that is superficial, tawdry and self-pleasuring (there is no beauty); and human beings who are slaves to their lusts (there is no freedom). What there is is raw sexual energy, violence, dehumanisation, struggle, abuses of power, and exploitation. Of course, directors like Scorsese (in CASINO, for example) or Coppola (in APOCALYPSE NOW [USA 1979] for example) are masters of showing this world to us, but Luhrmann's vision is in some ways more subtle and more shocking. There is a moral edge to Scorsese's exposure of a world of drugs, mafia violence, prostitution, gambling, and extortion in CASINO. The audience are to look upon this exposure from a certain critical distance; they are voyeurs but ethically superior. Luhrmann allows us none of the comforts of armchair moralism. We visually feast upon this scene. We are voyeurs but also participants in this presentation. This participation is one of the trademarks of Luhrmann's style of directing – the camera work is visceral.[1] We need to examine in more detail the relationships between this camerawork, the soundtrack and the dancing, in order to appreciate this participatory style.

The camerawork is complex and multidimensional in this sequence. As those who have seen the DVD extras know, the tango scene was shot from four cameras using a variety of perspectives: panoramic shots from above the dance-floor, tracking shots for Christian's walk through the dancers, close-ups, circling shots etc. Each camera frames the scene differently. Sometimes the frame is crowded to suffocation, bringing to us the smell of sweat, the heat of touch, the

*Shot 2: MOULIN ROUGE, DVD-Still*

1 For a discussuin on the bodily effects of films cf. Stefanie Knauss's article in this volume.

claustrophobia. Sometimes the frame is spacious, sounds echo cacophonously, though still there is a multitude of objects cluttering the frame. These different framings are spliced and edited to follow the rhythm of the tango. The effect is that we are never still, never in just one place, we are visually dancing about from one perspective to another. Into this tango, scenes from the gothic tower are intercut so that one scene comments upon the other (see shot two). To begin with, the scenes are tonally quite distinct – the physically and sexually charged tango cuts to the quieter tête-à-tête between the Duke and Satine. Eventually the violence that is always explicit in the tango scene and which the dancing and music heightens, even melodramatises, spills over to the attempted rape of Satine by the Duke, who has lost all self-control. Emotional control and its loss are important themes in the film; the loss of control can be redemptive (as with Satine giving in to her love for Christian) and destructive (as with the Duke's homicidal rages). The music, dancing and camera-work are important means for dramatizing this theme – the Dionysian frenzy of the cancan and balletic, Fred Astair and Ginger Rogers moment when Christian and Satine dance on the clouds, for example. That theme of control and its loss is played out in the tango scene through a complex parallelism between the dance, the emotions of the Duke and the agonies of Christian. Each character demonstrates a possession by a jealousy that borders on madness. Christian's song is an expression of the turmoil within both men at different times within the film. The point I am making here concerning audience participation is what I want to call the multi-layering of Luhrmann's filming. It is a multi-layering that is made all the richer by allusions to other films (the Hammer Horror genre), the earlier John Ford version of MOULIN ROUGE, paintings by Toulouse Lautrec, other famous vocal recordings (by Sting), for example. The multi-layering keeps the mind in play while the senses of sight and hearing and touch are overwhelmed by what is being presented. I include touch here even though the touching is more metaphorical than actual – we don't in fact receive any empirical perceptions of touch. But the dancing, particularly the sound of heals hitting the dance-floor do have a strong tactile element associated with them. It is like being hit, even assaulted – even if only in an auditory manner. The overall effect of this multi-layering is that the audience cannot disassociate itself from the unfolding spectacular narrative. In the early stages of the scene, when the multi-layering is being created the audience moves from intense engagement – with the dancers – to an observational distance – of the events in the tower –, from participant to voyeur. But as the scene progresses, with the inner violence of mind and outer violences of dance and rape, disengagement is impossible. We are drawn into the maelstrom, the madness of uncontrolled desire.

And here we start to engage the film theologically. For in the face of the betrayal of the transcendental aspirations, the transcendental values themselves indicate a level of desire in this Bohemian world to reach beyond the facades and fantasies of the tower, the huge elephantine brothel, the tawdriness of Moulin Rouge and Montmatre, and touch something authentic, real, about the human condition – particularly about love. Take that moment when Satine refuses the Duke and glances down at Christian in his agony (see shot three). It unleashes all the violence of desire in both the Duke and the tango. It is not a pure moment of romance, for the film is still playing with theatrical allusions and fairytale themes – the princess in the dark tower (only Satine is a whore), the balcony scene from Romeo and Juliet, the iconic portrait shots of Nicole Kidman's anguish (imitating frame shots that made Bette Davis, Vivien Leigh, Ingrid Bergman so famous) – nevertheless there is a desire to touch the true, a desire voiced in song. It is this desire to touch the true, to live the transcendentals of truth, beauty, freedom and love, in the midst of their evident and inevitable betrayal that constitutes the human tragedy. The tragedy lies in the impossibility of attaining what human beings most deeply long for.

*Shot 3: Moulin Rouge, DVD-Still*



This tragedy is right at the heart of Moulin Rouge and this scene in particular. In fact, it is at the heart of Luhrmann's filming as such and the sensual overloading that is a hallmark of that filming. It is as if Luhrmann is raging against cinematic mediation itself, wanting to overcome it by returning us to the immediacy of dramatic performance – where real actors and dancers, performing in real time, in real theatres, are co-present with their audience. This desire surfaces repeatedly throughout the film, voiced particularly by the director (Luhrmann), the director's avatar (the impresario Ziggler), and Satine. The human tragedy lies in this hopeless rage of the authentic against the inauthentic; the rage of trying to speak of truth, beauty, love, and freedom in a world sinking beneath the clichés and jargon of a culture glutted by its own mass production and its continual reproduction of fairy-tale endings. Even the authenticity of song, so key to the musical genre, can rarely rise above this mass production. Other than for the lover's lyric, "Come what may," all the songs in the film are recycled from elsewhere in the pop world. One might suggest Luhrmann is attempting to perform a sort of exorcism – of emotions, of theatricality itself, of escapist cinema musicals like THE SOUND OF MUSIC (Wise, USA 1965).

It is with the portrayal of human beings caught tragically between longings for values that they and the worlds they create forever betray that the film's 'theological' trajectories most fully emerge. They do so because the transcendental values advocated are profoundly related, historically, to those transcendental ideals that Christianity articulates and the children of the revolution (Lautrec et al.) comically turn into some Marx brothers routine. To understand what is clearly at stake here, let us return to the tango scene. For when the Argentinean emerges from the shadows to announce the dance from Buenos Aires, the camera observes him approach and the light catches the large silver crucifix around his throat. It is a significant detail especially when counterpoised with the image of Satine's exposed throat as she receives the diamond necklace from the Duke, and the prostitute in the tango who bares her naked throat before the men grouped around her like a sacrificial victim. The tango as performed in the film is a dance about animal sacrifice. It inflects, in a violent, cynical and sadistic manner, the *pasa doble* dance sequence in Luhrmann's STRICTLY BALLROOM. Satine is being sacrificed here for Ziggler's, and the Company's and her own baser ambitions. What is also being sacrificed is her love for Christian – although, as we discover at the end Satine does not go through with this sacrifice or the sacrifice of herself. As I said, at the beginning, with the tango the molten energy at the film's core surfaces. No more smouldering temptress – fires flare throughout this scene. The moment the crucifix flashes the film cuts to a medium shot of Christian – for the tango scene is an enactment of his crucifixion, his descent into the madness of jealousy, deception and betrayal. The forceful grating voice of the Argentinean as he opens the first bar of 'Roxanne' – elsewhere his voice is mellifluously operatic – emphasizes the tearing apart of the transcendentals love, beauty, truth and freedom. Together with the sharp aggression of the dance-steps, this rendition of the song magnificently cuts across the lyrical sadness of Sting's own recording. Christian's lyrics "Please believe me when I say I love you" struggle to rise above the destructive passion; the Duke dramatically embodies that destructive passion, unleashed when he tells Satine, in an agony of his own at her betrayal of him, "You made me believe you loved me." But Christian's passion is different. It is a passion expressed in a counter dynamic to the mythic formalities and energies of the dance. His is a slow, measured walking through, but then beyond the dance-floor to the outside and the base of the tower. His is a passion of non-resistance, of vulnerability unable to defend itself; he sings to himself, he walks in isolation, in abandonment. Until, that is, the moment where Satine says 'No' to the Duke.

What happens next, when viewed theologically, has to be appreciated in the wider context of the film's appeal to the Christian religion. When we first followed Christian into the Moulin Rouge, the camera swept us through the gates of Montmatre and the figure of a priest floated into the frame, warning of the sinfulness and evils of the place as if Christian was passing through the gates of Hell and descending into the multiple circles of the inferno. The priest's words echo those of Christian's own father. The portrayal of the father is hyperbolic and comic, but the portrayal of the priest is one of sad resignation. When interviewed, Luhrmann and his co-writer, Pearce, both talk of Christian as an Orpheus who descended into the underworld in search of his lost wife Eurydice; Orpheus whose voice and song could awaken the rocks, the trees and the stars. But we need always to recall Luhrmann's multi-layering technique. For the most famous 'Christian' in the history of literature is John Bunyan's, making his pilgrim's progress to the Promised Land through the shadows, temptations, despondencies and vanities of this world. The tonal shifts in the film's language, a language unique to Luhrmann, correspond to the different circles of significance. We begin with the superficial, pastiche, kitsch, and slapstick; we conclude with something bordering on tragedy – emotional and physical pain, madness, threats, attempted murder, and death. In terms of the plot, Christian like Orpheus, fails to free his love from the underworld. He fails to rise above the banalities, seductions and theatricality that threaten continually to engulf his song and his appeal to transcendental, eternal values. In fact, even song fails in the end. The last scene of the film leaves song and dance behind, Christian remains in Paris, trapped in his own memories and bereavement, tapping out pseudo-sophisms on his typewriter. "Above all a story about love. A love that will live forever. The end." Despite the background *adagio* these words barely raise themselves from the paper they are being typed upon. There is no freedom realised. It is death that has the final word. As with Orpheus, there is no return to the upper world. Theologically, given the crucifixion of Christian there is no resurrection. Even when the simple, underscored voice sings the closing bars of "The greatest thing in all the world is just to love and be loved in return", the camera is pulling out to the image of the stage and a conductor standing above the pit, with which the film opened, and the famous red curtains come down. If love has the last word it is, tragically, only in and through death. This parallels Luhrmann's dramatic conclusion to ROMEO AND JULIET, and announces again a radical departure from the 'fairy-tale' ending found in STRICTLY BALLROOM. In STRICTLY BALLROOM there is a resurrection. The ugly duckling Fran is united with her dashing partner who has creatively triumphed over the corrupt and rule-bound world of ballroom dancing. Their dancing brings the whole audience onto the ballroom floor, unifying the community.

Satine's death and Christian's decline into sad banalities bring the film to an end at the level of plot. It is as if Luhrmann senses his own failure to find a language in which the innocent, the ideal, the authentic can be voiced. The transcendental values, captured briefly only in the final duet between Satine and Christian – which begins by splicing the space of stage and auditorium, the spectacular Indian drama and the audience reception, but ends centre-stage – the transcendental values fade out. But at the level of cinema, something is achieved. The very inability to speak innocently, ideally, authentically is articulated; the failure does not deny the possibility, the hope, the longing which remains. There is no resurrection, despite Christian's crucifixion, but there is an exposure: the rampant consumerism that the Moulin Rouge theme-park announces exhausts itself; it is exorcised. In fact, in a very nineteenth century play on words that lies at the heart of that other great musical about prostitution *La Boheme*, consumerism is consumed in Satine's consumption. The move from the comic entertainment of the sleazy world of the Moulin Rouge to its exposure as corrupt and decadent is only made possibly by playing this world against the transcendental values being betrayed. So although the transcendental values are only realised momentarily they serve to open an alternative space for human longing; a utopic space that is conducive to practices of hope. At the ending not of the plot but the film credits a new note is sounded. When the curtain descends, there is a magnificent sweep of strings and, in flickering retro-cinematic form, a *piam memoriam* is announced. "In memory of Leonard Luhrmann." Leonard Luhrmann is Baz Luhrmann's father, who died suddenly as filming was about to begin. The stage and cinematic death spills over, when the curtain is drawn, into an actual death of someone loved and familiar (see shot four). But a new simplicity is born with the closing credits as a piano picks out a complex but haunting melody. That melody, too, will be overwhelmed by a full orchestral development, but cinematographically it is not with failure but with possibility that we end. There is no Christian symbolism in evidence here, but the ending, much more so than the cold, even callous news broadcast in the closing moments of ROMEO AND JULIET, follows what I want to call a certain Christic rhythm. I use the adjective 'Christic' to point to a narrative pattern linking this film to the death and resurrection of Christ as it was interpreted by the early church; a church who remained caught in a world that betrayed and denied their theological hopes and desires despite the resurrection of Christ. In this Christic rhythm the resurrection is not the triumph and erasure of the

*Shot 4: MOULIN ROUGE, DVD-Still*

crucifixion; it is the hope contrary to hope that Paul speaks of in his *Letter to the Romans*. The suffering, pain, and downright sordidness of Jesus Christ's death on the cross can never be forgotten; in fact the very way to redemption lies in facing the enormity of that event – and hoping for better things. Of course, in MOULIN ROUGE, there is no sacrifice. Satine has been dying from the beginning and Christian does not give up his own life for her. Nevertheless, Luhrmann remains profoundly interesting theologically because of his cinematic appeals to the Christian mythos, his tragic conception of the human condition, and the epic struggle in all his films to express "the greatest thing in all the world is to love and be loved in return." In one sense, this sentiment is the heart of the Christian Gospel: "This is my commandment, that you love one another as I have loved you." (Joh 15:12) But where Luhrmann differs from the Christian understanding of such love is exactly on the point of sacrifice: "No one has greater love than this, to lay down one's life for one's friends." (Joh 15:12) There is no sacrifice in MOULIN ROUGE, no room for it in the world it proposes; which raises the question of the effectiveness of the exposure of the shallow values of such a world. Luhrmann senses the possibility of the futility even of the exposure, I think. There is a postmodern reflexiveness about his theatrical treatment of theatre that suggests the exposure is one more move in an ongoing melodrama. It, too, could *just* be a piece of theatre. The slow *adagio* at the end rushes into a an up-beat and full orchestrated tempo. Nevertheless, the longing expressed in those transcendentals remain, articulating theological and metaphysical questions about the human condition.

Gerard Loughlin

# Video Divina

## Viewing Tarkovsky

Clive Marsh has drawn attention to the fact that in both church and cinema we have to do with affect, with the eliciting of emotion. Both film and liturgy stir us to feel, to experience fear and joy, sorrow and exaltation. And this common interest in stirring the viewer-participant to engage emotionally as well as cognitively in what is shown, leads Marsh to identify a 'spiritual' aspect to film watching, and most especially when it is regularly undertaken in the 'community' of the movie theatre.[1]

The cinema is spiritual when it becomes a ritual of self-reflection, when it takes place within the viewer's "life-structure" and engages his or her "inner life."[2] "Regular film-watching shapes a pattern of living. It [...] forms a major channel through which thoughts, feelings, and aesthetic and moral sensibilities are stimulated and developed. [...] [I]t proves a major way in which personal development happens."[3] One might almost say – though Marsh does not – that such regular and potentially life-changing viewing is akin to the Christian practice of confession, when self-interrogation leads to resolution and reform. But in the cinema this is undertaken by going 'out of oneself' into other, imaginary lives, and it is done without a necessary moment of absolution or forgiveness. It is a more purely interior transformation, with no required recognition of the others on whom one must depend in becoming other than oneself.



On Marsh's account, cinema going – when spiritual – is a practice by which the self is formed and reformed, constructed and reconstructed. But as Marsh goes on to note, such cinema going must be tutored by some sense of the other that the self is seeking to become.[4] For otherwise the viewer will be prey to all manner of unknown ideologies, to the 'demons' that always attend the viewing

1 Clive Marsh, *Theology Goes to the Movies*. London: Routledge, 2006.

2 Clive Marsh, *Cinema and Sentiment: Film's Challenge to Theology*. Milton Keynes: Paternoster Press, 2004, 122.

3 Marsh, *Cinema and Sentiment,* 134. See also Haines Lyon and Marsh's article in this volume.

4 Marsh, *Cinema and Sentiment,* 135.

of images.[5] Thus cinematic theology cannot avoid critique; a moment when it judges the lives that cinema tempts us to become, even if but momentarily. And that judgement can only be made through participating in something like the alternative vision that the church seeks to show in the 'cinema' of its liturgies.

## 1. Film and Liturgy

Film and liturgy work on us in different but related ways. Both seem to achieve their effects, when successful, through perfect timings and modulations, the changing of scene and tempi at the right moment to enliven or disconcert, to enflame or quieten the soul. No doubt the cinema – especially the modern cinema – is more proficient in such manipulation than the church, because more rigorous or purified in its means. It aims to remove as many distractions as possible from its viewing, its pictures filling the viewer's vision, its sounds obliterating all other noises. And apart from the odd glitch with projector or speakers, the cinema's showings are perfectly coordinated and always the same. Sacred liturgy, on the other hand, is faulted by the forgettings and vagaries of its participants, by their ability to miss a cue, fall out of step. The music may come in too late or too early, and the choir miss the note.[6]



But the liturgy can survive the disruption of its decorum, the distractions of an imperfect production. And unlike film, there is a sense in which sacred liturgy works every time, for its 'success' depends not on the will of its practitioners but on the faithfulness of its Lord. For even when worship fails to deliver a spiritual high, a felt experience of transcendence, this very failure betokens the originary human condition that the church teaches through its practices of confession, supplication and assurance of forgiveness. And the mere fact that the congregation has come together betokens the arrival of the one who comes in its gathering. But no such arrival can be promised in the cinema. The ultimate beauty of the liturgy consists not in its performance – though this can be beautiful – but in its constantly repeated structure: the invocation of God's gifts *and their arrival*.

And liturgy is never sentimental, for the story it invokes – the story of a life given for life – is utterly unsentimental. A sentimental liturgy would have forgotten that the church comes together to remember a death, and only has *hope* of the resurrection. It must forever pray that what will be may be so. Liturgy reminds us of the sorrow that must always attend the joys of this world.

5 Cf. Gerard Loughlin, *Alien Sex: The Body and Desire in Cinema and Theology*. Oxford: Blackwell, 2004, 35–63.

6 On the missteps of liturgy see Kieran Flanagan, *Sociology and Liturgy: Re-presentations of the Holy*. Basingstoke: Macmillan, 1991.

Every birth announces a death (even if one death promises life), and such a bitter-sweet message is not considered good box-office. However, while most films – and especially Hollywood films – abjure such hesitancy, this is not true of all; not even of all Hollywood films. Some films are open to the vision that is always given – for those with eyes to see – in even the most desultory of liturgical performances.

Cinema is a practice because in order to see a film one must become part of the 'vision machine' that produces cinematic sight. Viewers are placed between projector and screen, and taught how to see in the dark. The machine is both hard and soft, technical and social. It is both the mechanics of coordinated shadows and the discipline of common viewing (when in the movie theatre), an audience tutored in narrative iconology, in the art of reading sequential images. Viewers must not only become accustomed to the dark, but they must learn how to see a three dimensional world in the two dimensions of the picture frame, and continuous time in the fractured moments of a film's narration. And this looking does not come naturally. It has to be learned.

The apocryphal story has it that when in the Lumiere's L'ARRIVÉ D'UN TRAIN (1895), the locomotive came hurtling into the station, several members of the audience turned and ran. This story grants the film image an objectivity and obviousness that may actually succeed rather than accompany its viewing. For other stories of early cinema record consternation on the part of audiences, not because they were confronted by an oncoming reality but by a play of light and shade that they were unable to interpret as representation, but only experience as confusion. They had to learn how to look before they could see what they were being shown. In the same way we must learn how to look for the spiritual in cinema. We must learn the art of spiritual reading or *lectio divina*.



## 2. Memory and Contemplation

*Lectio divina* was at first the sacred page that was read. But with time it became the name for the reading of the page; just as *sacra pagina* also passed from object to action, from noun to verb. In this passage from the written text to its reading, the word became an action of the soul, or better, an action in the soul of the meditating monk. The biblical text was constituted as sacred scripture in and through its prayerful reading.[7] The text had to be transformed in and through the imagination of its reader, and this transformation was an act of devotion, and so ultimately an act of the divine in the devotee.

7 See Gerard Loughlin, *Telling God's Story: Bible, Church and Narrative Theology*. Cambridge: Cambridge University Press, 1999 (1996).

As action, *lectio divina* consisted in three parts, or three moments within a continuous but complex activity. First, the monk or nun had to read the text; second she or he had to memorialize what s/he had read, so that – thirdly – the text could be recalled and so more fully entered in meditation. The work of memory was particularly important for those who could not have the text always before them, but must later recall what they had earlier read. Thus even when reading was the reading of another, as when passages were read in the refectory, the nun or monk could still dwell upon – and so come to dwell within – the words of scripture when the latter were recalled in private devotion, in the sequestration of the cell.

Hugh of St Victor (d. 1142) likened memory to the gathering and storing of images for future meditation. The trick was to gather just the things that were necessary, "to gather brief and dependable abstracts to be stored in the little chest of the memory, so that later on, when need arises, we can derive everything else from them." Or – more strangely – we might think of the memory as our stomach, from which the 'abstracts' are to be regurgitated and tasted again. But the point is that the text lives on in the memory, and just those parts of it that will take us to the one "fountainhead" from which everything flows.[8] For the point of remembering was *meditatio*, and *meditatio* led onto *contemplatio*: the "seeing" of the "invisible things of God."[9]



One read in order to pray, in order to see what the scripture had to show. The thirteenth-century *Ancrene Riwle* (or *Ancrene Wisse*) reminds the anchoresses for whom it was written that they ought to pray less that they might read more, for "[r]eading is good prayer. In reading, when the heart feels delight, devotion arises. And that is worth many prayers. St Jerome said, 'Let holy reading be always in thy hand.'"[10] It was only later in the thirteenth century, with the rise of the university and the decline of the monastery as a site of learning, that the reading of scripture was divided between academic and spiritual interests, and the earlier *lectio divina* came to be known as *lectio spiritualis*, and opposed to more academic study of the Bible. Nevertheless, it is in the thirteenth-century illustrated Apocalypse that Suzanne Lewis finds an apt figure for the practice of *lectio divina* as spiritual reading, as reading for *vision*.

8 Hugh of St Victor, *The Didascalicon of St Hugh of St Victor: A Medieval Guide to the Arts*, translated and introduced by Jerome Taylor. New York: Columbia University Press, 1991 (1961), 94.

9 Hugh of St Victor, *The Didascalicon*, 214n56.

10 *Ancrene Riwle: The Nun's Tale*, translated by James Morton. London: Chatto & Windus, 1924, IV, 287; cited in Suzanne Lewis, *Reading Images: Narrative Discourse and Reception in the Thirteenth Century Illuminated Apocalypse*. Cambridge: Cambridge University Press, 1995, 235.

For the Apocalypse already figures the fruition of *lectio divina* by being the writing of a vision or series of visions, vouchsafed to the Seer on Patmos. "Look! He is coming with the clouds." (Rev 1:7)[11] The Apocalypse is first seen before it is written, and its reading will seek to reverse its writing, to render to the reader's eye what was seen before it was written, and is now seen again in the vision of the reader. And that this reading is undertaken for vision – for seeing what was shown – is signalled by the copious illustrations in the illuminated Apocalypses of the medieval period. The words were turned into images on the page, as if reading had already attained its destined end. But of course the images themselves became a text inviting interpretation and meditation. They invited reading. They invited a *video divina*, a practice of seeing that already presaged what was to come in the movie houses of the twentieth century. The illustrated Apocalypses are exemplary because they turned the text into images, written words into storyboards.

It is easy to forget that the medieval church that developed the practice of *lectio divina* was as much interested in meditating upon images as upon words. Even the Cistercians, who shunned the sensible and abjured the decorative,[12] began to relent as soon as the twelfth century drew to a close, as soon as St. Bernard of Clairvaux (1090–1153) was in his grave.[13] The library at Clairvaux would become one of the richest in medieval Europe. But it was not only in the decorated manuscript that monks and nuns encountered images. They met them in community and in privacy, in the choir and in the cell; in the seclusion of their memory.



Film also lives in memory. This was never more the case than when films could be seen only in the movie theatre. But even now, when they are available on DVD for repeated and frame-by-frame viewing, the film can still live only in the memory, which alone turns a temporal succession of images into a meaningful unity, an entity which exists only *between* what is seen and the one who sees. Thus the films that may shape and reshape our lives are themselves shaped and reshaped by the lives that see them. Like any text or image, a film is different each time it is viewed because viewed by people who are different each time they look.

The church teaches that since everything comes from God we may look for the "invisible things of God" in the visible things of God's making (i.e. everything). The world too is to be remembered, meditated and contemplated.

11 For Margaret Barker, the Apocalypse or Book of Revelation is the vision that was given to Jesus by God (Rev 1:1). See Margaret Barker, *The Revelation of Jesus Christ*. Edinburgh: T. & T. Clark, 2000.

12 See Caroline Walker Bynum, *Metamorphosis and Identity*. New York: Zone Books, 2001.

13 Janet Coleman, *Ancient and Medieval Memories: Studies in the Reconstruction of the Past*. Cambridge: Cambridge University Press, 1992, 170–72.

Thus the doctrine of creation authorizes the desire to see in cinema something more, but not other than what it shows. In cinema we may practice *meditatio* and *contemplatio*. But this looking through remembering requires practice. We have to learn how to dwell in the image – in the remembered film – so that we might come to see the invisible in the visible, and it is this art of *video divina* that Andrei Tarkovsky sought to teach in his films. It is the art of seeing something more *but not other than* what is shown.

## 3. Moving Air

The coming of the god is announced with the stirring of the air, with the bending of grasses in the field, the movement of leaves on the tree. We cannot see air, except as it moves things, though we can feel it on our skin, blowing against our face, ruffling our hair. Perhaps we can smell air, or is it only the lightest of things moving, perfumes and pollens, tickling the nose? Perhaps we can taste it, a clear or sultry air, or again is it only the tasting of things, sea-spray and fine earth? We certainly feel and hear air, as it brushes past us, rustling leaves and swaying grasses, announcing the coming of the god, and then, when the wind drops down, and the day becomes still and tranquil, the god's passing, or resting, very quietly close by.



One may recall those moments in the films of Andrei Tarkovsky, where natural elements – falling rain or wind-blown grasses undulating in waves – seem to presage a reality or significance beyond the articulation of either the films' characters or their viewers. One may recall the early scene in MIRROR (USSR 1974), where the narrator's mother, Masha (Margarita Terekhova), is sitting on a fence, smoking a cigarette, with the soft light of the setting sun coppering the leaves of the trees behind her. She is looking out across the field that is the very field below the house in which Tarkovsky spent his childhood summers, the house which had been destroyed but was rebuilt for the film.[14] The scene is the second in the film, the first after the main titles. From her seat on the "springy bar of the fence," Masha can look down the slope of the field to where people can be seen walking along the road from Ignatievo to Tomshino, though the road itself cannot be seen. Travelers can be recognized only when they have passed the bush in the middle of the field. "Somebody walking along the road vanished behind the bush. If he now came out on the left of the bush, then it was HE. If

14 Vida T. Johnson and Graham Petrie, *Andrei Tarkovsky: A Visual Fugue*. Bloomington and Indianapolis: Indiana University Press, 1994, 115; Andrei Tarkovsky, *Sculpting in Time*, trans. Kitty Hunter-Blair. Austin: University of Texas Press, 1996 (1986), 132.

it was on the right, then it was not he, and now he would never come back."[15] But it is not he; it is not the narrator's longed-for father, who is away at the war. It is a passerby (Anatoly Solonitsyn), a doctor who has lost his way.

The film's encounter between the stranger and the mother, waiting for her husband, closely follows Tarkovsky's novelized script for the film, "A White, White Day" (or "Bright, Bright Day"). But the film's meeting is lighter in mood while yet more resonate with unspoken possibilities and feared losses. In the script the doctor sits down on the grass before musing on the sentience of nature, but in the film he first sits on the "springy bar" of the fence, beside Masha, causing it to break and landing both of them on their backs, almost lying together like lovers. Masha jumps up and brushes down her clothes, but the doctor remains where he is, listening to the buzzing of insects that has suddenly grown loud on the soundtrack. Then he takes his leave, and starts back down the path, across the field towards the bush. "For a long time, mother followed him with her eyes. Then she slid off the fence and walked slowly home. A breath of wind sprang up and bowed the alder bush that grew by the fence."[16] But in the film, Masha is already off the fence when the doctor leaves, and as he goes she notices a speck of blood on his face and calls after him. And the breath of wind that springs up is more than a breath, more than a sudden flurry. It springs up out of the stillness of the late afternoon, and races across the field, from the distant bush, past the doctor, to break in the foreground, bending the alder and brushwood at the edge of the film frame. It springs up and races towards us, towards Masha, as she stands in the protection of the wood, at the edge of the field. The wind is both natural and unnatural, and a viewer cannot but feel that it invests the meeting of the waiting woman and traveling man with an import beyond its seeming inconsequence. It marks their encounter with some significance and fills the late afternoon with either blessing or foreboding. It is surely the sign of a presence, a symbol for something metaphysical. Yet Tarkovsky insisted that nature appears in his films as simply nature, as rain falling, fire burning, and wind blowing.



> Rain, fire, water, snow, dew, the driving ground wind – all are part of the material setting in which we dwell; I would even say of the truth of our lives. I am therefore puzzled when I am told that people cannot simply enjoy watching nature, when it is lovingly reproduced on the screen, but have to look for some hidden meaning they feel it must contain.[17]

---

15 Andrei Tarkovsky and Aleksandr Misharin, A White, White Day, (1968/1984) in Andrei Tarkovsky, *Collected Screenplays*, trans. William Powell and Natasha Synessios. London: Faber & Faber, 1999, 263–32 (268).

16 Tarkovsky and Misharin, A White, White Day, 269.

17 Tarkovsky, *Sculpting in Time*, 212.

## 4. Natural Symbols

Tarkovsky simply wants to bring the "real world" to the screen, "so that it can be seen in depth and from all sides, evoking its very 'smell', allowing audiences to feel on their skin its moisture or its dryness." He doesn't want them to be asking "Why? What for? What's the point?" He wants them to surrender to the "immediate, emotional aesthetic impression," to nature as it is in itself, brought into the cinema and placed upon the screen. We should trust what we see.[18]

> Nature exists in cinema in the naturalistic fidelity with which it is recorded; the greater the fidelity, the more we trust nature as we see it in the frame, and at the same time, the finer is the created image: in its authentically natural likeness, the inspiration of nature itself is brought into cinema.[19]

Tarkovsky records, perhaps with amusement, that audiences reacted with incredulity when he insisted that there are no "symbols or metaphors" in his films. "They persist in asking again and again, for instance, what rain signifies in my films; why does it figure in film after film; and why the repeated images of wind, fire, water?" Why indeed, for it is somewhat disingenuous of Tarkovsky to complain that he does not "know how to deal with such questions."[20]

For while it may take some time before a poetic filmmaker can or will say why a particular shot or camera movement was required, s/he had from the first an unspoken, intuitive knowledge – a deeper discernment – of what seemed necessary to produce the image, to undertake the arduous setting-up of lights and camera, of the machines and technicians that produced the illusion of wind, rain or fog. For rarely can a film director afford to wait upon the elements to disport themselves as required. Tarkovsky's nature is always premeditated because always constructed. The strange wind that disturbs the stillness of the evening is utterly real because the real effect of a helicopter, flying towards the camera, just out of shot. Like the words of a poet, Tarkovsky's nature has been carefully honed for its purpose.

And when pressed – pressing himself – Tarkovsky will admit that there are some metaphorical or symbolic moments in his films. He cites the last shot of NOSTALGIA (Italy/USSR 1983), when he brings the "Russian house inside the Italian cathedral."[21] Just after the collapse and presumed death of the film's protagonist, the Russian poet Andrei Gorchakov (Oleg Yankovsky) – perhaps in the 'moment' of his death – we see him seated on the ground outside his dacha, his

18 Tarkovsky, *Sculpting in Time*, 213.

19 Tarkovsky, *Sculpting in Time*, 212.

20 Tarkovsky, *Sculpting in Time*, 212.

21 Tarkovsky, *Sculpting in Time*, 213–14.

country house in Russia, the lost home that appears in so many of Tarkovsky's films. The poet rests his weight on one arm, and a dog sits to his left, and both look straight ahead at us the viewers, while the camera slowly tracks back to reveal that this strange and impressive setting – which we already recognize from the poet's dreams earlier in the film – is now situated within the ruined nave of an abbey church, its glassless windows reflected in a foreground pool.[22] Today this doubled landscape – the Russian inside the Italian – would be computer generated, and all the poorer for it. Like the wind and rain, Tarkovsky's dreamscape is utterly real, a constructed miniature landscape, with a scaled down model house, creating a false perspective. As the camera pulls back to show the full setting, snow begins to fall "as though in a dream,"[23] both in the middle and far distance, throughout the nave which now harbors the Russian countryside.

This scene, as Tarkovsky puts it, is a "constructed image which smacks of literariness;" a depiction of the dying Gorchakov's state of mind, caught by the past in the ruins of the present. Tarkovsky offered two contradictory readings of the scene. On the one hand it may figure the poet's dirempted world, torn between past and present life – as was Tarkovsky, filming in Italy while yearning for Russia and the life to which he did and did not wish to return.[24] Or it might figure not diremption but its mending, a "new wholeness in which the Tuscan hills and the Russian countryside come together indissolubly," merged into the being and blood of the poet, even as he feels that he must return to Russia. Tarkovsky worries that the scene may lack "cinematic purity," but feels that it is free from "vulgar symbolism," for it refers not to something outside of the scene, to something other than Gorchakov, but to the writer himself, who is in the scene.[25] The shot refers to itself. It is its own world.



22 The church is the twelfth-century Abbey of San Galgano in Tuscany.

23 Tonino Guerra and Andrei Tarkovsky, Nostalgia, (1978–82) in Andrei Tarkovsky, *Collected Screenplays*, trans. William Powell and Natasha Synessios. London: Faber & Faber, 1999, 471–503 (503).

24 "I have to say that when I first saw all the material shot for the film I was startled to find it was a spectacle of unrelieved gloom. [...] This was not something I had set out to achieve; what was symptomatic and unique about the phenomenon before me was the fact that, irrespective of my own specific theoretical intentions, the camera was obeying first and foremost my inner state during filming: I had been worn down by my separation from my family and from the way of life I was used to, by working under quite unfamiliar conditions, even by using a foreign language. [...] I was startled to find how accurately my own mood while making the film was transferred onto the screen: a profound and increasingly wearing sense of bereavement, away from home and loved ones, filling every moment of existence. To this inexorable, insidious awareness of your own dependence on your past, like an illness that grows ever harder to bear, I gave the name 'Nostalgia'. [...]" Tarkovsky, *Sculpting in Time*, 203–204, 206.

25 Tarkovsky, *Sculpting in Time*, 216.

## 5. Within the Image

Tarkovsky seeks to show the truth itself, rather than something else, which stands in for the truth. When Tarkovsky rejects symbolic readings of his work it is because he is thinking of the symbol as a stand-in, a substitute, and Tarkovsky wants something more immediate, something that does not point away from itself, but into which we are led. He wants something that is, as it were, a symbol of itself, and so not a symbol as we might ordinarily understand the term. Tarkovsky admits that when it rains in his films it is not just a case of bad weather, but nor is it a symbol of something other than rain. We should resist the temptation – strong though it is – to take Tarkovsky's gentle downpours as signs of God's grace, symbols of a more metaphysical event. The wind that blows across the fields and through the trees in MIRROR is not mere happenstance, but nor is it a symbol, a stand-in, for the "pervasive Holy Ghost, in Christian belief the third person of the Trinity alongside Jesus and God," as Mark Cousins is too quick to tell us in his history of film.[26] How then should we understand it?

Rain – or snow or wind or fire – appears in Tarkovsky's films in order to produce what he calls an "aesthetic setting in which to steep the action of the film," it appears in order to show us a world.[27] Tarkovsky tells us that he wants to put his own world on the screen, as he feels and sees it, "in its ideal and most perfect form." "I am recreating my world in those details which seem to me most fully and exactly to express the elusive meaning of its existence."[28] As Tarkovsky (with Aleksandr Misharin) put it, he hopes to answer – to *show* the answer to – a fundamental question, the question of MIRROR and of all Tarkovsky's films: "What did Man live for, what does he live for and what will he live for; by what great, secret powers, *invisible to our gaze* [...]."[29]



Tarkovsky – as he himself admits – is not consistent in his discussion of symbols. "However, it is for the artist both to devise principles and to break them."[30] When asked about the dogs that appear in his films – in SOLARIS (USSR 1972), STALKER (West Germany/USSR 1979)and NOSTALGIA (Italy/USSR 1983)

26 Mark Cousins, *The Story of Film*. London: Pavilion Books, 2004, 307. Cousins is also too quick in his theological note on the Trinity, since the Son and Spirit are the same 'substance' as the Father and so also God, and thus not 'alongside' but *in* one another.

27 Tarkovsky, *Sculpting in Time*, 212–13.

28 Tarkovsky, *Sculpting in Time*, 213.

29 Andrei Tarkovsky and Aleksandr Misharin, Proposal for the film "Confession", (1968) in Andrei Tarkovsky, *Collected Screenplays*, trans. William Powell and Natasha Synessios. London: Faber & Faber, 1999, 257–61 (261); emphasis added.

30 Tarkovsky, *Sculpting in Time*, 216. Here one might also think of those more recent dogmaticians, the Danish confessors of Dogme 95, the filmmakers Lars von Trier and Thomas Vinterberg. Cf. Richard Kelly, *The Name of this Book is Dogme 95*. London: Faber & Faber, 2000.

– he could retort that they were just dogs.[31] But on other occasions he does not hesitate to inform us about his intended symbols. Thus he tells us that the watering of the withered tree in the closing scene of THE SACRIFICE (Sweden/France 1986) is a "symbol of faith."[32] However, the fact that Tarkovsky can offer us two contradictory readings of the final shot in NOSTALGIA, suggests how his images escape any symbolic straitjacket, and not least the intentions of their maker, so that even he is uncertain of their import. Elsewhere Tarkovsky is led to affirm what we might think of as open symbols, images with no single meaning, reference or resonance, but suggestive of a multitude, intimating what cannot be put into words. "Symbols cannot be stated or explained, and, confronted by their secret meaning in its totality, we are powerless."[33] Whether we call them images or symbols, it is clear that Tarkovsky wants to produce pictures that are not mere transcriptions, but material visions, and so we are led back to his claim to have produced images that are neither symbolic nor mere verisimilitude, neither stand-ins nor mere "bad weather."[34]

## 6. Material Vision

At one level, of course, many of Tarkovsky's images are just of weather, of the elements by which we are buffeted. The reverse side of Tarkovsky's transcendentalism is a concern to show us the materiality of life, saturated with substance. 

> Rain is after all typical of the landscape in which I grew up; in Russia you have those long, dreary, persistent rains. And I can say that I love nature – I don't like big cities and feel perfectly happy when I'm away from the paraphernalia of modern civilization, just as I felt wonderful in Russia when I was in my country house [Myasnoye], with three hundred kilometers between Moscow and myself. Rain, fire, water, snow, dew, the driving ground wind – all are part of the material setting in which we dwell; I would even say of the truth of our lives.[35]

But even as Tarkovsky affirms life's materiality, he ascribes to it a meaning that goes beyond mere facticity. Rain, fire, water, snow, dew, and the driving ground

31 Johnson and Petrie, *Andrei Tarkovsky*, 38.

32 Tarkovsky, *Sculpting in Time*, 224.

33 Vyacheslav Ivanov quoted approvingly in Tarkovsky, *Sculpting in Time*, 47.

34 Natasha Synessios also argues that reducing the natural elements in Tarkovsky's films to symbols and metaphors "demeans his vision." Rather we should understand them as inviting us to "enter, ponder and observe the world unfolding on the screen; a world whose elements and matter are familiar, yet made strange." Natasha Synessios, *Mirror*, KINOfiles Film Companions 6. London: I.B. Tauris, 2001, 70.

35 Tarkovsky, *Sculpting in Time*, 212.

wind, are part, but not the entirety of truth. They appear in Tarkovsky's films as 'reality effects', but not as that term is normally used, as fabricated markers of contingency, apparent accidentals. Tarkovsky's images are their own reality, intensifiers of the world, productive of what he calls its elusive meaning.

And so, if we choose to take Tarkovsky seriously when he tells us that there are no symbols or metaphors in his films, and in spite of his statements to the contrary, we have to think of his images not as symbols but as icons. For icons – though perhaps deploying a symbolic language – are in no sense stand-ins or substitutes. They are just themselves; but disclosive of more than just themselves. And because they are disclosive – disclosive when venerated – they are venerable. Tarkovsky's ANDREI RUBLEV (USSR 1966/1971) famously ends with a color sequence of the great fifteenth-century painter's icons, and it is the theology of the icon that best helps us to understand Tarkovsky's attempt to produce non-symbolic 'symbols', images that resonate with what cannot be seen while yet fully in view. "Icon painting," Sergius Bulgakov writes, "testifies to the beyond and its aspects; it does not attempt to prove, it simply presents."[36]

In Tarkovsky's world the wind moving the grass is not symbolic of the god passing by, of a spirit drawing near, or of anything at all. It is simply the movement of the wind. But that is the movement of the god, for the religious imagination; not a sign of the god, but the god passing. The rain in Tarkovsky's films is not a sign of God's grace, it is God's grace falling, gently from heaven.[37] Perhaps we can say that when we enter Tarkovsky's world we have passed over to what in our world must still be symbolized. We are within the symbol, so that everything is as it appears, but what appears is just out of reach of what can be named, at least by us. And isn't this always the case with the appearance of the gods?



Tarkovsky's nonsymbolic symbols – that show only what is to be seen – are like representations without originals, like icons. For icons are images that have no model, in the sense that what they show cannot be seen except in the image itself. Thus an icon of Christ is not a portrait of the man Jesus, since the icon does not show us the man, but the incarnation of *deity* in the man, and deity is not visible. The icon is not just a picture of Jesus as he was, as he might have been if caught by a camera, but Jesus as he is, sitting on the right hand of the Father. He is the Christ who lives now, a mystical reality that is yet utterly concrete, mystical in its materiality, both in the consecrated elements of the Eucharist and

36 Sergius Bulgakov, *The Orthodox Church*, trans. Lydia Kesich. Crestwood (N.Y.): St Vladimir's Seminary Press, 1988 (1935), 143.

37 As Antoine de Baecque notes, Tarkovsky's earth is never without water, and its watering announces the 'essential'; that which is to be seen *in* the seen. "La terre de Tarkovski n'est cependant rien sans eau, l'eau lourde, bornée, bordée, où croupissent les nostalgies, comme l'eau du ciel, lueur de pluie qui annonce l'essentiel." Antoine de Baecque, *Andrei Tarkovski*. Paris: Editions d l'Etoile/Cahiers du cinéma, 1989, 21.

in the receiving church, which is Christ's body, as well as in the stranger who comes unbidden. Thus the icon that pictures divinity cannot refer us to anything else, to a yet more life-like image beyond itself; just as Jesus, in whom God is to be seen, does not refer us to anyone else other than himself. Thomas wants to know the way to God, to the Father, as if it might be somewhere else, when in fact it is before him already. "I am the way, the truth, and the life," says Jesus. "No one comes to the Father except through me. If you know me, you will know my Father also. From now on you do know him *and have seen him*" (John 14:6–7). Jesus is the icon of the Father, but all we can see is Jesus himself.

When watching one of Tarkovsky's films we might almost say that we are within the film as icon, within a series of images that are not metaphoric of some other, unseen images, but are rather a series of images in which the unseeable is shown. As already suggested, Tarkovsky's transcendent is utterly material, his beyond entirely immanent, up-close and so invisible; and this answers to the materiality of the icon, to the board and paint which catches the viewer's gaze and makes her look. The icon's claim to immanent transcendence is authorized by, and follows from, the logic of divine incarnation, by which matter is given to display its transcendent cause the more it is itself. To touch Jesus was to be touched by God.[38] The authorizing logic for daring to paint the divine was finely caught by Thomas Aquinas when puzzling over the corporeality of Gabriel, when appearing to the Virgin: a veritable icon of the divine blessing (Luke 1:26). For Thomas did not doubt the record of the evangelist, that the angel appeared to the corporeal eye, and not to the eye of the intellect, as might have been expected, when the tradition agreed that intellectual vision was superior to both spiritual and physical sight.[39] Thomas found the answer to his dilemma in the fittingness of corporeal vision for the announcement of the incarnation. For it "fitted in first with the message itself," since Gabriel "came to tell of the incarnation of the invisible God. It was appropriate then that an invisible being assume a visible form."[40] If God was to appear in flesh, his angel could do no less.



38 "We declare to you what was from the beginning, what we have heard, what we have seen with our eyes, what we have looked at and touched with our hands, concerning the word of life." (1 John 1:1).

39 Cf. Augustine, The Literal Meaning of Genesis, in *On Genesis*, trans. Edmund Hill, OP. New York: New City Press, 2002, 464–506 (Bk XII).

40 Thomas Aquinas, *Summa Theologiae*, Blackfriars translation. London: Eyre & Spottiswoode, 1969, *prima pars* 3a.30.3; See Janet Martin Soskice, Sight and Vision in Medieval Christian Thought, in: *Vision in Context: Historical and Contemporary Perspectives on Sight*, ed. Teresa Brennan and Martin Jay. London: Routledge, 1996, 29–43 (31).

## 7. Time-Pressure

Famously, Tarkovsky thought that film, and his films in particular, could incarnate time. Film gives us time that we would not otherwise have. As we watch the unfolding drama of a shot or series of shots, a "sculpture in time," as Tarkovsky called it, we are watching a temporal structure that has come from elsewhere, from nowhere, and manifested before us. And this manifestation has its own time or times; a rhythm of temporalities, of differently pressured movements. "The consistency of the time that runs through the shot, its intensity or 'sloppiness', could be called time-pressure: then editing can be seen as the assembly of the pieces on the basis of the time-pressure within them."[41] And the structure of edited time-pressures in Tarkovsky's films is rarely simple, even in his simplest scenes. It is often a folded, multi-layered dynamic, with several interrelated times within the same duration; a temporal palimpsest. In the scene where the mother and doctor meet there are at least three times folded upon one another. First, there is the present of the meeting, visible on the screen – the time it takes the doctor to approach across the field, talk with Masha and depart, and for the wind to come across the field, twice over. Tarkovsky wanted us to notice the time of his films – the time that it takes to watch them – and risked ever longer shots



in order to alert us to their passing, pushing us beyond the point at which we might become bored, to one where the time itself becomes freshly present: the falling rain really falling in the cinematic icon; the wind really blowing across the field of the image.

The scene of the meeting runs for about six minutes. But this diegetic time – which fills the viewer's present – is cast into the past by the narrator's recalling of the meeting even as we watch it, so that it is both past and present at the same time. Admittedly the narrator, Alexei (Innokenti Smoktunovsky), only introduces the scene. And it concludes, not with the narrator, but with Tarkovsky's own father – the poet Arseni Tarkovsky (1907–89) – reading one of his own poems in voice-over. But these unseen speakers – the real father and his fictionalized son, who never appears as an adult in the film – are enough to cast the scene into the past, to present it as a memory, and to let us know that the mother is herself given over to memory, to waiting for the return of her husband, the narrator's father. But this also complicates the scene, for whose memory does it show? The narrator's, who awaited his father? His mother's, who awaited her lover? The scene brings their past into the present. But as it runs on, its authorship is unsettled by subtle hairline cracks in the timeline, as if the memories of different people, or of different immediacies – those directly recalled and those appropriated from others, or imagined on the basis of pho-

41 Tarkovsky, *Sculpting in Time*, 117.

tographs or other mementos – have been interlaced, almost seamlessly. (And of course the screen image is constructed by Tarkovsky from his own memories and photographs of his parents and of himself as a child, when living in the home he has so lovingly rebuilt for the film.[42])

When the doctor asks Masha for a light for his cigarette, he seems to notice something behind her, and she, as he bends to light his cigarette from hers, turns around to look in our direction. The film cuts to a mid-shot of the young narrator, the five-year old Alexei (Filip Yankovsky), asleep with his sister in a net hammock, strung between the trees. It is an image of utter tranquility; of energy spent at the end of a summer's day. But the framing of the shot, together with the children's obliviousness to the adults' interchange, suggests that it cannot quite be what Masha sees on turning around to look into the camera. The shot has a very slightly different "time pressure" from the others in the scene. It is as if she has looked into the past, into another memory – whether her own or someone else's – of the summer days spent at the house among the trees. It also signals, somewhat slyly, that even if Alexei, the narrator, could have remembered this scene from his childhood, he was asleep when it happened.[43] It is a dreamed memory.

When the doctor departs, he leaves screen left – or more nearly bottom – and continues to talk with Masha from off camera. She calls to him about the blood behind his ear, and we cut to a shot of him in the field, and he seems to be further away than he could have walked in the time since his exit of the previous frame. Of course it may be accidental, but this slight, almost unnoticeable elision of time – a speeding of its flow – further serves to unsettle, however subtly, the simplicity of an otherwise purely linear scene.



## 8. Veneration

Yet we may say that not everyone is given to see what the icon has to show, that the prototype appears in the type only for the eyes of faith, when illumined by the light which comes from the icon itself, the emanating, circulating light of the Spirit, which shines forth in order to catch those eyes, to make her viewers look into the light, to lead them back to the effulgence of the divine glory. Finally that

42 See Giovanni Chiaramonte, The Image as Remembrance, in Chiaramonte and Tarkovsky, *Instant Light*, 119–30 (119–21); Andrei Tarkovsky, *Journal 1970–1986*, traduit de russe par Anne Kichilov avec Charles H. de Brantes. Paris: Cahiers du cinéma, 2004, 106–11.

43 Johnson and Petrie, *Andrei Tarkovsky*, 116. It is entirely appropriate that many of the first Russian viewers of the film – of Tarkovsky's own generation – saw not so much his or his characters' memories, but their own. See Tarkovsky, *Sculpting in Time*, 10–11; Johnson and Petrie, *Andrei Tarkovsky*, 133.

which is seen and the light by which it is seen are one and the same.[44] The divine appearing is dependent, co-dependent, on those who look; but their looking is called forth by that which they are seeking to see. And this circulating gaze finds its parallel in the compelled look of the cinema audience, each individual of which will see the film differently. Tarkovsky records that he once thought film presented an unambiguous, "total" image, "a total effect, identical for every audience," but that he was forced to admit that he was wrong, that the vision appears in the relationship between the screened image and the viewers by whom it is seen. One might say that the film appears not on the screen but in the space between viewers and viewed, in the reflected light of the screen that permits the screen image to be seen. Moreover, this relationship, which is neither screen nor eye, but the space between, is a movement of mediation, an interpretative flow which the cinematic iconographer excites by refusing or hiding sight.

> The basic principle – as it were, the mainspring – is, I think, that as little as possible has actually to be shown, and from that little the audience has to build up an idea of the rest, of the whole. In my view that has to be the basis for constructing the cinematographic image. And if one looks at it from the point of view of symbols, then the symbol in cinema is a symbol of nature, of reality. Of course it isn't a question of details, but of what is hidden.[45]



In the sense that Tarkovsky wished to exclude them, there are no symbols in his films because his images do not point away to something else, but only *into* themselves, into the *time* of their viewing, the duration where viewed and viewer meet and another 'reality' appears. And this art of the 'hidden' – which shows what is beyond or, better, *within* what is seen – works by withholding, by limiting its vision to a discrete range of repeated images. And this also is the practice of icon painting, which works with an "exceedingly limited scale of artistic means."[46] Moreover, by withholding images from the audience, Tarkovsky obliges his viewers to become co-producers of the film image, the cinematic vision, "on a par with the artist in their perception of the film." This is a cinema of 'reciprocity' in which the audience comes to share with the author in the "misery and joy of bringing an image into being."[47]

44 See Vladimir Lossky, *The Mystical Theology of the Eastern Church.* London: James Clarke & Co Ltd, 1957 (1944), 218; Loughlin, *Alien Sex*, 90–95.

45 Andrey Tarkovsky, *Time Within Time: The Diaries 1970–1986*, trans. Kitty Hunter-Blair. London: Faber & Faber, 1994 (1991), 65 (24 January 1973).

46 Bulgakov, *The Orthodox Church*, 142, 144.

47 Tarkovsky, *Sculpting in Time*, 20–21; Johnson and Petrie, *Andrei Tarkovsky*, 39–40. For similar co-production in the films of Nicholas Roeg see Loughlin, *Alien Sex*, 230–31.

An audience has to want to see what Tarkovsky has to show in order for it to come into view, just as the devout must pray before the icon if they are to see its wonders, if they are to catch sight of its showing. The devout must look with love – in love – and Tarkovsky desired nothing so much as that his films should have a loving audience. "I do nothing in particular to please an audience, and yet hope fervently that my picture will be accepted and loved by those who see it."[48] Tarkovsky would not seek to humor his audience, because he desired not adulation but devotion to his showings, just as the prophets, faithful to their visions, come to tell us not what we want but what we need to see.[49] "An image is an impression of the Truth, which God has allowed us to glimpse with our sightless eyes."[50]



48 Tarkovsky, *Sculpting in Time*, 170.

49 "As soon as one begins to cater expressly for the auditorium, then we're talking of the entertainment industry, show business, the masses, or what have you, but certainly not of art which necessarily obeys its own immanent laws of development whether we like it or not." Tarkovsky, *Sculpting in Time*, 170.

50 Andrei Tarkovsky in Chiaramonte and Tarkovsky, *Instant Light*, 16.

Stefanie Knauss

# The Sensuality of Sense

## Reflections on the Bodily Dimension of Filmic and Religious Experience

> Unlike most movie violence, the violence here [in SAVING PRIVATE RYAN] comes coupled with considerable emotional impact. This is the most intense modern war movie ever made [...] every casualty onscreen truly feels like in actual life, and the impact is staggering. The extended battle sequences are some of the most powerful moments ever put on film. From the very start, you can barely breathe as the action unfolds on the screen. Using discomforting handheld shots, various film speeds, and ample use of surround sound, the result is terrifyingly realistic.[1]



In research on the interaction between film and religion, a new phase has begun marked by publications such as *Film as Religion: Myths, Morals, and Rituals* by John C. Lyden[2] and *Cinema and Sentiment: Film's Challenge to Theology* by Clive Marsh[3]. Film – and other forms of mass media – is no longer understood to be simply a way for religion to publicise its message; religious motifs in films are no longer the only link between these two cultural spheres. Instead, film and media are increasingly recognised as having religious-like functions[4] (even if on a very basic, not explicitly religious level) and playing a major, constitutive role in the new forms of religion that have developed in our media society.[5] Going to the cinema has become a ritual alongside or as a replacement for religious services for many: in a short survey on German TV in December 2006, an interviewee stated that the family visit to the cinema has become a Christmas tradition just as strong or even stronger than going to church together on Christmas Eve. Cinema does not only provide a structure to holidays and workdays alike,

1 Williams, Madeleine: SAVING PRIVATE RYAN. http://www.cinematter.com/movie.php3?spr – accessed 06.08.2006.

2 New York: New York UP, 2003.

3 Milton Keynes: Paternoster, 2004.

4 Cf. Charlotte Haines Lyons's and Clive Marsh's article in this volume.

5 Cf. Hoover, Stewart: *Religion in the Media Age*. New York: Routledge, 2006.

but also offers food for thought and suggests possible answers to existential questions about the future, the meaning of love, life and death etc. – questions and answers that were formerly restricted to religious contexts and have now moved to secular media, and in particular to the stories provided by films. The huge success of films such as TITANIC[6] can be attributed to the combination of a touching, romantic story with more existential questions that occupy people of all times: the desire for deep, romantic love, the sacrifices we make for our beloved, the guilt of survival, the meaning of life, death and memory, the search for one's place in society, resistance against socially prescribed roles.

However, the impact that films have on their viewers, and the power with which they shape the audience´s ideas about themselves and society, cannot only be ascribed to the stories they tell, i.e. to the film narrative and content, but depends also, and maybe even to a larger degree, *on the way in which* the stories are told. The images and sounds, colours, movements, changes of light, the relationship between the objects in a frame are not just the wrapping for the story, but have a meaning in themselves, in that they affect the viewers in an immediate, intense and bodily way which leads to the deep involvement with the plot of the film that is needed to make it meaningful to its audience. Only fairly recently, however, has the affective and emotional experience of watching a film received scholarly attention,[7] and since then, it has become clear that it cannot be neglected in the dialogue between religion and film either:



> It is part of the task of theological interaction with film […] to offer an account of the embodied nature of film-watching. This is a constructive theological task which would inevitably draw on 'creaturliness', the givenness of the body, the sanctity of the body, but would need to offer such readings in a manner consistent with the film-watching experience.[8]

It is my hypothesis that the reflection on the bodily aspect of both filmic and religious experience can bring out new elements of the film experience *as* religious experience, which goes beyond a simple replacement of the more fundamental

6 Cameron, USA 1997.

7 Most of all in Vivian Sobchack's work, e.g. *The Address of the Eye: A Phenomenology of Film Experience*. Princeton: Princeton UP, 1992; *Carnal Thoughts: Embodiment and Moving Image Culture*. Berkeley: University of California Press, 2004; in a German-speaking context, Christian Mikunda has developed a film analysis based on Rudolf Arnheim's findings in the psychology of perception in: *Kino spüren: Strategien der emotionalen Filmegestaltung*. Wien: WUV-Universitätsverlag, 2002; most recently, the issue has been taken up in a collection of essays: Marschall, Susanne; Liptay, Fabienne (eds.): *Mit allen Sinnen: Gefühl und Empfindung im Kino*. Marburg: Schüren, 2006. One of the rare exceptions from the early times of film theory is Siegfried Kracauer: *Theorie des Films: Errettung der äußeren Wirklichkeit*. Frankfurt: Suhrkamp, 1985, 216ff. See also: Stefanie Knauss: Transcendental Bodies: Überlegungen zur Bedeutung des Körpers für filmische und religiöse Erfahrung. Regensburg: Pustet, 2008.

8 Marsh: *Cinema and Sentiment*, 97.

sense-making effect of religion by the momentary satisfaction that film might offer, in that it has a lasting relevance for the individual, its relationships to other human beings and to the world, and beyond. As will become clear, this is not a merely momentary, pleasurable experience that is (mis-)taken for a religious one, and would therefore be subject to Feuerbach's projection theory, but includes both the pleasurable and the painful, the immanent and the transcendent. This does not only give a new dimension to the understanding of film as religion, but also has an influence on the role the body plays in religious tradition.[9] Even though the body is an indispensable element in the relationship between God and human being, and in salvation in Christianity, it has increasingly been neglected in favour of a more spiritual understanding of salvation and the practice of faith. One of the attractions of evangelical churches and other new religious movements is certainly their greater emotional intensity especially in worship services, which affects their members in ways neither the average Catholic nor mainstream Protestant churches provide nowadays.[10]

Given the ambiguous presence of the body in current social discourses between idealisation and objectification, virtualisation and being seen as the last moment of authenticity, however, this "constructive theological task" (Marsh) is one with not only theological-religious implications, but also an impact on social attitudes towards the body, and on film studies' approach to the film experience.



In the following, I will combine an overview over the bodily aspects of media (in particular, film) experience and over the body's role in religion with an analysis of STRANGE DAYS (Bigelow, USA 1995), in which the religious aspects of the bodily film experience will be outlined. In the conclusion, these aspects will be elaborated on from the perspective of constructive theology.

## 1. The Sensuality of Film Experience

The question of what it means to be human in a mediatised, technisised world has become extremely virulent in recent years; an important part of this question is the inquiry into what the human body is and which relevance it has for human existence, whether it can be dismissed of totally or how it can be shaped to fit

9 In the following, I shall restrict myself to the Jewish and Christian traditions bearing in mind that in other religious traditions, it is a very different role the body plays. However, a closer analysis, e.g. of the body discourses of eastern traditions on the background of the particular bodiliness of films by Kim Ki-Duk, such as SEOM (THE ISLE, South Korea 2000), might be worthwhile.

10 Cf. Percy, Martyn: Sweet Rapture: Subliminal Eroticism in Postmodern Charismatic Worship. In: Hannaford, Robert; Jobling, J'annine (eds.): *Theology and the Body: Gender, Text and Ideology*. Leominster: Gracewing, 1999, 1–29.

the ideal. Therefore, it does not come as a surprise that the bodiliness of human beings is a major topic in a lot of media products (video art, film, photography) and analyses of the representation of the bodies in them.[11] What does come as a surprise, however, is how little attention has been paid to the role the body plays in the reception process of media products. Instead, the disembodiment and virtualisation of human interaction with the world is bemoaned by many who forget that even the most virtual chat or video game experience is, in fact, first of all a bodily, sensual experience (seeing, moving one's hands, hearing) – of course an experience of a different kind than a personal, bodily encounter with another person or a situation, but nonetheless, it addresses the recipient's body and leaves a mark on it, just like any other experience: "In fact, we are never disembodied. [...] Far from being left behind when we enter cyberspace, our bodies are no less actively involved in the construction of virtuality than in the construction of real life."[12] Not total disembodiment, but a transformation is therefore noticeable in the way bodies and their senses are involved in their interaction with the world and this makes necessary the study of the bodily aspect in media reception. In film theory, a study of the affective, emotional and cognitive moments of the reception process is required; not at the expense of psychoanalytic, cultural studies or other approaches to film studies, but as a complement to them.



For most people, the bodily dimension of film watching is subconscious, and only when brought to their attention, do they become aware of the literal meaning of phrases such as 'roller-coaster' or 'tear-jerker'. The bodily effect of a film is most obvious in the reception of pornography[13] which is produced with the intention to cause strong bodily reactions of sexual excitement. Watching a film becomes a bodily experience, a kind of interaction with the actors on screen in which the perceptions of touching, stroking, kissing, rubbing are more than just virtual and 'in your mind', but very physical in how they feel and which effects they have. Yet watching porn is not only a 'virtually real' sexual encounter, but also a moment in which the viewer becomes aware of her-/himself as a bodily being, with bodily reactions, which exceeds the sexual excitement and results in a wholistic knowing of oneself as embodied being whose relationships to other people have this embodied dimension too (to various degrees, depending on

11 Cf. e.g. Tasker, Yvonne: *Spectacular Bodies: Gender, Genre and the Action Cinema*. London: Routledge, 1993; Frölich, Margrit; Middel, Reinhard; Visarius, Karsten (eds.): *No Body is Perfect: Körperbilder im Film*. Marburg: Schüren, 2001.

12 Hayles, Katherine: Embodied Virtuality: Or How to Put Bodies Back into the Picture. In: Moser, Mary Anne; MacLeod, Douglas (eds.): *Immersed in Technology: Art and Virtual Environments*. Cambridge: MIT Press, 1996, 1–28, here: 1.

13 Cf. Williams, Linda: *Hard Core: Power, Pleasure, and the Frenzy of the Visible*. Berkeley: University of California Press, 1999.

the kind of relationship).[14] However, the bodily film experience is not restricted to the merely pleasurable or exciting; the experience of pain is not restricted to actual reality and cannot be used as a characteristic that could distinguish the real world from a virtual one, as it is suggested in THE MATRIX.[15] Film can be as painful as real life and can cause intense discomfort (e.g. in seeing the gory THE PASSION OF THE CHRIST[16] or the not gory at all, but no less intensely painful rape sequence in STRANGE DAYS). Although it is not the same as 'real life', film experience comprises the whole variety of emotional and affective reactions human beings are capable of.

The play between virtuality and reality, between the life on-screen and one's own existence off-screen is a constitutive part of the film experience and important for its impact on the viewers.[17] If the on-screen and off-screen space simply coincided, film would not have the visionary or critical effect it has by contrasting one's own life with the experiences of the film characters. Yet, if there were no overlap of the viewers' experiences with those of the characters on-screen, it would be impossible to follow the story, to empathise with the characters and to understand their reactions and decisions, and therefore, the film would remain irrelevant to the audience.

However, the body also sets limits to what is possible in the film experience: even though technology in a science fiction film such as STRANGE DAYS might be so far advanced that it is possible to experience other people's emotions as if they were one's own, in cinema, the viewers' physical reactions still need to be supplemented by their imagination, and yet always remain incomplete. In other words, there will always be a difference between one's own existence and the filmic world, no matter how close one can get by bodily involvement and imaginative efforts, there will be a lack of perfection, yet the promise for future completion.



The identification with the filmic world and its characters is not a matter of psychological mirroring only, as film studies have long posited, following Lacan's theory of the mirror stage during which a child recognises its own wholeness and identity in the image of the other body. Instead, the mimetic recognition of and empathy with the characters' perceptions provides an understanding of the film on which the intellectual analysis of motivations or results of actions

14 Cf. Williams, Linda: Pornographische Bilder und die 'körperliche Dichte des Sehens'. In: Kravagna, Christian (ed.): *Privileg Blick: Kritik der visuellen Kultur*. Berlin: Edition ID-Archiv, 1997, 65–97, here: 79.

15 Larry and Andy Wachowski, USA 1999.

16 Gibson, USA 2004.

17 Cf. Cohen, Alain J.-J.: Virtual Hollywood and the Genealogy of the Hyper-Spectator. In: Stokes, Melvyn; Maltby, Richard (eds.): *Hollywood Spectatorship: Changing Perceptions of Cinema Audiences*. London: British Film Institute Publishing, 2000, 152–164, here: 153.

is based. Jennifer Barker, following Vivian Sobchack's view of the film as a body, uses an even wider understanding of identification in that she shows that viewers do not only identify with characters in a film, but with the film itself: its turns and twists, speed and movement, ups and downs are comparable to bodily movements of muscle and viscera, and only as such are they understandable, and in return, provide an understanding of the viewer's own body: "In becoming absorbed by the film and absorbing it at the same time, the viewer takes on qualities of the film that the film already shares with the viewer. Simply put, we and the film become more like each other, but in doing so, we become more like ourselves."[18]

For Sobchack, the acts of seeing and being are mutually connected and both are closely linked to and even motivate knowledge: seeing and being become both modes of knowledge in film, not only about oneself, but also about the world in which one exists.[19] In her view, it is precisely the materiality of human existence which is constitutive for the transcendental character of film experience:

> [A]t the movies or elsewhere, as lived *bodies* we are always grounded in the radical materialism of bodily *immanence*, in the 'here' and 'now' of our sensual existence – and this no matter how different our cultural situations or differently organized and valued modes of 'making sense'. However, as *lived* bodies, we always also have the capacity for *transcendence*: for a unique exteriority of being – an *ex-stasis* – that locates us 'elsewhere' and 'otherwise' even as it is grounded in and tethered to our lived body's 'here' and 'now'.[20]



These bodily-yet-transcendental experiences are possible not only in the cinema, of course, but the bodily participation in the world of the film enables them in a unique way which I think is at least partially responsible for the religious relevance cinema and film have for otherwise religiously uninterested people.

While Sobchack's and Barker's phenomenological approach describe the relevance of the bodily involvement in the film experience for human existence as the curious paradox of being beyond and, in that, becoming even more oneself, Christian Mikunda takes a more psychological approach by analysing the way in which filmic techniques and forms influence the body.[21] He also finds a relevance of these experiences for the psychological development of the individual, yet without referring to the paradox of immanence and transcendence. Psychology

---

18 Barker, Jennifer: *The Tactile Eye*. PhD thesis UCLA. Los Angeles, 2004, 162.

19 Cf. Sobchack, Vivian: *The Address of the Eye*, 57.

20 Sobchack, Vivian: Embodying Transcendence: On the Literal, the Material, and the Cinematic Sublime. Unpublished paper presented at the Conference on Media Technologies, Sensory Experiences and the Making of Religious Subjects, Amsterdam, 31.03.2006.

21 Cf. Mikunda: *Kino spüren*.

of perception has shown, for example, that colours or sounds have a very bodily effect, causing a change in rates of heart beat, sweating etc., or that a certain positioning of objects within a frame can cause tension in the viewer. Similarly, camera movements such as pans or tracks, can induce a feeling of being in motion in viewers and change their sense of equilibrium and position in space. While these filmic codes have their function within the film either by making it simply more interesting (sensual) or in conveying a message (expressive),[22] the bodily effects they have are not only entertaining, but have psychological significance. That is, the viewers become more aware of themselves, and this awareness leads to a stronger self-confidence and sense of identity: "The emotional language of film is an expression of the basic human need for bodily perceptions. [All] physical phenomena in the language of film strengthen our body awareness."[23] Filmic codes thus have not only aesthetic relevance, but also a psycho-hygienic and identity-formative function.

Because experiences made in cinema are bodily and immediate, they leave a trace in the viewers even after leaving the cinema, and have an impact on their interaction with others and their approach to life and its existential problems. Antonio Damasio's research[24] on the interrelatedness between consciousness, emotions, rationality and the body has shown that the development of consciousness and the ability to make even supposedly purely rational decisions are strongly dependent on bodily sensations, emotions, which mark a certain situation and are afterwards recalled when a similar situation occurs (what he calls the *Somatic Marker Hypothesis*): "Acting at a conscious level, somatic states (or their surrogates) would mark outcomes of responses as positive or negative and thus lead to deliberate avoidance or pursuit of a given response option. But they may also operate covertly, that is, outside consciousness."[25] Cinema experiences which leave their mark in the bodies of viewers can therefore be seen to have – consciously or not – an effect on the recipients' future decision making and attitudes towards life.



Thus, thinking about the role of the body in the film experience has shown that it is relevant in three respects: first, the physical aspects of the film experience are important for the recipients' self, the development of self-awareness and self-identity as embodied individuals, but also as beings that exist in relation to others. Second, it also has an ethical relevance in that it plays a role for the interaction with other persons and the world at large through its influence on

22 Cf. Mikunda: *Kino spüren*, 293.

23 Mikunda: *Kino spüren*, 307 (translation S.K.).

24 Cf. Damasio, Antonio R.: *Descarte's Error: Emotion, Reason, and the Human Brain*. New York: Quill, 2000 (first published 1994); Damasio, Antonio R.: *The Feeling of What Happens: Body and Emotion in the Making of Consciousness*. San Diego: Harvest, 1999.

25 Damasio: *Descarte's Error*, 187.

decision-making processes by the ways in which existential or less important problems are somatically marked positively or negatively. Finally, the paradox of immanence and transcendence that is experienced in the physical involvement into a film is comparable to religious experiences *per se* in that it leads beyond the present without denying the human situatedness in the world.

## 2. The Body in Religion, Theology and Religious Practice

As God's creation and an indispensable part of human existence, the body has always played an important, yet ambivalent role in Judaeo-Christian tradition: on the one hand highly valued as a moment in the God-human relationship, God's revelation and the hope for salvation, the body is, on the other hand, also considered to be that aspect of humanity which leads us away from God through unruly passions, desires and needs which bind us to the world.[26] Theological reflections on anthropology have, therefore, tended to discuss more spiritual issues, and theological body discourses are mostly restricted to the discussion of sexuality (and therefore come with a certain negative bias). Even though bodily forms of devotion and worship (asceticism, the cult of relics, inclusion of bodily elements into the celebration of the sacraments etc.) have had their place in Christianity throughout the centuries, a tendency towards spiritualisation (in particular in the liturgy of the sacraments) can be observed. Studies in feminist theology and gender studies as well as a new 'body theology' have pointed out these developments and also shown the potential that there is in Christianity, nevertheless, for a new understanding of the importance of the body in religion.[27]



These can be found, in particular, by going back to the biblical concept of the body. However, to talk of *the* biblical concept of the body is somewhat misleading: as there is no single word in Hebrew for 'body', so there are a multitude of ideas about what the body is, what relevant role it plays in human existence and salvation. In the Old Testament, there is a strong sense of a body-mind-unity of the human being (expressed e.g. in the motif of the creation of humans out of dust and the breath of life) which includes and informs the relationship between God and human beings to a high degree: "[S]uch an anthropology

26 Cf. for body discourses in the early church: Heimerl, Theresia: *Das Wort gewordene Fleisch: Die Textualisierung des Körpers in Patristik, Gnosis und Manichäismus*. Frankfurt: Lang, 2003, 36.

27 Cf. e.g. Ammicht-Quinn, Regina: *Körper – Religion – Sexualität: Theologische Reflexionen zur Ethik der Geschlechter*. Mainz: Matthias-Grünewald-Verlag, 1999; Isherwood, Lisa; Stuart, Elisabeth (eds.): *Introducing Body Theology*. Sheffield: Sheffield Academic Press, 1998; Coakley, Sarah (ed.): *Religion and the Body*. Cambridge: Cambridge UP, 1997.

discovers in concrete bodies the symbolic, or better, the sacramental presence of God."[28] However, there is also the sense that the body, and in particular sexual relationships between human beings, but also food and cleanliness, have to be regularised by elaborate laws. This ambivalence is continued in the New Testament. Jesus' healing encounters with human beings show that salvation has a physical dimension, too, and will not be complete without the resurrection of the body at the end of time. Yet, the body is also considered by Paul as an appropriate metaphor for a life that does not take God as its origin, reason and goal. Even though the phrases, life "according to the flesh" and "according to the Spirit"[29] in his letters should not be understood as an anthropological dualism, the metaphors do make clear that the flesh is considered inferior to the spirit.

In the later history of Christianity, these two lines are continued: the body was, notwithstanding its leanings towards sin and damnation, an indispensable part of the *conditio humana* and therefore of human religious life and salvation. Practices such as an extreme asceticism, which could be understood as a negation of the human body and its needs, were also ways to prepare this body for its role in the salvation of the person, to cleanse it from its sinfulness and to make it worthy of being the location of the encounter with God. Thus, Tertullian's rigorous attitude towards the body gains new meaning: "his insistence on the control of the body was so rigorous precisely because he believed that it was directly through the body and its sensations that the soul was tuned to the high pitch required for it to vibrate to the spirit of God."[30]



Similarly, mediaeval mysticism reveals a surprising bodiliness (often combined with forms of asceticism such as fasting or sleep deprivation), in which the mystic's experience of the presence of God is expressed in a physical, often sexual, language which certainly is more than a metaphorical way of describing the undescribable, but instead a sign for the paradoxical way in which the physical and immanent can become a means to encounter the transcendent and divine.[31] This vogue of bodily mysticism can be better understood in the context of mediaeval and late mediaeval theology which put a stronger emphasis on the humanity of Christ. This is reflected in the arts of the time, e.g. in crucifixion scenes where

28 Schroer, Silvia; Staubli, Thomas: *Body Symbolism in the Bible*. Collegeville: The Liturgical Press, 2001, 4.

29 Rom 8:6f (RSV).

30 Brown, Peter: *The Body and Society: Men, Women and Sexual Renunciation in Early Christianity*. New York: Columbia UP, 1988, 76.

31 Cf. e.g. Milhaven, J. Giles: A Medieval Lesson on Bodily Knowing: Women's Experience and Men's Thought. *Journal of the American Academy of Religion* 2/57 (1989), 341–372; id.: *Hadewijch and Her Sisters: Other Ways of Loving and Knowing*. Albany: State University of New York Press, 1993; Dinzelbacher, Peter: *Christliche Mystik im Abendland: Ihre Geschichte von den Anfängen bis zum Ende des Mittelalters*. Paderborn: Schöningh, 1994.

Jesus is represented as a suffering and dying human being, in contrast to the victorious, raised Christ of Romanesque art.[32] Even though more female than male mystics have described their experiences in bodily terms, this is not a gender-specific phenomenon. Theresia Heimerl has demonstrated that social contexts, education and personal disposition influenced the ways in which the presence of God was experienced more than gender.[33] Rupert of Deutz, for example, described his experience of Christ's presence in these terms: "I embraced him and kissed him long. I felt how gladly he admitted these signs of my love, because kissing, he opened his mouth so that I could kiss him more deeply."[34] Hadewijch of Antwerp's description of her loving encounter with Jesus is quite similar: "He came himself to me, and took me entirely in his arms, and pressed me to him; and all my members felt his in full satisfaction, in accordance with the desire of my heart and my humanity."[35] In these physical experiences of kissing, touching, holding, smelling, tasting, in painful or pleasurable sensations, the mystics made the experience of God's presence, and were imparted a knowledge about God and the relationship between humans and God that exceeded all rational and intellectual knowledge. In a time when bodily knowing was not yet inferior to rationality, the bodily experiences of asceticism and mysticism were seen as natural ways of relating to God: "In such piety, body is not so much a hindrance to the soul's ascent as the opportunity for it."[36]



It is not surprising that these forms of mysticism and other bodily forms of devotion died out gradually with the onset of Early Modernism: a new mechanical view of the body and the subsequent body-mind dualism have made the body unlikely to serve as the locus of the encounter with the divine. The state became increasingly concerned with disciplining the bodies of its subjects,[37] whereas, in a kind of division of labour, the church concentrated on the soul.

32 Cf. Dinzelbacher: *Christliche Mystik*, 94f.

33 Cf. Heimerl, Theresia: *Frauenmystik – Männermystik?: Gemeinsamkeiten und Unterschiede in der Darstellung von Gottes- und Menschenbild bei Meister Eckhart, Heinrich Seuse, Marguerite Porete und Mechtild von Magdeburg*. Münster: LIT, 2002, 289.

34 "[Ich] umarmte ihn und küßte ihn ganz lange. Ich fühlte, wie gern er diese Zeichen der Liebe zuließ, da er selbst unter Küssen seinen Mund öffnete, damit ich tiefer küssen könne." (Rupert of Deutz: Os meum aperuit; quoted in W. Berschin's translation in: Dinzelbacher: *Christliche Mystik*, 104 [translation S.K.].)

35 Hadewijch: Vision 7; quoted in M. Columba Hart's translation in: Milhaven: *Hadewijch and Her Sisters*, 16.

36 Bynum, Caroline Walker: *Fragmentation and Redemption: Essays on Gender and the Human Body in Medieval Religion*. New York: Zone, 1991, 194.

37 Cf. Foucault, Michel: *Discipline and Punish: The Birth of the Prison*. New York: Vintage Books, ²1995; Foucault, Michel: *The Will to Knowledge. The History of Sexuality* Vol. 1. New York: Vintage Books, 1990.

This led to a greater spiritualisation of faith and its practice (intensified by the Reformation and its greater focus on the word of the scriptures[38]). Apart from some forms of popular piety, the body no longer played a large role in either religious practice or in teaching (apart from teaching on sexual ethics), and this view is in general still valid for today's Christianity. Yet, central topics of Christian theology are directly linked to the body: creation, incarnation and the resurrection of the body, and it is worthwhile to reconsider them from a more 'bodily perspective'.

The creation stories of Genesis, in particular Gen 2, make clear that the human being as a unity of body and spirit, is God's creation and is wanted by God as bodily being. Neither the body nor the mind are superior, instead their inexplainable combination in the human being makes humans so particular among all other beings. As a bodily, physical being, the human is connected to the world, and through their bodies, humans relate to each other. And only in this relationality (to other human beings, to God, to the world around them) is their humanity fulfilled.[39] Being created in God's image as a being of body and spirit, all human beings have the same dignity and are to be respected in their physical and psychological well-being.

In theology, the most fundamental aspect of Christianity, the in*carn*ation of the Word, has somewhat receded to the background in its literal meaning: God became flesh, became a man in body and mind, without being less God, and through the incarnation, the human constitution as body and mind becomes the indispensable moment of salvation. God takes on a body in order to become close to human beings in their flesh; salvation happens within the structures and conditions of human existence and nature, not outside of it, and if we are saved, it is in our existence in body and mind. In Jesus Christ, the body becomes the point of encounter between God and human, and it gains a new dignity and value in the economy of salvation. While God's incarnation and bodily living and suffering in the world makes possible the healing of human beings in their bodies, it also points towards the fact that in the body of every person, the image of God can be found, and that the care for other human beings in their bodiliness is a way to encounter God, for whatever we do to others, we do to God.[40] For Elisabeth Moltmann-Wendel, the incarnation is a sign that we – and in particular women, who for a long time have been identified with body and



38 Cf. Bottomley, Frank: *Attitudes to the Body in Western Christendom*. London: Lepus Books, 1979, 173. A slightly more positive view of the role of the body in Protestant Christianity is posited by David Tripp in: The Image of the Body in the Formative Phase of the Protestant Reformation. In: Coakley: *Religion and the Body*, 131–152.

39 Cf. Sattler, Dorothea; Schneider, Theodor: Schöpfungslehre. In: Schneider, Theodor (ed.): *Handbuch der Dogmatik* Vol. 1. Düsseldorf, Patmos, [2]2002, 120–238, here: 159.

40 Cf. Mt 25:40.

nature and therefore considered to be inferior to men (reason, culture) – are called to salvation and life eternal with and in our bodies, in their beauty, with their scars, pains and pleasures.[41]

Because the body is such a constitutive element of human nature, it cannot be imagined that it does not play a role in the resurrection: if it is to be 'me' who is to enter the eternal life, this must include – in some form or another – my body and my physical experiences too. Reflections on the resurrection are therefore strongly linked to ideas about identity and subjectivity, about what it is that makes me 'me' and the meaning of life and death. Speculations on the resurrection have never dismissed the body and the importance of bodily experiences, but have come to various conclusions as to the form it will take – metaphors such as the body as a vessel that is broken in death and will be put together in the afterlife, or that of a seed that has to change form and yet remains the same, reflect the two main lines of thought on the issue in patrology.[42] Origen took a slightly less materialistic approach in that he posited that the continuity between the earthly and the resurrected body would be guaranteed by the *eidos*, a kind of genetic code, which is the same in both.[43] Increasingly, the soul was perceived to be that element that guarantees the identity of a person before and after death, and so the emphasis was moved from the resurrection of the body to the immortality of the soul in theological reflections.[44] However, this demonstrates the continuing importance the body has in Christianity in spite of its ambivalent attitude to it, that belief in the resurrection of the body has never been abandoned: "For however absurd it seems [...] it is a concept of sublime courage and optimism."[45] And it is a concept that opposes social and religious tendencies towards an idealisation and/or negation of the human body, and makes one think about the role of the body for human existence, in this life and in the next.



Given the influence that Christianity's view of the body had and still has on social discourses on bodiliness, it is important for theology to take a stance in current body discourses and, in going back to its roots in the Bible and to such fundamental elements of the Christian faith as creation, incarnation and resurrection, develop a more positive and wholistic view of the body and its indispensable role for human existence, religion and social interactions. With

41 Cf. Moltmann-Wendel, Elisabeth: *Wenn Gott und Körper sich begegnen: Feministische Perspektiven zur Leiblichkeit*. Gütersloh: Gütersloher Verlagshaus, 1989, 32f.

42 Cf. Bynum, Caroline Walker: *The Resurrection of the Body in Western Christianity, 200–1336*. New York: Columbia UP, 1995, 6f.

43 Cf. Bynum: *Resurrection of the Body*, 65f.

44 Cf. Greshake, Gisbert; Kremer, Jacob: *Resurrectio mortuorum: Zum theologischen Verständnis der leiblichen Auferstehung*. Darmstadt: Wissenschaftliche Buchgesellschaft, 1986, 243.

45 Bynum: *Resurrection of the Body*, 343.

this, Christian theology would also contribute to the contemporary uncertainty as to what human existence means, and which part the body plays in it, uncertainties that lead to such extremes as objectification or body cult, virtualisation or body modifications as ways to come to terms with the paradoxes of human existence.

One of the moments in which the body as perceptive organ and constitutive element of human existence and identity becomes particularly obvious is the film experience because of the extreme bodily immediacy of the reception process. In the following analysis of STRANGE DAYS, some aspects of this experience will be pointed out, and the interrelatedness of bodily, filmic and religious experience will be illustrated.

## 3. A "Breathless Joy Ride": STRANGE DAYS

The reviews of Kathryn Bigelow's film STRANGE DAYS point out its bodily effects quite clearly: Janet Maslin from the *New York Times* calls it "a troubling but undeniably breathless joy ride [...] with [...] high-voltage visual style,"[46] Franz Everschor's review talks about its stimulating effect achieved through the use of filmic technologies by which viewers can not only empathise with the world of the screen, the characters and their emotions, but feel and experience them themselves.[47]



The strong bodily, emotional involvement of the viewers by the film is not untypical for the genres of film noir, action and science fiction film and romance, of which this film is a compound. But other than the typical commercial Hollywood film, Bigelow achieves a distancing effect by combining strongly involving filmic codes with disruptive elements and a certain media criticism embedded in the story: a new recording and 'viewing' technology called SQUID makes it possible not just to see and hear what has been recorded, but to experience the emotions, to repeat the *experience itself* of the person who recorded. In the plot, such a clip showing how a regime-critical rap musician was murdered by a cop is passed on to the clip dealer Lenny (Ralph Fiennes) who, with the help of his strong friend Mace (Angela Bassett) does not only succeed in hunting the murderers down and passing the clip on to the chief of the LAPD, but is also saved by Mace from his own clip-induced nostalgia over his former girlfriend, Faith (Juliette Lewis), and alienation from real life, and learns that he is really

46 Maslin, Janet: New, Improved Virtual Reality, 1999. http://movies2.nytimes.com/mem/movies/review.html?title1=STRANGE%20DAYS%20(MOVIE)&title2=&reviewer=Janet%20Maslin&pdate=19951006&v_id= – accessed 08.05.2006.

47 Everschor, Franz: STRANGE DAYS, http://cinomat.kim-info.de/fdarchiv/fdkritiken.php?nr=12460&ref=such – accessed 08.05.2006.

in love with Mace. Tied in with this fairly straightforward action/romance plot is a story of a perverse rapist and murderer who connects his victim to his own SQUID recorder so that she feels how he is turned on by her fear while he rapes and kills her. Through these – difficult to bear – sequences, the viewers themselves are challenged in the voyeurism of their media consumption; and in the characters hooked on the virtual reality of these clips – instead of real life – and behaving like drug addicts on the search for the better – and eventually fatal – trip, the relation of reality, fiction and media, and the importance of the encounter with reality (physical, bodily reality) is pointed out.

When Bigelow describes her own experience of Sam Peckinpah's western, THE WILD BUNCH (USA 1969) as "I was breathless, transformed,"[48] this is an observation that is also applicable to her own film. Particularly intensive is the impact of light, camera movement, motion and acoustic codes in her film that are used so expertly that they leave the viewers worn out and changed by the experience.

Especially in the SQUID sequences, the audience is enabled to undergo the same ambivalent experience as the recipients of the clips – it is a seemingly authentic, and yet not quite authentic experience: the SQUID sequences are all shot from a strictly subjective perspective (given that they are recordings of what a particular person goes through) so that that person's face or body is only seen in mirrors or at the edge of the screen, e.g. when they look at their hands. But this unusual perspective and limited range of vision make every camera movement (i.e. body movement) even more intensive and provide for intense shock effects as well as disharmony because of the unusual framing of objects. In one scene, the effect is particularly striking when hands in white gloves appear at the bottom of the frame, set against a darkish-blueish background and so both disrupt the set-up of the image and cause tension by the light-dark contrast so that the overall effect of the image on the viewer is one of disquiet and unsettlement – exactly what is intended in a scene which shows the perverse rapist entering Lenny's house while he is in there, asleep. Hand-held camera and shaky images as well as sudden pans (e.g. when a character looks behind her to watch out for pursuers) cause a high frequency of changes in the image which have to be processed by the viewers and therefore keep them alert and tense: "we share not only the angle, but also the modality of the characters' vision and, therefore, their feelings of fear and anxiety."[49] However, at the same time that



48 Quoted in: Struck, Wolfgang: Körpereinsatz 1: Fundstücke – Art World – SET UP. In: Kienast, Welf; Struck, Wolfgang (eds.): *Körpereinsatz: Das Kino von Kathryn Bigelow*. Marburg: Schüren, 1999, 17–24, here: 17.

49 Rascaroli, Laura: Steel in the Gaze: On POV and the Discourse of Vision in Kathryn Bigelow's Cinema. Screen 3/38 (1997), 232–246, here: 234.

these sequences are highly involving and energetic, they also have an alienating effect because viewing habits are disrupted, and also because even the most subjective camera perspective does not – and could not, without becoming unviewable – represent real human vision and movement. Thus, the perspective of the SQUID-sequences "binds us tightly into the action. But at the same time, this perspective is oddly impersonal."[50] The limits of media are thus illustrated – and made *palpable* – in the seemingly limitless medium of SQUID.

Not only the SQUID-sequences, but also the 'real-life' scenes in the film, are affecting. In particular, light-dark contrasts have a strong impact on the viewer and are used to either point out particular elements in the frame (e.g. the rapist's white gloves) or have a physically activating and unsettling effect that reflects the tension prevalent in the dystopian setting of the film (a Los Angeles reminiscent of the race riots of 1991), in which flames flicker across the streets, helicopter searchlights stroke over the city and the coloured lights of the clubs express the breathlessness of the night. Thus, the viewers are able to experience what Lenny describes to Mace while driving through the city: "It's going to be a big night. Can't you feel it? The energy in the air? There's money to be made, dreams to sell." In one scene, the physical effect of Bigelow's use of lighting in the film is particularly impressive: Lenny is being beaten up in a dark basement with just one neon light dangling from the ceiling. The irregular flashes of the light swinging on its cord now and again hit the camera and cause visual 'blows' on the eyes of the spectators, similar to those that Lenny receives on his body. 

Contrasts are used not only in the lighting, but also in the sudden, and effective, changes from motion to stillness, e.g. in a chase scene which ends in a subway station. Here, the tension of the chase down the stairs (shaky camera, fast movement and cuts, objects flashing across the screen, high-pitched screams etc.) is prolonged when the victim disappears among the people on the platform, a train pulls in and she still does not appear. While her pursuers look for her, the viewers hold their breath – maybe literally – waiting for what is to come. When she suddenly bursts out of her hiding place and gets into the train just before the doors close, the pursuers try to grab her, shoot at her and pull her hair, the noise, speed of movement and action are even more intense because of the moment of relative quiet just before and the viewers are physically affected in a similar way to the woman in her escape and run for the train. Just like the woman sits shivering in the train, the viewers are exhausted and the tension is slow to dissolve.

50 Shaviro, Steven: "Straight from the Cerebral Cortex": Vision and Affect in STRANGE DAYS. In: Jermyn, Deborah; Redmond, Sean (eds.): *The Cinema of Kathryn Bigelow: Hollywood Transgressor*. London: Wallflower Press, 2003, 159–177, here: 163.

Sound is used in a highly nuanced way to cause shock and anxiety, underline the atmosphere of a situation or even change it, and to build up the peculiar spatial sensations of the SQUID-sequences where surround-sound is used to high effect. Coming unexpectedly and from different directions, the acoustic stimuli cause a bolt of energy in the viewer which can be explained by evolutionary psychology as an orientation reflex: "In a knee-jerk reaction, the individual turns towards the stimulus, while its organism automatically activated all its energies for the possible emergency (escape, attack). This bolt of energy is experienced as an emotional state."[51] Often, a subtle change in the soundtrack can create a new atmosphere: when Mace enters the basement where Lenny is beaten up, a slightly new rhythm makes the music much more energetic and optimistic, signalling to the viewer that everything will be all right, now that Mace is here so that the still intense stimuli of the following fight can be 'enjoyed' relaxedly.

All of the filmic codes – and the above mentioned are just some examples of an aesthetically very complex film – are used with a perfection that guarantees that the viewers participate in the anxiety, fear and tension, but also the love and hope the characters in the film experience.



In spite of its dystopian setting, and references to the apocalypse (e.g. the final battle between Good and Bad, the murdered rap musician Jeriko One as the apocalyptic prophet), the film remains in the here and now: the apocalyptic disturbances, and the hoped-for renewal of society happens in the presence and immanency of the world, in the solution of social conflicts, in intersubjective relationships and in the immediacy of pain and violence,[52] not only to the characters, but also to the viewers. Bigelow's use of filmic codes does not allow for cinematic escapism into a world where pain is not an issue, or if it was, it would not influence the viewers, and everything was possible and allowed. Instead, in a nearly agnostic defiance, the film establishes a strong ethical message and impact precisely through the negative and positive emotions it transmits to its recipients: the norms by which human behaviour is judged to be right or wrong, are inner-worldly, related to inner-worldly social situations and human interaction. Ethical principles are no longer based on religious norms or universal truths,[53] but on the immediacy and often physicality of intersubjective relationships, in pain, love and violence: the responsibility for one own's acts, the reality principle and the avoidance of (media-induced) passivity, the establishment of just living conditions for all.[54]

51 Mikunda: *Kino spüren*, 158 (translation S.K.).

52 Cf. Valentin, Joachim: *Zwischen Fiktionalität und Kritik: Die Aktualität apokalyptischer Motive als Herausforderung theologischer Hermeneutik*. Freiburg: Herder, 2005, 380.

53 Cf. Bauman, Zygmunt: *Postmodern Ethics*. Oxford: Blackwell, 1993.

54 Cf. Valentin: *Zwischen Fiktionalität und Kritik*, 380.

Because of their bodily involvement, the viewers become aware both of the threats of a violent, ruthless society, the need for norms that protect individual rights and safety (both bodily and mental), and of the problematics of a media use that controls interaction with reality. Most extremely in the SQUID-clips, but also in the rest of the film, the viewers are forced into roles and situations beyond their everyday experience. The changes between the perspective of victim and perpetrator make it even clearer to the viewers that they have to take a stance in the ethical issues raised. Because the scenes of violence and breaches of personal rights are so uncomfortable that they leave a negative marking on the viewers, the suffering with the victims of rape and violence in a bodily way (i.e. empathising, rather than sympathising with them) establishes an ethics that takes the body and bodily integrity of persons as its origin and norm. On the other hand, the exemplary character of Mace who is guided by ethical responsibility, loyalty and compassion,[55] is marked positively by colour code, music and frame design (she often takes a balancing position in the set-up of an image), as well as by the narrative.

An ethics based on the immediacy of the body, however, requires that one becomes aware of its relevance for one's own identity and for intersubjective relationships and the encounter with and orientation in the world. The virtual world of the clips in the film and the failure of the characters who are hooked on them show clearly that a life that is predominantly influenced by second-hand experiences is incomplete and unfulfilled, even though it might be tempting to make these experiences without exposing oneself to risk. The film does not teach its lesson simply theoretically, but makes it palpable by drawing the viewers into the world of the clips and transmitting emotions to them, but then disrupting the identification and pushing the viewers back into their reality: experiences are not possible without taking the responsibility for what one does, to oneself or to another. This responsibility is the consequence of the human freedom to choose and to act so that the film's emphasis of the need to take responsibility also points out the human condition of being free, yet accountable for one's acts.



Laura Rascaroli has called Bigelow's work and in particular her visual style a move towards a "transcendental vision."[56] Drawing her viewers into the film physically, by the visual and acoustic codes used, the filmic experience becomes an experience of transcendence of the here and now. The borders between the viewer's body and the film's as well as the characters' bodies are dissolved in the effect the film has on them: in moving with the film, feeling with the cha-

55 Cf. Lane, Christina: The Strange Days of Kathryn Bigelow and James Cameron. In: Jermyn; Redmond (eds.): *The Cinema of Kathryn Bigelow*, 178–197, here: 193.

56 Rascaroli: *Steel in the Gaze*, 237.

racters, the filmic and spectator reality collapse. However, this transcendence is rooted very much in the immanence of bodies: it is experienced in the body, and in reflecting on the film experience, the importance of bodily experiences for human existence and interactions becomes obvious. The immediate bodily impact of the film emphasises the necessity to take responsibility in the world, and to contribute to making it a better place for all embodied, human beings. While in the agnostic world of the film, the horizontal dimension (relationship between human beings) is emphasised, a theological reflection of the film can take this one step further and read these human interactions as an important aspect of the God-human relationship (vertical dimension): both are, from a Christian point of view, inseparable.

Paying heed to the physical impact of this film, therefore, shows that bodily experiences are a major part of human existence without which a full development of one's capacities is impossible. While thus being important for the individual's identity and self-consciousness, the bodily film experience also makes clear that an ethics of respectful intersubjective interaction in a world in which universal norms have failed or are no longer convincing has its origin and base in the bodiliness of all human existence and is motivated by one's own constitution as a body-mind unity. This is not 'told' to the viewers, but instead made palpable through the use of filmic codes which both encourage empathy on an intense physical level, and disrupt it in order to allow for critical distancing and reflection.



## 4. Some Constructive-Theological Reflections

For a constructive theology, the questions of the constitution of the 'hearer of the word' (Karl Rahner) and of the conditions for an experience of God's presence pose themselves in a new way in a media society. The ability to hear God's word has been understood as being intrinsic to human beings and deducible from their constitution (i.e. as beings existing in a *body*-mind unity) since Rahner's anthropological turn. Given that the human person is constituted in body and mind, the bodily dimension cannot be dismissed from religious experience and practice. Rahner sees the awareness of one's own finiteness as the precondition for reaching beyond and asking about the infinite: "In radically experiencing its finiteness, [the human] reaches beyond this finiteness and experiences itself as a being of transcendence, as spirit."[57] Thus, the finiteness and immanence of the human embodied existence moves the individual to transcend this immanence

57 "Indem er seine Endlichkeit radikal erfährt, greift er über diese Endlichkeit hinaus, erfährt er sich als Wesen der Transzendenz, als Geist." (Rahner, Karl: *Grundkurs des Glaubens: Einführung in den Begriff des Christentums*. Freiburg: Herder, 1984, 42f. [translation S.K.].).

and stretch out into the beyond, which again can only be experienced under the conditions of the human constitution in body and mind. Therefore, all bodily experiences, including aesthetic experiences such as the reception of film or other works of media and art, can be understood as including elements of a religious experience in the quest for the absolute and in the gift of its presence.

In creation and through his incarnation, God has made possible, in particular, the relationship between himself and human beings by taking human bodiliness not as a necessary evil, but making it the origin and condition for a free and personal relationship with God. Only when the person has developed a sense of self-identity (which includes the awareness of the body and the integration of the bodily and mental dimensions of the human) can such an I-Thou relationship with God be established which characterises the Jewish and Christian idea of God/human relations, and is also prerequisite for an existence in freedom and responsibility in relation to God and to other human beings.[58] Created bodiliness is also the condition for intersubjective relationships – the fundamental relationality to the other through which human existence finds its fulfilment – and in this, the experience of the absolute Other, God. Thus, "the human being has an at least implicit *experience of God* in that existential self-transcendence, which occurs in the act of the *love of one's neighbour*."[59] The relevance of the bodily dimension of human existence for salvation is brought to its highest point in the hope and belief that human bodiliness is included in the economy of salvation and that the human person will be saved in its concrete and individual existence as body-mind unity.[60]



The paradoxical relation between immanence and transcendence, which marks all religious experience, is also characteristic for the bodily film experience, and in becoming aware of this aspect, the viewers acquire a new sensitivity for this paradox in other spheres of their lives: while the world of the film becomes experienceable through the bodily involvement in it, it always remains *other* to one's own situation in the cinema, and yet the experience of an *other* world is possible only in the very immanence of one's body. Thus, the experience of transcendence in film is not escapism from the troubles and imperfections of this world, but in being bodily, it is always bound to one's concrete existence, an experience of transcendence under the conditions of human existence, and including and evoking all of its positive and negative aspects.

Viewing films is thus not only an intellectual exercise, in which various models of sense-making and concepts of life are presented and afterwards evaluated for

58 Cf. Rahner: *Grundkurs*, 37.

59 "[...] der Mensch in derjenigen existenziellen Selbsttranszendenz, die im Akt der *Nächstenliebe* geschieht, mindestens implizit eine *Gotteserfahrung* macht." (Rahner: *Grundkurs*, 437 [translation S.K.], emphasis in the original.)

60 Cf. Rahner: *Grundkurs*, 262.

their relevance to one's own life. Most of all, it is a sensual experience which leaves its mark on our bodies, and makes sense through our senses in that it points us both to ourselves, our embodied existence and individuality, and beyond the limitations of our situatedness in the here and now, by transcending exactly the experiencing bodies and giving us a larger perspective of our existence, of our sense in life, at the same time making clear that this is not all there is to human existence.

After a history of the neglect of the body – not to speak of its negation – in Christian theology and practice, the awareness of the bodily dimension of film viewing contributes to a conscious reintegration of the body in human existence: forms of bodily knowing (e.g. the immediate, non-discursive understanding of a film sequence because of the emotions it evokes) and relating (e.g. in the empathy with film characters) can regain the relevance they have lost due to the rationalism of the Enlightenment both in religion and in society, and thus contribute to an enrichment of human existence in all its dimensions.

Alexander Darius Ornella

# Networked – Subjectivity Revisited

> The media's the most powerful entity on earth. They have the power to make the innocent guilty and to make the guilty innocent, and that's power. Because they control the minds of the masses.[1]

## 1. Media as a Fundamental Part of Human Experience

Today, our world and our everyday lives are increasingly entangled with media and communication technology.[2] *Welterschließung*, social interaction, constitution of subjectivity, and the staging of the self increasingly take place in an electronically mediated world. In this context, media are not simply tools that can be used without influencing their users. There is an interrelationship – or to be more accurate, an interdependence – between media and society as well as between media and users. This interdependence and the pervasion of our daily lives by media and technology in general are not only difficult to escape from – if that were possible at all – but affect the whole of our human existence. What Katherine Hayles states about the relationship between humans and intelligent machines, namely that "what we make and what we (think) we are coevolve,"[3] applies as well to the relationship between humans and communication technologies: what we do with media and communication technology and what we think we are coevolve.



Taking Hayles seriously, we have to ask ourselves how media influence our self-understanding, our relation to the world and to our fellow human beings, who we are, and what it means to be human. Today, media play a substantial role in the constitution of (human) subjectivity. Depending on the level of interaction with media, they question and restructure subjectivity, either fragmenting it or emphasizing its dynamic and fluid character.

---

1 Malcom X, 1963, http://www.ifla.org/faife/litter/origin/m.htm, accessed February 8, 2007.

2 In this paper, I use a broad understanding of 'media'. Furthermore, as most (new) media are computer-based and technological advancements, it is increasingly difficult to distinguish between media and technology.

3 Hayles, Katherine N., *My Mother was a Computer. Digital Subjects and Literary Texts*, Chicago: The University of Chicago Press, 2005, 216.

In my paper I do not focus on a single medium, but rather on a key feature many modern/new media have in common: the networking of people, information, locations, societies, economies, and cultures, and the alienation this can cause.[4] First, I will introduce my theoretical approach and explore the relationship between media networks and subjectivity. Then, using the NETWORKING TV advertisement by Apple as my tutor text, I argue that, in today's society, subjectivity is defined through participation in network processes. In my conclusion, I will explore the consequences of the 'mediated' and 'networked' subject for theology.

One of the biggest problems in the discussion of subjectivity, however, is that authors only rarely state which concepts of subjectivity they refer to or criticize and in which historical context and philosophical tradition they situate their critique of and their attempts to redefine subjectivity today. Thus, for the purpose of this paper and in particular with regard to the theological approach to subjectivity in the final section of this paper, I refer to this term as a sense and understanding of the self and a self-conception that is constituted through and acquired with the help of media and communication technology. It is essentially fragmented, patchworked, and fluctuating.



## 2. Media as a Challenge to Autonomous Subjectivity

It is not a new phenomenon, and not necessarily a phenomenon of media society, that the traditional understanding of the subject as stable, free, and autonomous is challenged.[5] In fact, feminist theory, literary and cultural studies, post-modernism and post-structuralism have challenged this kind of autonomous subjectivity over the last few decades. What exactly is understood as 'subjectivity' and which aspects are criticized often varies, however.

Media – and technological advancements – have always been important for human *Welterschließung* (the disclosure and discovery of the world), *Welterkenntnis* (learning about the world) and the human horizon of being (*Seinshorizont*)

4 Manuel Castells mentions several effects the information technology revolution and the changes in society and economics have: the emergence of the network society, data collection and privacy concerns, flexibility and instability of work, the instant sharing of information, decentralization, individualization, and the effects of 'being connected/disconnected'. Cf. Castells, Manuel, *The Rise of the Network Society. The Information Age. Economy, Society and Culture*, Vol. 1, Blackwell: Oxford, reprint 1999; Castells, Manuel, *The Power of Identity. The Information Age. Economy, Society and Culture*, Vol. 2, Blackwell: Oxford, reprint 2001, 1.

5 To be more accurate, the critiqued focused on what has been called a 'stable, free, and autonomous' subject in philosophical thinking. I would, however, question, whether the free and autonomous subject of philosophy really reflected the experience of, for example, subordinates and servants. Could it not be that the deconstruction of the free subject is only a realization of what has always been the human experience?

and have thus contributed to social and cultural changes and transformations.[6] Nowadays, with the omnipresence of media and communication gadgets, a permanent flow of information and an increasing number of places that offer multimedia info screens and 'elevator music', media have become an integral part of what it means to be human. The ability of the individual to deal and interact with all these communication technologies we are immersed in has become fundamental to how subjectivity is understood and what a subject can contribute to society.

The simultaneous availability and easy accessibility of many electronic media (internet, TV, radio, telephone) as well as social and economic changes have transformed the traditional and static sender-receiver hierarchy of communication processes into a fluid and mutable relationship. Jürgen Habermas, for instance, argues that mass media allow for social control but they also have an enfranchising potential.[7] Interaction on multiple levels and between different actors is made possible and often encouraged by electronic media, thus strengthening the free and autonomous subject – or so it seems. The impression emerges that the subject is able to make informed decisions and participate in public decision-making processes. Interactivity suggests that an individual and his or her opinions are being taken seriously by those in charge of decision-making processes and enables individual subjects to group together and voice their concerns – successfully or not – against those in power in the network society. Further, electronic media also enable subjects to form social ties and communities that correspond to their interests and are not limited to specific places.[8]



Interactivity, however, especially on multiple levels, with multiple channels and varying contexts at the same time opens the possibility of multiple subjects inhabiting a single human body (e.g. online identities, the 'Digital Me'[9]), can cause stress, disorientation, and be a source of "contradiction in both self-representation and social action."[10] The spread of communication networks and the

6 Cf. Assmann, Jan, *Das kulturelle Gedächtnis. Schrift, Erinnerung und politische Identität in frühen Hochkulturen*, Beck: München, 2nd ed., 1997, 23; cf. Assmann, Aleida, Vier Formen von Gedächtnis. Von individuellen zu kulturellen Konstruktionen der Vergangenheit, in: *Wirtschaft & Wissenschaft*, Vol. 9, Nr. 4, 2001, 34–45, http://www.stifterverband.de/pdf/wiwi_401_assmann.pdf, accessed October 14, 2006.

7 Cf. Habermas, Jürgen, *Theorie des kommunikativen Handelns II. Zur Kritik der funktionalistischen Vernunft,* Frankfurt/Main: Suhrkamp, [4]1987, 573.

8 Cf. Hampton, Keith N., Networked Sociability Online, Off-line, in: *Castells, Manuel (ed.), The Network Society. A Cross-Cultural Perspective*, Cheltenham/UK: Edward Elgar Publishing, 2004, 217–232.

9 Cf. Heim, Michael, Access to the Digital 'We', in: *.copy – Zukunftsmagazin der Telekom Austria*, 12, http://wai.telekom.at/Content.Node/copy/12/copy12_1.1.pdf, accessed June 14, 2006.

10 Castells, Manuel, *The Power of Identity*, 6.

possibility of accessing them almost anywhere at anytime[11] lead to an expansion of both the human mind and the human body. Further, the developments in pervasive computing and microelectronics will increase the blurring of boundaries between humans and machines, humans and media, the inner self and machinic life.[12] In the future, nanotechnology, i.e. miniature machines that can be inserted into our bodies for surgery and that can inhabit our bodies might make any of these boundaries obsolete.

## 3. Networked Subjectivity

Media and technology connect people from all over the world with each other and with different societies, cultures, and economies. They broaden our horizon, and the way in which they network people and how people participate in those networks formed by communication technology have to be seen as important sources for the constitution of subjectivity. Thus, in the global „network society,"[13] a society that is shaped by the processes of various networks and the interaction with those networks, "both subjectivity and reality itself are increasingly entangled with communication media."[14] This means that subjects are shaped, defined, and constituted by their ability to participate in and interact with the different networks and communication technology that are present and operate in our society.



A network typically consists of nodes and the links between them. What a network is, or nodes are, in particular, depends on the specific context. In the network society, there are different networks operating, e.g. the network of politics, of economics, of communication. All these networks are today – in some way or the other – shaped by media and communication technology.[15] A node, then, can either be an individual actor or institutions and organizations. According to Manuel Castells, a network can be understood as a set of nodes that operates by the binary logic of inclusion and exclusion, or being connected

11 Except a large part of the world's population, especially in less-developed countries. Cf. Castells, Manuel, Information Technology, Globalization and Social Development. *United Nations Research Institute for Social Development (UNRISD) Discussion Paper* No. 114, September 1999, http://www.unrisd.org/unrisd/website/document.nsf/(httpPublications)/F270E0C066F3DE7780256B67005B728C?OpenDocument, accessed June 14, 2006.

12 Cf. Castells, Manuel, Informationalism. Networks, and the Network Society. A Theoretical Blueprint, in: Castells, Manuel (ed.), *The Network Society*, 3–45; Hayles, Katherine N., Computing the Human, in: *Theory, Culture & Society*, 22, 2005, Nr. 1, 131–151, here: 140.

13 Cf. Castells, Manuel (ed.), *The Network Society. A Cross-cultural Perspective*, Cheltenham, UK: Edward Elgar Publishing, 2004.

14 Hayles, Katherine N., *My Mother was a Computer*, 86.

15 Cf. Castells, Manuel, Informationalism.

or disconnected. The inclusion of a single node is dependent on its ability to contribute to the network's goal. While all nodes are important for the proper operation of a network, once a specific node is no longer required for or does no longer contribute to the communication processes, it is automatically excluded from the network. "Nodes only exist and function as components of networks. The network is the unit, not the node."[16]

In the network society, the static sender-receiver hierarchy is transformed and more and more processes and aspects of everyday life include communication technology. News from around the world is available online, errands can comfortably be 'run' from home, e.g. shopping, price comparisons, and administrative paperwork. In this context, the subject becomes a node of communication networks but can never be sure of his or her own position in a network nor of his or her relationship to a network. Subjectivity depends on the subject's ability to participate in the communication processes and contribute to the network's goals. Often, individual subjects only become aware of their dependence when they are no longer able to participate in the communication processes either because they cannot satisfy the requirements (e.g. lack of knowledge, skills or financial means), or a rupture in the communication process occurs which they do not know how to deal with and which leads to disorientation and uncertainty; or the communication process has simply changed and they are no longer able or willing to support existing structures. In all these cases, subjectivity depends on whether or not an individual knows how to successfully deal with communication technology and is able to incorporate it into his or her daily life.



Further, networks, especially those that are either formed or influenced by media, are usually decentralized and rather uncontrollable – this at least seems to be the case from the perspective of an individual subject.[17] Even though today a single media tycoon (e.g. Silvio Berlusconi, Rupert Murdoch) or a single media conglomerate often owns and operates various media products that – from the outside – seem to operate independently, media often develop a momentum of their own that is hard to predict due to complex market relations and media-society-recipients interactions. Examples are the release of pictures from Abu Ghraib or Berlusconi's – admittedly tight – defeat in the 2006 elections in Italy in spite of the fact that he owns or has a share in major Italian media labels.[18]

16 Ibid., 3.

17 Cf. Schulz, Walter, *Subjektivität im nachmetaphysischen Zeitalter. Aufsätze*, Pfullingen: Verlag Günther Neske, 1992, 275ff.

18 I am aware that the topic of 'politics and media' would require a more in-depth discussion. Berlusconi's close defeat is a good example for the ambivalent role of media in political life: media have a strong influence on people and their opinions, they can shape their users' ideas, but owning and controlling media is not a guarantee for success either. For a commentary on Abu Ghraib cf. Zizek, Slavoj, Between Two Deaths. The Culture of Torture, http://www.lacan.com/zizektorture.htm, accessed June 14, 2006.

Power structures in the network society are complex and developments, often hard or impossible to predict. Not least, these complex, unpredictable processes lead to an unstable, fragmented, multiple, and ever-changing subjectivity because not even those in power can be sure of their status and thus of their subjectivity as structures in a network can often change rapidly.

Change, however, can happen over a longer period of time too. Thus, Castells' understanding of a network, especially his principle of inclusion/exclusion, requires critical evaluation. Castells' remarks give the impression that inclusion/exclusion works on an either/or, i.e. a binary, basis. As long as a node is able to contribute to the goals of a network, it is a part of it; otherwise it is excluded from the communication process. However, inclusion/exclusion has to be seen as a gradual process over a shorter or longer period of time. Understanding the principle of inclusion/exclusion as a process helps one to analyze the complex relationship between a single node and the network as a whole. It emphasizes the effects the network has on the specific node as well as the success or failure of a node to contribute to the network. Further, Castells seems to overemphasize the network as a whole over a single node, especially with regard to power structures within a network. While Castells attests that "any communicating subject [can] act on the communication network"[19] and that this opportunity to influence the network depends on the context, i.e. "on the pattern of power present in the configuration of the network,"[20] resistance itself can, according to Castells, only take place within and as a network. "It is the characteristic of the network society that both the dynamics of domination and resistance to domination rely on network formation and network strategies of offense and defense."[21] Castells is certainly correct to point out that the feeling the individual might have of not being able to influence power structures and control the world is a source of fragmentation and disorientation for the single subject, and resistance is often enacted most effectively as a group. However, in his theory, the subject seems to be completely disempowered, since even resistance depends on the ability to participate in network structures. In Castells' concept, resistance appears to be merely another variety of power. Those who are excluded from a network are not even able to put up resistance anymore.



As mentioned above, media and communication networks have always played an important role in our knowledge about the world *(Welterkenntnis)*. In fact, today's media networks promise to deliver experience of reality/the world and *Welterschließung* at the click or push of a button. Media experience, however, is necessarily always fragmented, partial, and selective and thus leads to a frag-

19 Castells, Manuel, Informationalism, 12.

20 Ibid.

21 Ibid., 35.

mented subjectivity. According to Castells "local experience remains fragmented, customized, individualized. The socialization of society – the construction of a shared cultural practice that allows individuals and social groups to live together [...] – takes place nowadays in the networked, digitized, interactive space of communication, centered around mass media and the Internet."[22] This holds true first and foremost in developed, so-called 'first world' countries. To account for media networks as a global phenomenon, it is important to consider the impact of the presence/absence of media on knowledge and *Welterkenntnis* in less developed countries, especially in their relationship to the west. The economic, financial, and educational prospects for societies and people, especially children, in the developing world increasingly depend on their capacities to use and access communication technology. There are several initiatives that try to overcome the so-called 'digital divide', for example Computer Aid International or the critically received OLPC (One Laptop per Child) initiative, founded by Nicholas Negroponte,[23] all stressing the importance of 'being connected' for developing countries.

What is said about the socialization of society also applies to the socialization of the individual subject and its attempts to make sense of the world. Media and communication technology is often used to stage, define, and express oneself. Who someone is, and in particular how someone is perceived by others, depends on which technology he or she uses and how it is used. The deliberate usage of the iPod, for example, is often part of the user's self-understanding and self-definition.[24] Mark Poster states that "[s]ubject constitution in the second media age occurs through the mechanism of interactivity"[25] with and through media and communication technologies. It is the network and how one participates in that network that defines human subjectivity. People who choose to participate will advance and contribute to the shaping of networks;[26] the others will have to surrender to these processes. Participation, however, often is not a matter of choice, but remains beyond the control of the individual subject. As the communication process in society is proceeding, new ways of communicating with each other are developed and new technological tools and gadgets are pushed onto the market. People who cannot or do not want to keep up with these de-



22 Castells, Manuel, Informationalism, 30.

23 Cf. http://www.laptop.org/, accessed February 19, 2007.

24 Cf. Brown, Jeffrey, *Apple's iPod. A Technological, Cultural Phenomenon*, http://www.pbs.org/newshour/bb/media/jan-june06/ipod_05-15.html, accessed October 15, 2006.

25 Poster, Mark, *The Second Media Age*, Cambridge: Polity Press, reprint 1996, 33. In contrast to the 'first media epoc', that was characterized by a broadcast model, Poster understands the second media age as characterized through a decentralized model of communication, cf. ibid.,18.

26 Cf. Castells, Manuel, Informationalism, 12.

velopments will become increasingly alienated from the communication process and thus from society.

The Apple Commercial NETWORKING[27] reflects this effect of the communication network on its participants. The advertisement illustrates how easy it is to set up a link between a Mac and another medium, be it a PC, a digital camera, or a printer. The main message of the spot is "Everything just kind of works with a Mac."[28] Other gadgets, such as a PC, might be difficult to configure, but with a Mac the user is ready and set to go. For my purpose, the way the communication process develops and is portrayed in the commercial is a helpful way to understand how subjectivity is constituted through the interaction – or lack thereof – with a communication network.

> Mac: "Hello I'm a Mac."
>
> PC: "And I'm a PC. We've got a little network going here and it was very easy to set up."
>
> Mac: "We speak each other's language."
>
> PC: "We share an internet connection and all sorts of things we do together ... Who now, who is this now? What's ah?"
>
> Mac: "Oh this is that new digital camera from Japan that just came out."
>
> Mac: "Hajimemashite (nice to meet you)."
>
> Camera: "Hajimemashite (nice to meet you)."
>
> Mac: "Yoroshiku onegaishimasu (welcome)."
>
> PC: "Wait wait wait. You speak her language?"
>
> Mac: "Oh yeah absolutely! Everything just kind of works with a Mac."
>
> Mac: "Arigatou (thank you)."
>
> Camera: "Ne ne ne daren taku pokunai?"
>
> PC: "Bongiorno. Hello!"[29]



The ad starts with two men – one in his twenties wearing casual clothing, the other, probably in his thirties, wearing a suit – holding hands. The younger guy represents a Mac, the older, a PC; the PC and the Mac holding hands represents the link – or network – between the two. In the beginning of the advertise-

27 Apple, NETWORKING. TV Commercial, http://video.google.com/videoplay?docid=6088040155514961953&q=apple+networking, accessed June 14, 2006.

28 Apple TV advertisement NETWORKING.

29 Japanese quotes taken from http://www.duncans.tv/2006/apple-get-a-mac, accessed February 9, 2007.

ment, with no other participants but the two, the communication process and information/data exchange works without any problems whatsoever because the Mac and the PC "speak each other's language." All of a sudden, however, a new participant enters the arena: a young, attractive Asian woman representing the latest digital camera from Japan.[30] With the appearance of the digital camera, the structure of the network and thus the communication and information flow changes. The Mac and the digital camera instantly start talking with each other in Japanese. The PC is a bit puzzled and asks "You speak her language?" The Mac answers "Oh yeah, absolutely! Everything just kind of works with a Mac." What is interesting in the spot is that the person representing the PC becomes more and more alienated as the new medium or new technology, represented by the Asian woman, is introduced and the communication process changes. Towards the end, even though the PC still holds hands with the Mac, the Mac is much closer to the Asian girl, because they speak each other's language, i.e. they are media-apt and therefore connected, whereas the link to the PC becomes loose and fragile.

As long as the PC is strongly connected to the network, he is sure of his own subjectivity. As soon as the link becomes loose, he becomes puzzled and disoriented – as can be seen by his facial expression. The PC cannot prevent the introduction of a new medium or communication technology. He (or it) can try to learn to speak the new language (learn how to deal with the new medium), but he cannot prevent the distribution itself. Nor can he control the way the 'cool' computer and the 'cute' Asian camera interact with each other. In the advertisement, the PC fails to speak the new language[31] and thus experiences disorientation and alienation from the network.



The process of alienation is rooted in the ambiguity and complexity of networks. In a network, the role, position, and self-understanding of a subject can change rapidly. Media and communication technology, e.g. communication networks, can facilitate communication, enhance user experience, contributing to a rich and satisfying interaction with media and other human beings. While *Welterschließung* and *Welterkenntnis* have always – at least to some extent and for some people – depended on media and networks, it is the omnipresence and flood of images, texts, videoclips,[32] i.e. information, that dominate how we experience ourselves and our world today. As the Apple advertisement shows, networks promise to connect tools, people, society, location, events, and cultures. Networks, however, can also disrupt user experience and self-assurance when

30 It is important to be aware of possible fetishizations of Asian women in the west.

31 I am aware that there is a religious-like/ideological war between Windows supporters and *NIX (including MacOS) supporters.

32 E.g. shopping malls, public transportation, multimedia home entertainment centers.

the user looses control over what kind of information is accessible when, where, and for whom or when, where, and how to stop the steady flow of information.[33] As is obvious in the Apple advertisement, a network does not take heed of individual users' abilities or inabilities, but tries to guarantee this steady flow of information reconfiguring its nodes and its structures. This reconfiguration and the principle of inclusion/exclusion is a process, not an either/or state of being. The constitution of the individual subject, then, depends on how one is able to participate in and handle the flow of information, and how the individual subject is represented (or misrepresented) by information, e.g. in databases. Katherine Hayles is right that "information increasingly determines the constitution of subjects."[34]

In today's communication networks, not only information itself but a steady and permanent flow of information from multiple media sources at the same time are essential for our experience, our knowledge about the world and our relation with it, and thus our self-understanding. Media, communication technology, mediated experience, as well as this very flow of information increasingly dissolve the boundaries between the 'the real' and 'the virtual' and outrank 'real life' experiences. This dissolution of reality and the focus on the process of the network are also depicted in Apple's TV advertisement. Apple's networking spot features three persons – or media tools – forming a network; the background is completely white. Even though this simplicity is typical for Apple's 'iconography', we can read it as: what matters are media and the networks they form. Life is all about being connected. The network is real, it is *the* reality. The featuring of real human subjects representing media products, namely a PC, a Mac, and a digital camera supports the interpretation that human life in today's mediatized culture evolves in a networked context and interaction with communication technology, i.e. being connected, is a fundamental aspect of today's self-understanding. This, in combination with the setting in white space, expresses the complexity of the human-media relationship, which has both an enfranchising and a disorienting potential. It emphasizes that human subjectivity is increasingly defined by its ability to interact with media as well as the tendency of media users to ascribe human characteristics to media and communication technologies.[35] By portraying computers and digital media as human subjects, the advertisement proposes that the developments in media and communication technology might pose the question of a machinic subjectivity some day in the not so far away future. Hayles sees these future issues thus:



33 Cf. Schulz, Walter, *Subjektivität im nachmetaphysischen Zeitalter*, 273ff.

34 Hayles, Katherine N., *My Mother was a Computer*, 71.

35 Cf. Reeves, Bryon/Nass, Clifford, *The Media Equation. How People Treat Computers, Television, and New Media like Real People and Real Places*, Stanford, CA: CSLI Publications, 1996.

"What it means to be human finally is not so much about intelligent machines as it is about how to create just societies in a transnational global world that may include in its purview both carbon and silicon citizens."[36]

## 4. Theology and the Networked Subject

Faced with these challenges, I do not endorse a pessimistic attitude towards media or technology, or think of media as determining society or what it means to be human. Instead, social and technological changes should be seen as "new opportunities for reconstructing the mechanisms of subject constitution."[37] Theology cannot afford to either exclude itself from this discourse, ignoring today's mediatized context, or be excluded from it by not taking seriously enough the way more and more humans interact with each other through communication technology. Theology is an academic discipline that reflects the fundamental questions of humanity (Who are we? Where do we come from? Where are we heading towards?) and thus necessarily has to deal with media as the context in which the processes of subject constitution take place. The individual – especially in today's western world – is fundamentally connected to media and communication technology as the context in which he or she raises those questions essential for human self-understanding. As such, theology has to address this context and the relationship between the context and the individual as well as how these questions are asked and tried to be answered. Theology also reflects on religious practices. Today, religious identity is often informed by the subject's search for religious or spiritual values in the media, by religious media events as well as the commodification of religion through media. Further, religion and religiosity themselves can be a source of identity formation and subject constitution in a world that is complex and ever changing.[38] Understanding religious practices as media practices can help theology to understand and address the networked subject's longing for meaning.



But why use the term 'subjectivity' at all, especially because it is contested both in a philosophical as well as a theological context? The philosophical objections have been briefly touched on in the beginning of this paper. Theology itself has had a very ambiguous relationship to the concepts of 'subject' and 'subjectivity'. Augustine, philosopher and theologian, and the Jewish-Christian tradition mark the beginnings of the occidental philosophy of subjectivity. In

36 Hayles, Katherine N., Computing the Human, 148.

37 Poster, Mark, *The Second Media Age*, 19.

38 Cf. Castells, Manuel, *The Rise of the Network Society*; Castells, Manuel, *The Power of Identity*.

fact, Klaus Müller called Augustine the first philosopher of subjectivity.[39] Augustine marks the beginnings of his quest for God with his *dictum* "si enim fallor, sum."[40] Only by acknowledging his very existence, the 'I', is Augustine able to turn to God as the Other, the vis-à-vis. Only by looking into himself, only by taking the 'I', the first person, as the point of departure, is Augustine able to find God as well as that which completes the 'I': the otherness of God:[41] "Noli foras ire, in teipsum redi; in interiore homine habitat veritas."[42] With the emergence of the free and autonomous subject that did not need any transcendent reference or transcendent otherness, e.g. in Kantian subjectivity, Catholic theology became increasingly skeptical of the concepts of 'subject' and 'subjectivity' and has often welcomed the criticism of the autonomous subject found in various schools of thought.[43] Cardinal Ratzinger, for example, argued for the dissolution of the term subjectivity because – for him – it expressed a solid, independent, and egotistical 'I'. In contrast, he states that many sources contribute to what we call the self.[44] Ratzinger's view is supported by a networked subjectivity insofar as it is constituted through interaction and the complex processes in a network. It is not egotistical but fundamentally shaped by the relations in which it is enmeshed.



Abandoning the term 'subjectivity' altogether, however, does not seem to be reasonable. In fact, in the last 70–80 years there have been voices in Catholic theology (e.g. Maurice Blondel, Karl Rahner, Hansjürgen Verweyen, Thomas Pröpper) that call for a reconsideration of this rather skeptical regard of the term 'subject', not without taking seriously the criticism that, for example, postmodern philosophers and feminist theory have raised.

While the term 'subjectivity' is indeed a contested one, it expresses a rich if ambiguous history of human experience as well as philosophical thinking. As Flusser points out, one would loose too many of these implications, knowledge, and insights, and the awareness of the problems of subjectivity we have accrued up until now, if one gave up the terminology.[45]

39 Cf. Müller, Klaus, Subjekt/Subjektivität, in: Franz, Albert, Baum, Wolfgang, Kreutzer, Karsten (eds.), *Lexikon philosophischer Grundbegriffe der Theologie*, Freiburg: Herder, 2003, 384–386, here: 384.

40 Augustine, *De civitate Dei*, XI 26.

41 Cf. Taylor, Charles, *Quellen des Selbst. Die Entstehung der neuzeitlichen Subjektivität*, Frankfurt/Main: Suhrkamp, 1999, 238ff.

42 Augustine, *De vera religione*, XXXIX 72.

43 Cf. Müller, Klaus, Subjekt/Subjektivität, 384–386.

44 Cf. Ratzinger, Josef Cardinal, *Zur Gemeinschaft gerufen. Kirche heute verstehen*, Freiburg: Herder, 1991, 33.

45 Cf. Flusser, Vilém, *Vom Subjekt zum Projekt*, *Schriften*, Vol. 3, Düsseldorf: Bollmann, 1994, 23.

The concept of the networked subject is able to provide a framework for theology to take seriously the multiple sources that contribute to the constitution and *information* of the individual as well as the role and importance of media and technology in these processes. Further, it can help to understand the complexity of the relationship between communication networks and the self. This framework, understood as an interdisciplinary approach including media theory, sociology, cultural studies, and (social) network theory, can help to answer crucial questions, such as: Who participates in this world of mass media and why? Who is not able to or does not want to participate and why? What effects do media have on the individual subjects? Finally, what does the relationship between those two look like?

Links between a theological and a mediatized understanding of subjectivity can be established using Dieter Henrich's understanding of the term. Henrich refers to subjectivity as knowledge about oneself and as a process that is based upon this very knowledge and in which the subject continually modulates and remodulates its relationship to the world *(Weltbeziehung)*.[46] In fact, both knowledge about the world, and knowledge about oneself correspond to each other and are fundamental in the constitution of subjectivity. From the individual subject's perspective, knowledge about the world provides the context in which he or she finds herself placed and is the source to draw from when reflecting about one's role within and one's relationship to that context. This very knowledge about the world and about oneself also includes the ways in which the individual is linked to others, and to the world, as well as his or her role in the world. Flusser states that "[o]ne is, who or what one is, only insofar and to that extent, as one knows something."[47] Media play a crucial role in reality perception as well as in epistemical processes. Knowledge and experience mediated by communication technology and networks, however, is always partial and leading to what Robert Jay Lifton calls a "protean self"[48] addressing the fluidity and mutability of contemporary subjectivity. Thus, a theological reevaluation of the term 'subjectivity' based on Henrich's definition necessarily has to consider the partiality of knowledge and the self caused by media as an integral part of human experience



In the Apple commercial, knowledge and experience play a crucial role in determining the status of the subjects within the network, too. As the commu-

46 Cf. Henrich, Dieter, *Versuch über Kunst und Leben. Subjektivität – Weltverstehen – Kunst*, München: Carl Hanser Verlag, 2001, 31.

47 Flusser, Vilém, *Vom Subjekt zum Projekt*, 36: „Man ist, was man ist, nur in jenem Maß, in dem man etwas weiß" (translation A.O.).

48 Cf. Lifton, Robert Jay, *The Protean Self. Human Resilience in an Age of Fragmentation*, Chicago: The University of Chicago Press, 1999.

nication process in the network portrayed changes, so do the relations among the participants as well as their position in the network. Part of that transformation can be attributed to the knowledge about the world, i.e. the context (the network), the experience of the subject and its ability to apply that knowledge in the specific situation. Whereas the PC does not have the required knowledge to stay an integral part of the communication or even understand the fundamental changes the network has undergone, the Mac has what it takes to be a part of the transformation. This seems to correspond with Henrich's definition of subjectivity as knowledge about oneself (and the world) as the basis of the subject's relation to the world. Through his knowledge, the Mac is able to stay an active participant in the communication process and alter and remodulate his relation to the other participants in the network. The Apple advertisement thus poses various questions and challenges for theology. Theologically speaking, the human being is fundamentally a *Beziehungswesen*, i.e. a relational being. Relationships to God, to fellow human beings, and the world are essential to what it means to be human. Today, these relational links are lived in and through media and communication technology to a major extent. For a theological understanding of the human being, the relationship between God and humans as their creator is essential. Mediatized and networked subjectivity can help theology to come to a better understanding of the context in which relationships evolve and – to some extent – depend on and address ethical questions such as what happens to an individual and its relationships when the knowledge required to participate in communication processes is not available for whatever reason. Networked subjectivity as being constituted by the context and the relationships the subject finds him- or herself in might help theology to understand how the individual subject perceives media as a transcendent *(transzendental)* context through which mediatized subjectivity can thrive but is also fundamentally dependent on.



Further, the networked subject supports what Ricœur has called the critique of an overrated *cogito*,[49] that stands for an absolute 'I' without a relationship to the other. Ricœur's thoughts on the *cogito blessé* – the wounded *cogito* – show that the self is shaped through its context and constituted through interaction.[50] Subjectivity – in its continual constitution through media and communication networks – can be thought of, according to Ricœur, as a process of philosophical (and theological) inquiry that has the determination of the self as a goal rather

49 Cf. Orth, Stefan, *Das verwundete Cogito und die Offenbarung. Von Paul Ricœur und Jean Nabert zu einem Modell fundamentaler Theologie*. Freiburg: Herder, 1999, 219f.

50 Cf. Hiller, Doris, Das Ich des Glaubens. Theologische Überlegungen zur Kategorie der Subjektivität im Anschluß an Paul Ricœur, in: Dalferth, Ingolf U., Stoellger, Philipp (eds.), *Krisen der Subjektivität. Problemfelder eines strittigen Paradigmas*, Tübingen: Mohr Siebeck, 2005, 241–259, here: 245.

than its origin.[51] Subjectivity understood in this communicational and networked context means an open and dynamic process that corresponds to a (theological) eschatological perspective (already-not yet). The Apple commercial expresses this open process portraying the PC's subjectivity and self-understanding as fundamentally connected to both how the network changes structures of interaction and how the PC itself tries – but fails – to alter communication patterns. This understanding opposes any form of self-positioning (*Selbstsetzung*), taking seriously Ricœur's critique of the traditional philosophy of subjectivity. As the Apple spot illustrates, networked subjectivity is (and is only) constituted through interaction with communication networks expressing the fundamental ambiguity of both human existence and media processes. From the perspective of the subject, the act of constitution is both active and passive. On the one hand, she or he is constituted through media and their transformation processes; on the other hand, the way the subject interacts with the networks shapes both the subject and the network. The networked subject – as a node of a network, not its center – finds itself between the two poles of 'I' and otherness. She or he is thus decentered – a thought that is important in Ricœur's thinking – and can lead to a new understanding of what it means to believe from a Christian perspective. The creed, for example, expresses the most fundamental truths of Christianity rather than focusing on the faithful 'I'. In omitting the 'I' for the most part, it is able to, according to Karl Barth, speak about the human essence most perfectly. It is, however, the 'I', the faithful subject, that speaks and that marks the beginning of the *symbolum*.[52]



Today, subjectivity can be understood only as contextual, relational, and networked. What it means to be human is – to a large extent – shaped by media and communication technology. A fundamental aspect of these technologies is that they are able to network people across time and space and that they play a crucial role in the *Welterschließung*. The networked subject – in his or her ambiguity – can provide an important framework for theology to reconsider its evaluation of the term 'subjectivity' and, more importantly, provide a basic understanding of the context of the contemporary *conditio humana*. Trying to bring both the *homo medialis* as networked being and the *homo religiosus* (as a *homo aestheticus*) together can help theology to understand how media contribute to human self-understanding. The *homo medialis* does not only reflect today's human experience, but is both the addressee of and the respondent to the Trinitarian communication network.

51 Cf. Orth, Stefan, *Das verwundete Cogito*, 222.

52 Cf. Hiller, Doris, Das Ich des Glaubens, 241f.

Florian Kröppel

# Different Rites of Initiation – Different Heroes[1]

Two men, one old, one young, are in a boat far out in the middle of a lake. After a short argument, the older one pushes the younger into the water. The younger one lashes about, swallows a lot of water, finally sinks to the bottom of the lake. But he does not die. When he is back on solid ground, his life starts anew.

This scene from HIGHLANDER (Mulcahy, USA/UK 1986) is a typical example of how mainstream film represents the transformation of a 'normal' person into a hero. This transition is an extremely important element in mainstream film. While analysing the extremely successful and influential film MATRIX[2] I was first struck by this kind of transformation of the hero. The main character exhibits strong soteriological facets: he has been born to save the world. Yet in order to fulfill his mission, he has to become a new person: he has to die and be born again. In this film, the hero's initiation is shown through a series of impressive images that are highly symbolic. After repeatedly watching the film, I realised that there were clear aesthetic and narrative parallels, even on the level of dialogue, to other successful mainstream films, an observation which lead me to pursue the reflection of this moment of transformation some more.



The stories told in film are distinctly different from everyday life: they talk about the unusual, that which is worth being told. In order to fit into this unusual story, the protagonist has to change, too. This transformation which occurs internally has to be made visible to the audience, usually in scenes which are called scenes of initiation. These are used regularly in commercial films, and therefore, I will focus in this article on the questions of which images are chosen to serve as representations for the hero's transformation, and which actions express the transition from 'normal' to 'heroic'. Finally, I will analyse what the form of the initiation scene says about the overall content of the film.[3]

One might question the value of these issues within the framework of a discussion about *theology* in a media society. Yet, it is the task of theology to

1 Translated by Stefanie Knauss and Barbara A. Emmel.

2 Larry and Andy Wachowski, USA 1999.

3 These questions are discussed in more detail in my MA thesis: *Taufe im Film: Initiationsrituale und ihre Bedeutung für den kommerziellen Film*. Diplomarbeit, Graz University 2006, on which this article is based.

reflect on faith and its foundations, God's revelation, within the context of our time and society, including culture and media, which then conversely are used to publicise the results of this reflection. Even extremely commercialised art forms, such as mainstream cinema, are open to theologically relevant questions and religious themes. The sense-making options and possible answers to existential questions (about good/evil, love, death, success etc.) offered in film, and the concepts that viewers bring with them to the cinema, converge there and are developed into a new narrative by which one can structure one's life, after "the end of grand narratives" (Lyotard).[4] How this is done, and which motifs from the religious sphere are used to achieve this sense-making function of film, is one question that theology has to deal with today in a dialogue between theology and the arts in all forms.

## 1. Filmic Structure

Mainstream film builds around a narrative structure, a 'plot', which Bordwell defines as "a chain of events in cause-effect relationship occurring in time and space."[5] The plot can also be called that chronological sequence of images, whose content is defined by characters and external circumstances. These elements are spliced together into a 'story' through the recipient's abilities to abstract and fill in the empty spaces left open in the narrative.[6] This is possible because humans have been surrounded by stories for their whole life, and most people who go to the cinema may not only have similar previous experiences with stories, but also have similar expectations as to what a story should be and do. In short: recipients create their own film, but (mostly) they follow general rules.



During this constructive process, viewers invest attention, thought, interpretation – all of which are efforts for which the film has to recompense them in the form of entertainment, thrill, excitement, and also in the attempt to provide answers to incipient (but often unexpressed) questions. Thus, entertainment can be defined as "a process of reception (and its characteristics) which is marked by the fact that the affective and visceral benefits experienced by the viewer are greater than his or her cognitive, affective and visceral investment, with this

4 Cf. the article by C. Marsh/Ch. Haines Lyons in this volume on what people do with the films they watch.

5 Bordwell, David; Thompson, Kristin: *Film Art. An Introduction*, New York: McGraw-Hill 1993, 65.

6 The difference between plot and story can be illustrated by the flashback: although the early event is told later on in the plot sequence, this does not change the chronological sequence of the story.

investment not exceeding a certain limit."[7] One might add that the investment should not be below a certain limit, either, or else the audience will become bored. An active and interdynamic participation of the mind and its senses is needed for a successful reception process, even with the most commercial of films. In fact, the most successful commercial films pay careful attention to audience reception and participation through their attention to the normative traditions of story making, such as the rising action, climax, falling action and resolution of the problem (i.e. the fairly set rules of the classical dramaturgical structure).

For the analysis of the narrative structure of film, Vogler's twelve-stations model of narrative proves to be useful.[8] Vogler's work is based on Joseph Campbell's reflections on the structure of myths in *The Hero With a Thousand Faces*, and applies Campbell's principles to mainstream films. The hero's journey is made up of twelve 'stations' which show an overall cyclical form.

After the hero's initiation, the building of the conflict and ultimately the conflict's resolution, the hero returns to his or her beginnings but in a changed way: having developed, matured and gained knowledge about him- or herself and the world. Beginning and end are distinguished by a new quality the hero has acquired in the course of his or her adventures, an 'elixir', which provides satisfaction to the audience and dissolves the tension that lies at the heart of the film and that functions as its impetus. A prologue is prefixed which functions as self-legitimization for the narrative or myth.[9] The 'narrative cycle' of the action is paralleled by the 'personal cycle' of the protagonist and antagonist. The personal cycle can be understood as the means by which a character changes and grows, a process that – as will be shown – is not linear but moves forward suddenly at particular points in the narrative, the so-called plot points. It is just these plot points that are of particular relevance for a theological discussion of mainstream film.

Given that myth and film share very similar structures, one might assume that they have similar functions for the audience, too. The function of a myth is to provide answers to important questions about human life, and to order and stabilise the world which – in many religions and cultures – is seen to be always on the verge of sliding into chaos. Myth, therefore, has an obvious reli-



7 Eder, Jens: *Dramaturgie des populären Films. Drehbuchpraxis und Filmtheorie*, Hamburg: LIT 2000, 20 (translation S.K. and B.A.E.).

8 Vogler, Christopher: *The Writer's Journey. Mythic Structure for Writers*, Studio City, CA: Wiese 1998.

9 Cf. Wessely, Christian: *Von Star Wars, Ultima und Doom. Mythologisch verschleierte Gewaltmechanismen im kommerziellen Film und in Computerrollenspielen*, Frankfurt: Lang 1997, 61f.

gious function which is reinforced by the interdependence of myth and ritual.[10] Additionally myth has a clearly pragmatic dimension: one does not only act *on* a myth, but is also acted upon *by* a myth.[11] Film achieves this sense-making function not only through its structure, but also through the identification of the audience with the protagonist, his or her world and the problem or question posed to him or her. The filmmaker will therefore aim at promoting audience identification in his or her film.

## 2. The Meaning of Moments of Disruption and Rupture in Film

At the beginning of a film, time, place and characters are introduced (in the exposition). The author or filmmaker uses this first opportunity to steer the sympathy and/or antipathy of the audience according to his or her purposes by showing the protagonists in actions that reflect their character and personality. Even though these beginning sequences may contain problems that are posed to the characters, these characters are still taking part in everyday life without any essential and existential questions cropping up. Any fundamental questions about the sense of existence do not come up until a disruption or rupture has occurred, and everyday life can no longer go on as it was. It is at this point that life will have changed in fundamental ways.



This is also the point at which film and religion meet. A film moves its audience, touches the viewers, in the very moment of disruption: this is the moment when something unexplainable happens, when higher powers seem to be at work, and the transcendent enters immanent, everyday life. These may include experiences of ecstasy, revelation, or ones associated with the moment of death. Without this disruption or rupture, transcendence and salvation cannot be experienced. If salvation is indeed a fundamental need of humans, and this need can be satisfied by film, it is important to pay attention to the moment of rupture in film. The term 'rupture' itself expresses the intensity of the experience and is stronger than a simple disruption; rupture means that there is no way back, neither to the safety of the everyday, nor even to the crisis that caused the rupture in the first place: "this crisis is the sign for soon-to-happen cataclysms, perhaps even a definitive end, the beginning of the end of the world in a small way, a personal mini-apocalypse."[12] If at the beginning, the protago-

10 Cf. Lang, Bernhard: Ritus, Ritual, in: Cancik, Hubert et al. (eds.): *Handbuch Religionswissenschaftlicher Grundbegriffe* (HrwG), Kohlhammer, Stuttgart 1998, 451.

11 Tworuschka, Udo: Mythos, Mythologie, in: Drehesen, Volker et al. (eds.): *Wörterbuch des Christentums* (WdC), Gütersloher Verlagshaus Gerd Mohn, Güterloh 1988, 851.

12 Kirsner, Inge: *Erlösung im Film. Praktisch-theologische Analysen und Interpretationen*, Stuttgart: Kohlhammer 1996, 44 (translation S.K. and B.A.E.).

nist has been a 'normal' person, one with whom everybody in the audience can identify (because the 'normal' person is similar to us), by the end she or he has been transformed into a hero, a condition necessary in the accomplishment of his or her mission.

Inge Kirsner writes of the identification between audience and protagonist in cinema: "By means of the (partial) identification (or critical confrontation) of the viewer with the protagonist, the viewer participates in the crisis and experiences the 'salvation' alongside his or her representatives on the screen."[13] In order for viewers to develop and maintain an identification with the *transformed* protagonist, they too have to undergo a transformation to a degree.

Classical narrative structure defines quite strictly when the moment of rupture should occur in the course of a narrative, but how it is represented lies in the artistic freedom of each respective filmmaker. The difficulty, however, is that the moment of rupture itself is invisible, and the transformation of the protagonist is an internalized process and not accessible by the audience. "In film, internal processes can be made visible solely through the not-yet and not-anymore, but what is essential remains invisible."[14] Thus symbols and symbolic actions are the only way to attempt to make the invisible visible.

This interface between the visible and the invisible represents yet another point of contact between film and religion: the intention of religious communities is to make visible as far as possible the experience of the divine by means of rites and rituals: "The rite is a systematic regularised act in which a person, alone or in a group, visibly maintains the relationship with the feared or worshipped numen. As such, the rite is a recurring feature of religious customs, grounded in the present and history of salvation of the respective sacred community and accepted as such in secular society."[15] Furthermore, ritual is in its symbolism a re*action* to a self-revealing divine whose revelation is verbalised through myth. "In myth, the rite is given sense and explained. And vice versa: myth is continuously recreated in the drama of the repetitions of the rite. Rite and myth are mutually interdependent entities."[16]



Which ritual, however, would be an appropriate choice in order to represent the transformation of a normal person into a hero? It is my hypothesis that rites of initiation which express the transformation of a boy into a man or a girl into a woman, and an incorporation into the group are the ones used most successfully to visualise this transformation, to make accessible this existential, yet invisible moment, and thus to motivate viewer identification in mainstream film.

13 Ibid., 258 (translation S.K. and B.A.E.).

14 Ibid., 259 (translation S.K. and B.A.E.).

15 Körber, S.: Ritus, Ritual, in: WdC, 1082 (translation S.K. and B.A.E.).

16 Ibid (translation S.K. and B.A.E.).

Given that the hero's mission is the central moment of the narrative, the question can always be posed as to whether the respective rite of initiation chosen by the filmmaker is well suited to the exact mission. If it is possible to establish a pattern between the rite of initiation used and the mission of the hero, one can ask whether any given specific rite is chosen purposefully because the filmmaker is aware of its meaning, associations and function in any given religious community and seeks to transfer this awareness onto the audience. Even though this pattern is not necessarily applicable to the whole of film history, it is an interesting observation that those films that have had a significant influence on popular culture have made use of this formal and narrative element, and that the inclusion of a certain rite of initiation into the narrative of the film has apparently added to the quality and success of the film.

However, before analysing the initiation scenes in ONCE UPON A TIME IN THE WEST, RAIDERS OF THE LOST ARK and HIGHLANDER, it is necessary to take a closer look at the meaning, structure and form of initiation rites from the perspective of religious studies in order to better understand their use and function in these films.



## 3. Rites of Initiation

Initiation (Latin *initiare*: 'to begin, introduce, initiate') means a rite or action through which a person is introduced to a new environment, age group, stage of life, etc. For methodological reasons, I distinguish between three kinds of initiation: archaic initiation; initiation in mystery cults such as the cult of Mithras; and initiation in the monotheistic religions. According to Van Gennep, all three rites of initiation – in spite of all differences between them – consist themselves of three phases: rites of separation, liminality and re-incorporation.[17]

Archaic rites of initiation are used to introduce a boy, a girl or a whole age group into the world of adults. In these particular rites, the aspect of spatial separation is particularly emphasised: the boys may live in far-away camps, the girls may live in special houses. During the initiation process, the children learn about the traditions and taboos of their tribe or clan. Bodily castigation, inurement, circumcision or other bodily markers and/or ritual fights are part of the rite of initiation. Often, the climax of the period of isolation, and thus the ultimate rite of liminality, is the encounter with an ominous being which devours the initiate who is then reborn. The recognition of this monstrous being as a member of the tribe concludes the initiation. Such a symbol or symbolic being expresses both the life-threatening and life-giving aspect of social structures.

17 Cf. Turner's reception of Van Gennep's work in: Turner, Victor: *The Ritual Process. Structure and Anti-Structure*, Berlin: De Gruyter 1995, 93.

The re-incorporation is marked by ritual purification and eventually ritually donning new clothes. The successful initiation or transformation is greeted with collective satisfaction and joy and celebrated in an obligatory festival.[18]

Initiation in the various mystery cults is carried out in different ways than the rituals described above. And, in fact, these cults are so orientated towards initiation that they can be called cults of initiation. Mystery cults were secret cults (in contrast to the public cult of the state) which aimed at introducing the divine into the world and making it accessible to the individual through the reenactment of the death and resurrection of their chosen god in ritual acts. In these dramatic acts, the primordial myth of the god became the cultic present and reality: "The initiate hoped to reach ecstasy and enthusiasm through the initiation into the mysteries so that he or she could symbolically step out of themselves and the divine could enter them; the aim was change, salvation, resurrection, rebirth. Thus symbols played an important role in this process."[19] Well known cults of this kind include the cults of Attis, Isis and Mithras, in addition to the Eleusinian Mysteries (after 700 BCE).

Given the secretive nature of cults in general, procedures or detailed accounts of the respective initiation rites are not generally available, even though some actions and their meanings are known, e.g. for the Eleusinian Mysteries. Central to the rite of initiation were special cult objects kept in a basket which were believed to have been given by the god being worshipped. One action involving these objects required the initiate to open the basket, touch the objects and put them into a different vessel. The opening was understood as the descent into the underworld, whereas the touching of the objects was thought to bring life after death. In some cults, initiation involved a stage of preparation, such as a period of fasting before the ritual act. Other elements include the laying on of hands, a bath of purification, the dressing in new clothes.[20] In all cults, the initiation was not performed once in a lifetime, but could be repeated regularly: the close connection to the divine, and the membership in the elitist group, which was achieved by the rite, was transitory and had to be regularly strengthened and reinforced.



In monotheistic religions, rites of initiation include, in Judaism, circumcision, bar mitzvah and bat mitzvah; in Islam, circumcision; and in Christianity, baptism and confirmation. Because of its relevance for western mainstream film, the ritual of baptism and its possible historical influences will be presented in some detail here.

18 Cf. Grohs, E.: Initiation, in: HrwG, 238f.

19 Lurker, Manfred: *Die Botschaft der Symbole in Mythen, Kulturen und Religionen,* München: Kösel 1990, 57.

20 Cf. ibid., 58.

Baptism is the most characteristic Christian ritual. It has been practised ever since apostolic times and even today is acknowledged by all Christian denominations. The baptismal practice of the early church is documented in the New Testament. According to Acts 2:38, baptism was a normative feature of missionary activity (for example, Peter's) and the rite of incorporation into the Christian community: "Repent, and be baptized every one of you in the name of Jesus Christ that your sins may be forgiven ..."

Why did the Christians begin to baptise so soon after the Easter event? Was it because of Jesus Christ's command to baptise (Mt 28:19)? For most exegetes, among them Gerhard Barth, the formality of Mt 28:19 and its trinitarian structure suggest that it is part of a much younger tradition.[21] Since it is unlikely that the baptismal practice of the early Christian community can be traced to an explicit command of Jesus, it is therefore more likely that the water rite of John the Baptist served as an example to the early church.[22] In Christian baptism, the following characteristics of John's act of baptism have been retained: it is a single and singular event in the life of a Christian, it is not a self baptism, but requires a baptist or baptiser. The precondition for baptism is a willingness to convert; the important consequence, the forgiveness of sins. Ultimately, baptism is a condition for salvation in the imminent Last Judgement.[23]



What differentiates this rite most from the others described above is its function as preparation for the approaching Judgement Day. Initiation is not restricted to the individual or a group, but has a cosmic, even apocalyptic character: baptism and salvation at the end of times are closely linked. For the early Christians, this aspect of salvation and reconciliation could easily be related to Jesus' death on the cross. After Pentecost, the Christian baptism acquired its characteristic traits: it is a baptism in the name of Jesus by which the candidate receives the gift of the Holy Spirit.

Following Van Gennep's internal structure of the initiation ritual, the ritual of liminality is also equally central to baptism, the death of the old person and rebirth as a new person: "Therefore we have been buried with him by baptism into death, so that, just as Christ was raised from the dead by the glory of the Father, so we too might walk in newness of life." (Rom 6:4)

Three forms of initiation have been presented thus far: the rites of initiation of archaic cultures which are marked by a very physical symbolic act (e.g. circumcision, injuries, fight); the initiation of mystery cults which is performed

21 Cf. Barth, Gerhard: *Die Taufe in frühchristlicher Zeit*, Neukirchen-Vluyn: Neukirchner Verlag 1981, 13.

22 Cf. ibid., 43.

23 Cf. Ostmeyer, Karl-Heinrich: *Taufe und Typos. Elemente und Theologie der Tauftypologien in 1. Korinther 10 und 1. Petrus 3*, Tübingen: Mohr-Siebeck 2000, 88–102.

repeatedly throughout life and which connects the individual to the divine through sacred objects and introduces him or her into an elitist, sometimes secret society; and finally, Christian baptism which recreates the individual and is necessary for one's salvation in the Last Judgement. Common to all three is the internal structure of separation, liminality and re-incorporation.

The following film analyses concentrate on the use of rituals of initiation and their function within the narrative structure and reception process, and the question of how the 'message' of the film and the form of initiation used are interrelated.

## 4. Initiation in Mainstream Film

### 4.1 Once upon a Time in the West

After the financial and critical success of Sergio Leone's "Dollar Trilogy" with Clint Eastwood as protagonist, Leone went on to begin a new project, the ultimate Western, titled Once upon a Time in the West (C'era una volta il West, Leone, I/USA 1968), which was at once both operatic yet brutal and reprehensible. A railroad company mogul hires a group of killers under the leadership of Frank (Henry Fonda). In order to gain the desired land, they kill a farmer and his family just before the farmer's wife (Claudia Cardinale), who has been away, arrives back at the farm. This young woman decides to live at the now deserted farm, where she is protected by two renegades. One of them is rather taciturn and communicates mostly through a haunting melody he plays on his harmonica, which earns him his name, Harmonica (Charles Bronson). In the end, the unscrupulous mogul is killed and, just before the final duel between Harmonica and Frank, Harmonica's true identity is revealed: he is the brother of one of Frank's victims who was killed decades ago. After Harmonica has killed Frank and avenged his brother, the lonely avenger rides west, in spite of a tempting offer by the widow.



Harmonica's initiation as hero many years ago is shown in a flashback during the final duel: in the middle of the desert, a man is shown hanging from a decrepit gate. His feet just reach his much younger brother's shoulders on which he is propped, still alive. As long as the boy (the hero-to-be) remains standing, his brother will live, but as soon as he collapses, his brother will die. Frank, the antagonist, oversees the lynching. Finally exhausted from supporting his brother's weight, the boy collapses, a bell fastened at the rope rings, and his brother is dead. Just before this happens, Frank has placed a harmonica into the boy's mouth from which the boy produces, just before his brother's death, a long haunting sound, a kind of death song for his brother. As the boy lies prostrate in the sand, the mob rides away. A hard cut in the film brings the audience back to the duel between Harmonica and Frank.

### *The Initiation*

Like other sources of initiation rites in culture, film also builds around the same kind of tripartite structure of separation, liminality and incorporation.

In this film, the *separation* is symbolised by a common motif of place, the desert. It represents a contrast to urbane or fertile areas in which human civilisation has developed. A character placed in the desert symbolises one who is no longer part of this civilisation, is most likely close to death and on the threshold of the next world. In his initiation, the boy who would be later called Harmonica is tied up and immobilised by the weight of his brother on his shoulders. Captive as such in the desert, he is far removed from his normal everyday environment.

If the setting represents the ritual of separation, the story is *liminality* turned into film: death and a return to life are made visible. Both film and ritual face the difficulty of how to represent death: it can either be symbolic; or really occur and then be overcome, as in fantasy film; or be delegated to another person. If  another person dies in the place of the hero, the relationship has to be a very close one, involving an older, wiser person, such as a father or a mother. This is exactly what happens here: the older brother, who was a father figure to the much younger brother, dies when the boy breaks down under his weight. The moment of death is emphasised by the use of a slow-motion shot of the falling boy while the dead man himself remains outside of the frame. This is a clear hint that the child is the protagonist, and that his brother's death will have repercussions for his whole life. Just at this moment of death, when his brother dies in his place, the boy is transformed and becomes an avenger with only one aim and purpose in life, to hunt down and kill Frank, who in this moment becomes the ultimate antagonist, the hunted.

*Re-incorporation* happens in the cut back to the duel scene. Harmonica returns to the group of farmers he has been a part of for the whole film. Even though this scene, too, is set in the desert, it now is a civilised landscape in which railroad workers are busy with the new tracks that will bring even more civilization to the area.

In Once upon a Time, the separation motif dominates virtually the whole of the initiation process throughout the film. It is first symbolised by the barren landscape and the isolation of the boy who is immobilised and, because of the harmonica, speechless. The motif of death is drastically expressed in the character of his brother whose death the boy experiences physically and perhaps even considers himself responsible for. His isolation continues throughout the entirety of the film: he comes from nowhere, and even though he is himself somewhat in love with the widow and tempted by her offer, his isolation is so great that he chooses instead to ride off into an unspecified future on his own.

All of these elements hint at a relationship between this scene of initiation and the archaic rites of initiation: both are marked by the emphasis of aspects of physical pain and isolation, and by the transformation of a boy into a man taking his position in society (in this case, that of an avenger).

### *The Hero*

The hero is a loner whose goal is mostly important for himself, even though the community (here specifically the widow) profits from his success. The audience can participate in the hero's personal fate only by means of major abstraction (the individual evil is the structural evil and vice versa). Tarantino's KILL BILL VOL. 2 (USA 2004) works similarly. 'The bride' is a lonely revenger who is buried alive after a fight she lost. The audience sees her in a most hopeless situation – or so it seems. After having fought her way out of the grave only through the most strenuous of physical exertion, she continues her mission of revenge. Other lonely heroes in film history have lost a member of their family or been injured physically or psychologically by their enemy, e.g. in MAD MAX (Miller, AUS 1979). Without further (ritual or cultic) elaborations of his or her initiation, this kind of hero remains the stubborn revenger or avenger whose only sense in life is to punish the guilty. Any usefulness of his or her actions to society, beyond the personal satisfaction of a desire for revenge, is purely marginal and accidental in his or her life.



## 4.2 RAIDERS OF THE LOST ARK

With the character of Indiana Jones (Harrison Ford), Steven Spielberg (director) and George Lucas (script, producer) created one of the most famous action heroes of modern pop culture. Indiana Jones is an archaeologist who, in the 1930s, fights villains (mostly Nazis) with a whip and pistols and rescues rare treasures, rather than quietly sitting at home and doing his research at university. The treasures have mostly religious or at least cultic relevance, even though 'Indie' does not himself appear to be a religious person. In RAIDERS OF THE LOST ARK (USA 1981), Indiana Jones is looking for the ark on behalf of the American intelligence service, because there are rumours that Hitler is close to finding it. Hitler's finding it would create a serious problem because, according to a tradition, whichever army carries the ark with it will supposedly be invincible. In Cairo, the archeologist Jones finds the ark, but is quickly forced to hand it over to the apparently superior German army. When the Nazis open the ark, they are killed by its supernatural powers. Jones and his erstwhile girlfriend Marion (Karen Allen) survive, but the ark disappears.

The hero's initiation happens in a complex construct of three scenes which correspond to the three phases of the initiation, but which in and of themselves also show a tripartite structure. Each scene contains a partial initiation which is then fully concluded by the end of the third scene.

### The Initiation

The first scene is predominantly a scene of *separation:* after Indiana Jones has acquired the certain objects (an amulet and a staff) necessary to find the treasure and a map room where the exact position of the ark can be discovered, he descends into this map room, a cave with a circular opening at the top, with the help of his friends. Although he was part of this group during his former deeds, this action now isolates him and he is on his own. The isolation of the hero is reinforced and his return is made more complicated when his friends outside the cave have to leave their post.

During this time of isolation in the map room, Indiana Jones is shown the position of the ark by a beam of light. Thus the motif of gaining insight, literally an illumination, is foregrounded in this scene. From now on, Jones is one of the very few, and right at this moment even the only one, who knows where the ark is. His return from the cave, with the help of the community, shows that this scene in and of itself is a scene of initiation, including the typical three aspects of separation, liminality and re-incorporation into society.



The second scene of initiation occurs a few minutes later in the film: reunited with his group and with their help, Indiana Jones digs out a block of stone which, when pushed aside, reveals a larger and darker cave protected by a wooden figure. The bottom of the cave is alive with snakes. Indiana Jones and his closest ally climb down into the dark cave. A strong motif representing death accompanies this descent, which is reinforced by the fact that, as the audience has been told earlier, Jones has a mortal fear of snakes. In order to fulfill his mission, he has to face his innermost fears in this moment of *liminality.* Despite the snakes, the pair look for and find the ark without further difficulty. The darkness of the cave is vanquished when the golden artefact is taken out of its hiding place. Both touch the object and thereby establish a connection to the divinely given object. This clearly resembles the rites of initiation in mystery cults. But just a moment later, the ark has to be yielded up again to the enemies and is taken out of the cave. Although his ally makes it out of the cave, Jones' girlfriend is in turn pushed into the cave and the entrance is closed with the two of them now trapped in the cave. Alone with the snakes, the two frantically look for an exit and use the wooden statue to break down a wall in the cave. Interestingly, the transformation of the hero is paralleled by a transformation of the antagonistic power (at least in part) when a French archeologist takes pity on Jone's girlfriend. This refers to the darker powers' ability to change just as well as the good, as is typical of classical myths.

The third scene can be seen as a rite of *incorporation:* behind the wall, there is a passageway lined by mummified dead bodies. In the imagery of myth, this represents a kind of exit from the underworld, a way out of Hades. The two push through the narrow corridor and, after the hero has pushed away another block of stone, they are returned to their community and are back among the living.

All three scenes (the map room, the discovery of the ark, the escape from the snake-infested cave) show an internal structure typical of initiation rites: separation, liminality and incorporation, although one element is dominant in each scene. For example, the themes of isolation and separation are the strongest in the map room, where the hero is isolated, experiences an illumination and then returns to the outer world. In the middle scene, the central themes and images are the cave, the discovery and touching of a sacred object, even though moments of separation (descending into the cave) and incorporation can be found here as well (delegated to his friend who succeeds in leaving the cave). The final scene is obviously mostly a scene of return and incorporation with the encounter of death – an aspect of liminality here – being marked by the mummies at the side of the passage and the plunge into utter darkness.



These three scenes and the order in which they occur point clearly to a distinctive initiation rite, that of the mystery cult. First of all, the initiation is repetitious, because the object can be exchanged. This makes it possible to continue the series of films without the logic of the story suffering or the films becoming overly boring. Not surprisingly, there are similar scenes in the later Indiana-Jones-films. Secondly, the climax of the initiation is the touching of the sacred object which was central to the Eleusian Mysteries and other mystery cults, too. As in the mystery cults, the communal aspect is also emphasised in the film: Jones is with his friend in the cave, and later escapes from it with his erstwhile girlfriend.

### *The Hero*

Central to the initiation in mystery cults is a repetition of the initiation over time, the touching of an object and the gaining of a particular insight. The hero acts not out of merely personal interest, as in ONCE UPON A TIME or KILL BILL. As in all mystery cults, the community plays an important role: in this case America is the larger group or entity that will be saved from evil. Fighting against Hitler's troops on behalf of the American intelligence service, Jones is part of society and 'does his bit' for the war effort. The intelligence service can be understood to hint at the secrecy of the mystery cults in contrast to the state cult. Other heroes of this type can be found in the STAR WARS trilogy or the LORD OF THE RINGS films. Thus, in summary, if a community, or a part of it, is threatened and a hero sets out to save it, his or her initiation will most likely follow the pattern of the initiation rites of mystery cults.

## 4.3 HIGHLANDER

In Russell Mulcahy's action film HIGHLANDER, nearly immortal warriors battle throughout the centuries. The last one to be left over is to win a dubious 'prize', mortality, and the ability to read the thoughts of others. The protagonist is the warrior Connor MacLeod (Christopher Lambert) who lives in 20th century New York as Russell Nash. The audience is introduced to the beginnings of his career as an immortal in the Scottish Highlands and his fight against one antagonist, the Kurgan/Victor Kruger (Clancy Brown), whom he finally kills and thus wins the right to live as a mortal being.

The ways of the immortals, how to die, and, most importantly, how to fight with a sword (the magic object) are all initially taught to a young Connor by his mentor, Ramirez (Sean Connery). In the central of five initiation scenes, which occur throughout the film and which are closely interconnected by motifs and characters, Connor's own immortality is eventually revealed to him.



### *The Initiation*

The *separation* of the hero from society is shown in a scene of its own which precedes the initiation proper: Connor is frolicking with his wife on a field when suddenly Ramirez appears riding on a white horse. A storm comes up and Connor ends up physically isolated through a series of events: first he is separated from his wife and his clan, and then he is truly and fully isolated kneeling on a hill with bolts of lightning passing through his body. His anguish and his cries clearly portray the agony of the beginning of his initiation.

When Ramirez begins his training of Connor, they are in a boat, thus symbolising that the initiation is happening away from the hero's everyday environment. The scene described at the beginning of this paper follows. Connor's fall into the water represents the rite of *liminality.* As a voice-over, Ramirez's voice can be heard: "We call to you, O Heavenly Father!"[24] After Connor realizes his immortality, he comes back up to the surface. In the meantime, Ramirez is back on shore and is grilling fish while Connor can be seen coming out of the

24 Translation of the German dubbed version by S.K. and B.A.E.

water in the background. With this meal (typical as a closure of initiation rites), the *incorporation* of the initiate into society is to be celebrated. Connor comes closer and pulls his weapon in an attempt to kill Ramirez from behind, an action required in myth of a student learning to overcome a higher and antagonistic power. But Connor's attempt fails (as it must, for Ramirez knows of and is expecting it), and Ramirez begins his teaching in earnest. From now on, teacher and pupil are connected by the actions of the rite.

The rite of initiation used in this film shows all of the characteristics associated with Christian baptism as ritual:

- The main symbol of the Christian baptism is water, obviously present in the setting in the lake. The life-threatening aspect of water (the death of the old person) is emphasised through Connor's drowning.
- Christian baptism is not a self-baptism but requires the presence of a baptiser. In this story, this role is carried out by Ramirez, who represents the mythical archetype of an older and wiser mentor.
- Christians are traditionally baptised either in the name of Jesus Christ, or by virtue of the trinitarian formula. A film which does not want to show the incorporation of a person into the Christian community, but rather his or her transformation into a hero, will most likely not refer to the name of Jesus Christ. However, in this film, a residue of Christianity is noticeable in Ramirez' rather unmotivated exclamation on the way back to the shore: "We call to you, O Heavenly Father!" Because of its formulaic character, this phrase can easily be associated with the baptismal formula.
- During baptism, the candidate receives the gift of the Holy Spirit, which is represented here by the scene in which Connor kneels with bolts of lightning passing through his body. Coming from heaven, the lightning serves as a symbol for the spirit which is described as fiery tongues in the Bible.
- Water as a symbol is highly complex and ambivalent: it is both life-threatening, dangerous and wild, and life-giving, cleansing, and renewing. In baptism, all these aspects are bound up together: the old person dies, and the new one is born, cleansed from all sins. Through his 'baptism', Connor's former life is brought to an end, and he is reborn as a new person, an immortal warrior.



## *The Hero*

In many ways, Connor MacLeod represents a Christ character:[25] He was sent by a super-natural power (fate, a mission that cannot be rejected), he has su-

25 For a differentiation between Christ-like film characters, cf. Sofia Sjö's article in this volume.

per-human powers (he is virtually immortal), and he came to save humanity (in contrast to classical heroes sent to save a definable group, or even themselves). His battle against the Kurgan is neither made up by any desire for personal revenge, nor serves the interests of a particular (or secret) community, but rather is a selfless effort for the sake of humanity. Should Connor lose this battle, *all* of humanity would suffer in the 'realm of darkness'. In order to fit such a mission of cosmic, apocalyptic dimensions, the 'normal' person has to undergo a rite of initiation which contains an eschatological element. Baptism which rescues from the Last Judgement and eternal death can be seen as a rite of initiation which includes this aspect and therefore prepares the hero for his apocalyptic mission. Other examples from film history are the initiation of the hero in DOGMA,[26] MATRIX , ALIEN[3] [27] or less obviously, in HELLBOY,[28] STRANGE DAYS[29] or MONONOKE HIME.[30]

## 5. Conclusion



The interrelationship between mainstream film and religious ritual which has been analysed in its relevance for the narrative structure of a film and its impact on the audience demonstrates that there is both a religious heritage still alive in society and a religious need, even if implicit and anonymous. If this were not the case, filmmakers would refer to other formal elements in order to build their stories. Yet instead, the fact that they do use different initiation rites in order to convey various aspects of their stories, and rely on the audience being able to decypher these codes and their meaning, shows that religion – even if not in its classical forms – is very much alive and important for the popular culture of a supposedly secular society.

Initiation scenes are included in the most popular and successful films for a reason; in fact, they contribute to the success of the films to a large degree: initiation scenes are important structural elements on the narrative level of the story, and they enable the audience to identify with the hero and his or her mission. Thus, the viewers do not only become involved in the film, but are actually initiated along with the hero and transformed themselves. And similar to the mythical hero who gains knowledge about the world in the course of his or her adventures, the audience is offered answers to the questions about 'life and the universe' which they have brought along with them to the cinema.

26 Smith, USA 1999.
27 Fincher, USA 1992.
28 Del Toro, USA 2004.
29 Bigelow, USA 1995.
30 Miyazaki, J 1997.

Media hypes around films such as The Passion of Christ[31] or The Da Vinci Code,[32] and the increasing interest in pastoral work that includes popular media products clearly show that the dialogue between theology and film/media has to be included in the theological agenda. And if theology wants to be relevant to people today in its thinking about God and his relationship with humanity, these 'new' texts in which existential human needs, desires and ideals are expressed, have to be taken seriously and systematically reflected upon.



31 Gibson, USA 2004.
32 Howard, USA 2006.

# ./plug-ins

Herwig Rehatschek, Werner Bailer, Helmut Neuschmied,
Sandra Ober and Horst Bischof

# A Tool Supporting Annotation and Analysis of Videos

## 1. Introduction

Since the early 1990s, the Institute of Fundamental Theology of Graz University has investigated the relationship between theology and media, especially film, in the context of its research focus Theology – Aesthetics – Visual Arts – Film – Culture. It is also a member of the International Research Group *Film and Theology*.[1] An important focus of its research has been the detailed analysis of videos with respect to religious symbols. In addition, it explores the relationship between media and society, media and the construction of reality, the rise of the religious in media society, and the body as a site for religious experiences in films. Research in this area is not only performed by Graz University but also on an international level. Several well-known academics and institutions, for instance, are Peter Horsfield, an Australian theologian, Stewart Hoover and the research center at the University of Colorado at Boulder,[2] or the Center for Religion and Media at New York University.



In order to effectively perform research in the area of theology and video (film), efficient video annotation tools are needed.[3] The main genre of interest for institutions like the Institute of Fundamental Theology are feature films. Unfortunately, especially in this genre, practically no tools exist to support the researcher with video annotation tasks. 'Video annotation' in this context refers to adding high level semantic information (usually in text form) to the video stream. The advantage is that annotation makes hidden information explicit and facilitates the analysis of the video. Due to the lack of tools until now, the first research work at the institute has been performed with a simple video recorder, a big pile of paper with annotations to specific parts of the film referenced by time codes and a lot of spooling. This is very time consuming. The main reason for the lack of tools in the feature area is that this genre is of minor interest for

1 Cf. http://www.film-und-theologie.de.

2 S. M. Hoover, K. Lundby, Introduction. Setting the Agenda, in: S. M. Hoover, K. Lundby (eds.), *Rethinking Media, Religion, and Culture*, Thousand Oaks: Sage, 1997, 9.

3 Cf. Christian Wessely's article in this volume.

broadcasters and archives. In comparison to news and sports material, the reuse of parts of feature films is very complicated due to copyright restrictions. In the area of sports and news, the level of reuse is considerable, therefore commercial systems with a high grade of automation already exist in this area.

However, those systems are not really suitable for the detailed analysis of feature films since most tools only support global annotations valid for the entire content, e.g. film title, abstract, actors, etc. For a detailed analysis of a film, however, the researcher has to be able to work with smaller units, such as shots and scenes, be able to annotate them (temporal and spatial annotations) and relate them to each other. Temporal annotations describe a film segment which is defined by a start and end time code. These segments can either be a scene or a shot, but also any arbitrary part of the film (e.g. the appearance of a specific person or object or annotations referring to locations etc.). Spatial annotations describe the content of one frame, and hence the semantic decomposition of the image by describing the persons and objects present in this single frame.

A crucial aspect in the design of an efficient annotation tool is its ability to support the researcher (or 'human annotator') in usually time-consuming tasks by offering as many automatic features as possible. Annotations to be performed



fully or at least semi-automatic may include shot detection, camera movement, extraction of relevant key frames, extraction of color similarity features, object detection, object recognition, and transformation of spatial annotations into temporal ones. Spatial annotations can be transformed into temporal ones by object tracking, i.e. by following objects automatically. A person, for example, may be marked by a rectangle in one frame and then automatically be tracked forwards and backwards. This will relieve the annotator from the tedious task of marking one and the same person in hundreds of frames and save valuable time.

In this paper, we introduce our Semantic Video Annotation Tool (SVAT) application which enables efficient annotation combined with a set of automatic annotation plug-ins. All metadata of the tool is stored in the ISO standard MPEG-7[4]. There are usually two main stages in the process of video annotation: structuring of the video into a list and hierarchy of segments, and the addition of annotations of various types to these segments. Both steps can be supported by automatic tools. The complexity of automatic annotation and the need for user intervention is related to the level of the feature to be annotated. Low-level features are those that can be derived directly from the audiovisual data (e.g. "15% of the screen area is black", "the actress's voice has a fundamental frequency of 250Hz"). Thus, their description is unambiguous and can be easily automatized. The higher the level of the feature, the more semantics it conveys

4 ISO/IEC 15938:2001.

and the harder it is for an automatic annotation, as additional knowledge is required. This knowledge can be the prior knowledge of the viewer (knowledge the viewer already possesses, e.g. we recognize a table because of our everyday experience), domain knowledge (expert knowledge in a specific domain, e.g. for a referee in a soccer game, a ball rolling across a line between two goal posts is an important event), or contextual knowledge (knowledge we gather from accompanying actions and the context, e.g. we recognize the robot R2D2 in the end of a given STAR WARS film because it was introduced in early scenes of the film). The need for acquiring, representing, and using this additional knowledge complicates the automation of annotation for high-level features.

The problem of describing semantics is especially evident in terms of content structuring. Segmenting a video into shots is a comparatively simple task, which can be performed satisfactorily with automatic tools. This is due to the fact that the concept 'shot' has a very clear definition. This is no longer true, however, for larger units, such as scenes. A scene is often defined by the unity of time and place;[5] for example, the unit of continuous action at a location or following a character (with exceptions to this continuity in some cases),[6] and is required to be homogenous in style (positioning of actors, visual axis, etc.).[7] This definition is already somewhat fuzzy from a technical point of view. Additionally, we have to be aware that when we speak of place and time, this refers to the place and time perceived by the viewer. There may be subsequent shots that have no objective spatial or temporal relation, but if montage is used to make the viewer believe that the action is taking place at the same location or at the same time, the viewer will perceive the separate shots as being part of one scene. If we see content analysis as reversing the authoring process, shot detection merely reverses the technical act of cutting, while scene detection requires reversing the creative process of montage. Thus, content structuring is one of the tasks that cannot be fully automated, but tools can support the researcher in order to increase the efficiency of the manual process.

In the following, we first review related work. In section three, we describe the main parts of our video annotation tool. Section four presents the results of our work and offers some conclusions, while section five focuses on further developments.



5 Merriam-Webster's *Collegiate Dictionary*, 11th edition, 2003.

6 R. Arnheim, Film als Kunst, in: *Texte zur Theorie des Films*, 3rd ed., Stuttgart: Reclam, 1998, 189f.

7 D. Arijon, *Grammar of the Film Language*, Los Angeles: Silman-James Press, 1991, 20ff.

## 2. Related Work

There is a large amount of work dealing with the description of audiovisual media, but most of it concentrates on two genres: news and sports broadcasts. One reason for this phenomenon is the commercial relevance, as segments of sports and especially news content are frequently reused after their production (e.g. when the Concorde crashed, hours of ad hoc programs had to be filled with archive documentation material of the Concorde, because only a one minute sequence from the actual crash existed) and initial airing, so that they are valuable assets for broadcasters. Segments from feature films are hardly reused in other contexts, so that a detailed annotation is commercially not interesting. Further, compared to feature films, news and sports broadcasts have very clear dramaturgical structures, which makes the automation of segmentation (for example of news stories) more feasible.[8] There are only a few works dealing with general segmentation in feature films, most of them using rather simple features like dynamics (film tempo),[9] or defining "computable" units of the content[10] that do not necessarily coincide with scenes or sequences. There are, however, many low- and mid-level content analysis tasks that can be successfully automated (cf. Section 3.1), and even approaches for the automatic detection of some types of scenes that have clear visual or audio patterns, such as dialogs.[11]



With the advance in image processing, information retrieval, and database management, content-based image retrieval (CBIR) has been actively studied in recent years, which has resulted in a number of systems and techniques, both in academic and commercial domains. The goal of such a system is to find, given a specific image, the closest matches to that image in the video which itself can be seen as a large set of images, by looking at the image content. Many such systems exist but IBM's Query by Image Content (QBIC)[12] and Virage's VIR engine[13] are probably the best-known commercial systems. The user can specify

8 W. Kraaij and J. Arlandis, TRECVID-2004 Story Segmentation Task: Overview, *Proc. of TRECVID Workshop*, Gaithersburg, Nov. 2004.

9 B. T. Truong, S. Venkatesh and C. Dorai, Film Grammar Based Refinements to Extracting Scenes in Motion Pictures, *IEEE International Conference on Multimedia and Expo*, Lausanne, 2002, 281–284.

10 A. Hanjalic, R. L. Lagendijk and J. Biemond, Automated High-Level Movie Segmentation for Advanced Video-Retrieval Systems, *IEEE Trans. on Circuits and Systems for Video Technology*, vol. 9, nr. 4, June 1999, 580–588; H. Sundaram and S.-F. Chang, Computable Scenes and Structures in Films, *IEEE Transactions on Multimedia*, vol. 4, nr. 4, Dec. 2002, 482–491.

11 G. Haberfehlner, *Development of a System for Automatic Dialog Scene Detection*, Diploma Thesis, Fachhochschule Hagenberg, 2004.

12 Flicker M., Sawhney H. et al., Query by image and video content: The QBIC system. *IEEE Computer*, 28(9), 1995, 23–32.

13 Virage, http://www.virage.com.

a number of parameters prior to the searching. CBIR systems are applications often specialized in processing large still-image databases. The techniques applied in this scenario can also be used for image retrieval in videos because a video can be seen as a large set of single images. Most of these CBIR systems rely on the use of low-level image information, such as color,[14] shape,[15] and texture[16] features, to search for images in the video database. Recently, content analysis methods have focused on temporal information using motion features. With the help of the motion content, a hierarchical structure is built for a given database for indexing and retrieving video shots. In general, using motion features for representing video content is useful for some parts of a video, which have certain types of motions. However, within the motion class, there may be many subclasses that cannot be satisfactorily separated by motion features.

Recent studies in CBIR have focused on the approaches based on relevance feedback, which tries to bridge the gap between the high-level concepts and low-level feature representations by modeling the user's subjective perception from the user's feedback.[17] High-level concepts can be learned offline (i.e. preprocessing, before – and not during – the search takes place), and can be utilized and refined based on the user's specific interest during the on-line retrieval process. Relevance-feedback-based systems have two major limitations. These approaches estimate the ideal query parameters only from low-level image features. Due to the limited power of these features in presenting high-level semantics, it may not be effective in modeling user's perceptions. The feedback information provided in each interaction contains high-level concepts which can solely be used to improve the current query results for a specific user.



One well-known object retrieval approach in videos is known as *Video Google* and was popularized by J. Sivic.[18] The task is to search for further similar appearances of the requested object in the entire video. The object is selected by defining a region of interest within a frame of the video. Because the region of

14 R. O. Stehling, M. A. Nascimento, A. X. Falcao, On Shapes of Colors for Content-Based Image Retrieval. In: *ACM International Workshop on Multimedia Information Retrieval* (ACM MIR'00), Los Angeles, 2000, 171–174.

15 D. S. Zhang, G. Lu, Generic Fourier Descriptors for Shape-Based Image Retrieval. In: *Proceedings of the IEEE International Conference on Multimedia and Expo* (ICME'02). Lausanne, Aug. 2002, 425–428.

16 L. M. Kaplan et al., Fast Texture Database Retrieval Using Extended Fractal Features. In: *Proceedings of IS&T/SPIE Conference on Storage and Retrieval for Media Databases*, 1998, 162–173.

17 L. Goldmann, L. Thiele, T. Sikora, Online Image Retrieval System Using Long Term Relevance Feedback, *CIVR 2006*, LNCS 4071, 2006, 422–431.

18 J. Sivic, A. Zisserman, Video Google: A Text Retrieval Approach to Object Matching in Eideos. In: *Proceedings of the IEEE International Conference on Computer Vision*, 2, 2003, 1470–1477.

interest is not limited, the user can search for similar appearances of an arbitrary object. To speed up the search process, the video is analyzed in a thorough and time consuming offline pre-processing task without any user action needed.

The task of content annotation is to enrich the audiovisual content metadata, i.e. data *about* the content, and data that *describes* the content. The metadata can be extracted from the content itself or come from external sources (e.g. scripts). Content analysis can thus be seen as reversing the authoring process,[19] during which an audiovisual material is created based on information about the content to be produced (e.g. script, storyboard, scene sketches). Three perspectives for analyzing audiovisual content have been proposed:[20] layout (e.g. shot structure, camera motion), content (e.g. people and objects appearing) and semantics (e.g. scenes, named events). These three perspectives also correspond to the levels of features that can be extracted from audiovisual content, ranging from low-level features describing layout to high-level features describing semantics. The automatically extracted features can be used to support a human annotator, when an efficient annotation tool is available that visualizes the extracted features. Those manual annotation tools proposed in literature, which are relevant in the context of this work, are discussed in the following section.



The *Deconstructor*[21] is an online film analysis tool which assists the exploration of cinema's visual syntax through its arrangement and organization of shots. The Deconstructor can be used to view and dissect film scenes into a series of shots, allowing one to focus on examining the components of the whole in order to layer and juxtapose variables along the time line. One can view film scenes, extract a series of shots from the scene, and provide a description of each shot by considering the common variables such as shot type, time and angle. This information is then used to visualize the shots using a graphical representation of their descriptions. This aims to provide a sense of score for each scene, material that probes further analysis, and helps the user to identify rhythms and cycles.

*Anvil*[22] is a publicly available research tool for exclusively manual video annotation. The annotation scheme is generic and customizable. Customization can be done by specifying a set of attribute-value pairs which are used to attach the metadata. The structuring possibilities are simple definitions of annotat-

19 N. Dimitrova, Multimedia Content Analysis: The Next Wave, *Proc. of International Conference on Image and Video Retrieval*, Urbana-Champaign, July 2003, 9–18. C. G. M. Snoek and M. Worring, Multimodal Video Indexing: A Review of the State-of-the-art, *Multimedia Tools and Applications*, 25(1), Jan. 2005, 5–35.

20 C. G. M. Snoek and M. Worring, Multimodal Video Indexing.

21 The Deconstructor: An Online Film Analysis System, http://ccnmtl.columbia.edu/projects/feature_pages/133-deconstructor.pdf.

22 http://www.dfki.de/~kipp/anvil.

able frame sequences. Its original purpose was to annotate gesture and speech semantics in videos. To give an overview of the annotations in a specific time interval, *Anvil* has a so-called annotation board. This sub-window shows tracks of different data types like sound, spoken words, gesture descriptions, etc. The *Anvil annotation tool* aims at annotating parts of a video.[23] The weaknesses of *Anvil*, however, are its limited structuring possibilities and the need for explicit types for the annotations.

The *M-OntoMat-Annotizer*[24] is a public semantic annotation tool that was developed in the context of the *aceMedia* project.[25] Basically, it enables the user to attach metadata to videos or images. The basic idea of the tool is to extract low-level MPEG-7 descriptors and link them automatically to ontologies and semantic annotations in order to annotate high level semantics. Descriptors in the MPEG-7 standard are evaluations of video frames or individual images.[26] An example would be the dominant color in a region of interest in a frame or an image. At the time we evaluated the *M-OntoMat-Annotizer*, it did not support the manual structuring of videos. Instead, it concentrated on generating descriptors of images or frames. These descriptors are analyzed and associated with ontologies by an internal knowledge base which is an automated process. The *M-OntoMat-Annotizer* has a very different approach to video annotation. Structuring features in this tool are barely useful because it generates the structure by linking the descriptors with matching ontologies. The main feature is the automatic linkage between technical descriptions of the video and ontologies.



The *VideoAnnEx annotation tool*[27] allows the user to annotate shots in a video. The annotation data is stored in an MPEG-7 file. Each shot in the video can be annotated with static scene descriptions, key object descriptions, event descriptions, or other lexicon sets of descriptions. This restricts the annotation possibilities to the content of the lexica but keeps the annotations simple and consistent.[28] The *VideoAnnEx* tool takes an MPEG video and an optional MPEG-7 annotation file as its input. In case the annotation file is not found,

23 M. Kipp, ANVIL – A Generic Annotation Tool for Multimodal Dialogue, *Proceedings Eurospeech*, 2001. M. Kipp, *Gesture Generation by Imitation – From Human Behavior to Computer Character Animation*, Boca Raton, Dissertation.com, 2004.

24 http://acemedia.org/aceMedia/results/software/m-ontomat-annotizer.html.

25 http://acemedia.org/aceMedia.

26 K. Petridis, S. Bloehdorn, C. Saathoff, N. Simou, S. Dasiopoulou, V. Tzouvaras, S. Handschuh, Y. Avrithis, Y. Kompatsiaris, and S. Staab, Knowledge Representation and Semantic Annotation of Multimedia Content, *IEE Proceedings – Vision, Image, and Signal Processing*, June 2006, Volume 153, Issue 3, 255–262.

27 http://www.research.ibm.com/VideoAnnEx/usermanual.html.

28 C.-Y. Lin, B. Tseng and J. Smith, VideoAnnEx: IBM MPEG-7 Annotation Tool for Multimedia Indexing and Concept Learning, *Proc. of ICME*, Baltimore, July 2003.

*VideoAnnEx* creates the file by performing shot boundary detection. The shots can also be detected by the *IBM CueVideo Shot Detection Toolkit.*

From this review of the state-of-the-art, the necessity for a specific tool tailored to the needs of film analysts in terms of locating/analyzing religious references can be directly derived. According to our knowledge, none of the existing tools supports a flexible spatio-temporal annotation feature in combination with an effective navigation interface and sufficient automatic analysis features to support the analyst in his or her work.

## 3. Semantic Video Annotation Tool (SVAT)

In this chapter, we introduce our Semantic Video Annotation Tool (SVAT) application which supports spatio-temporal annotation. The sections below describe a typical annotation workflow from the user's perspective. This workflow typically starts with preparatory steps (i.e. preprocessing) where several features needed in subsequent steps are fully automatically extracted. This is described in section 3.1. In the second part of this chapter (section 3.2), the manual annotation process is described which utilizes the automatically extracted features.



### 3.1 Preparatory Steps and Automatic Annotation Assistance

In a first preparatory step of the annotation workflow, the global description of the source video data has to be specified and an automatic analysis process has to be started. A separate tool, the Media Analyze Tool (see Figure 1), has been developed for this. During the automatic content analysis, the characteristic camera motion, shot boundaries including dissolves, relevant key frames, several image similarity features, and the features which are required for locating similar image regions in the video are extracted. The automatically extracted metadata is described in detail in the following sections. The result is a first metadata description of the video which is saved in the XML metadata standard MPEG-7. The content analysis is a very time-consuming process. Therefore, the automatic analysis can be started for several videos and then the process can run over night.

#### 3.1.1 Shot Boundary Detection

Shots are the basic building blocks of the visual modality of a video. Shot boundary detection algorithms identify both abrupt (hard cuts) and gradual transitions (such as dissolves, fades, wipes, etc.) and produce a decomposition of the timeline into shots (shot list). As shot boundaries are the natural limits of most visual features (such as camera movements, objects), their detection is

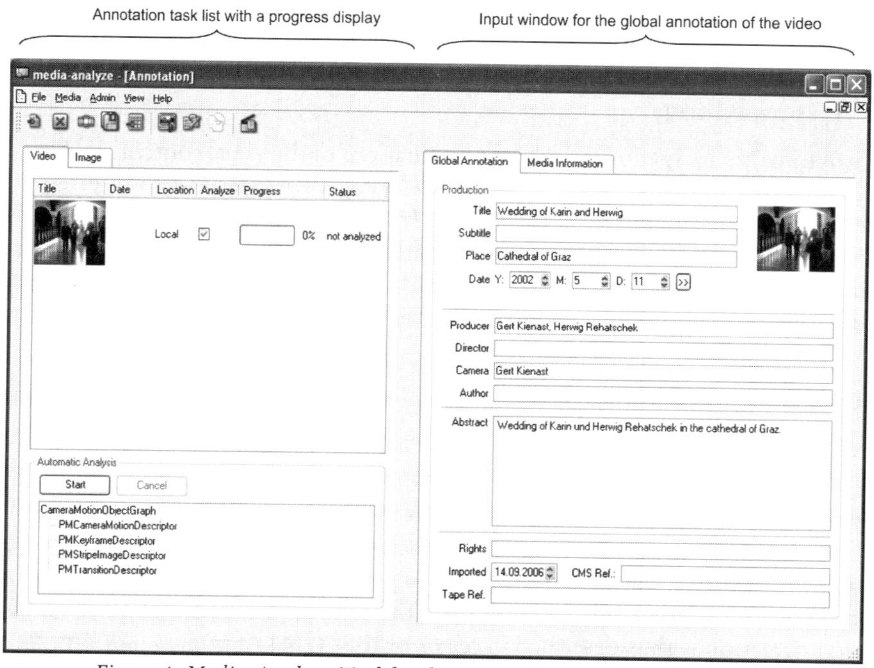


*Figure 1: Media-Analyze Tool for the automatic extraction of metadata*



an important prerequisite for further automatic content analysis. The visualization of the shot supports the user in efficiently navigating through the video and accessing certain time segments within the video. Shots are also an important basis for manual annotation, as many annotations are shot-based and knowledge about the shot structure facilitates building higher-level content structures such as scenes, sequences or chapters. In our semantic video annotator, an improved version of the algorithm described by Bailer et. al. is used.[31]

### 3.1.2 Key Frame Extraction

Key frame extraction tools identify a number of frames in each shot, which are used as representative proxies of the shot's content and support effective navigation within the video. The selection of key frame positions is based on the visual activity in the visual essence, i.e. the more object and/or camera motion, the shorter the time interval between two key frame positions. At least one key frame is extracted at the beginning of a shot. Key frames are an important means for efficient representation of the visual content of a shot and support navigation

31 W. Bailer, H. Mayer, H. Neuschmied, W. Haas, M. Lux, W. Klieber, Content-Based Video Retrieval and Summarization Using MPEG-7, *Proc. of Internet Imaging V*, San Jose, Jan. 2004, 1–12.

in the content. The extracted key frames are visualized in a special view of the SVAT which is located near the bottom as shown in Figure 4.

### 3.1.3 Stripe Image

Stripe images are spatio-temporal representations of the visual content and hence an effective way to navigate within video footage. A stripe image is created by extracting one column from each of the frames of the video and putting them together in temporal order. This visualization clearly shows shot boundaries as discontinuities, and allows a user to easily track camera motion and movements of larger objects. The extracted stripe images are visualized in the stripe image view of the SVAT tool (as can be see at the bottom of Figure 4).

### 3.1.4 Camera Motion Detection

The camera motion detection algorithm[32] identifies segments containing salient camera movements and describes this motion both qualitatively and quantitatively. The original camera motion, however, cannot be reconstructed unambiguously from the analysis of the video, since, for example, it is not possible to discriminate a translation of the camera (e.g. a track left) from a rotation (e.g. a



pan left), if the scenery is far away from the camera. The result of camera motion detection is thus described in terms of four types of camera motion (pan, tilt, zoom, roll) and a rough quantization of the amount of motion. Camera motion annotation can guide the user and support manual annotation. In addition, camera motion also conveys some semantics of the content. For example, zooming in on an object or person can be an indicator of its importance.

### 3.1.5 Object Recognition and Image Retrieval in Video

Automatic object and image retrieval in video material is an essential and necessary part of any annotation tool because manually searching for objects in a video is a time-consuming and annoying task. Supporting semi-automatic annotation, this computer-aided object retrieval should be easy to use, very fast and the results should be as accurate as possible. The retrieved images should be presented in a ranked list of key frames just as web search engines list their results in terms of relevance. After verification of the result whereby very little user interaction is necessary, the correctly found key frames can be annotated automatically. The resulting object recognition and video retrieval module was implemented as a plug-in for the SVAT tool.

The retrieval of an object in a video is a challenging task because an object's visual appearance may vary within the video due to changes in perspective or

32 W. Bailer, P. Schallauer, G. Thallinger, Joanneum Research at TRECVID 2005 – Camera Motion Detection, *Proc. of TRECVID Workshop*, Gaithersburg, Nov. 2005.

lighting, or the object may be partially occluded. To overcome these problems, several approaches have been developed based on a weak segmentation of the image instead of segmenting the image semantically in object foreground and background. Currently this 'local approach' to object recognition is very popular. The basic idea is to 1. detect a set of discriminative interest points (key points); 2. describe the local image region around the key point in a (possibly) invariant manner using a so-called descriptor; 3. use the set of descriptors for matching and recognition (basically a voting algorithm that counts the number of matches).

In our application, we detected Difference-of-Gaussian key points and computed SIFT descriptors introduced by Lowe[33] as local low-level features for every frame in the video. These key point locations are very precise and repeatable, because SIFT uses subpixel localization and multiple scale key point identification. This method is highly scalable because it is possible to add more local feature detectors and descriptors; for example, the 'maximally stable extremal regions' of Matas et al.[34] where areas are selected from an intensity watershed image segmentation. This, of course, increases the time required for the initial analysis of the video but the process runs totally offline and offers better results to users' queries. To use only high-quality features, all detected features of a key frame are tracked through some contiguous frames. Those features which can be tracked successfully are marked as stable and will be used in the later indexing step.



To facilitate fast image retrieval, a data structure known as 'inverted file structure' is applied which is also used in text retrieval approaches.[35] This inverted file structure is comparable to an ideal book index where key words list all positions in that document in which the word occurs. To obtain visual words, in analogy to text retrieval, we quantize the low-level feature descriptors detected in key frames into clusters for building a visual vocabulary. At the moment, tree-like vocabularies are very popular due to the great speed-up compared to vocabularies which use simple lists of visual words.[36]

The first step commonly taken for video processing is to split a given video into shots. The advantage of shot detection is to guarantee that at least one frame per shot is indexed and therefore objects can also be located in very short shots. We suggest defining those frames with the highest number of detected low-level features within every shot as key frames and to index them for later

33 D. G. Lowe, *Distinctive Image Features from Scale-Invariant Keypoints. International Journal of Computer Vision*, 60, 2 (2004), 91–110.

34 J. Matas, O. Chum, M. Urban, T. Pajdla, Robust Wide Baseline Stereo from Maximally Stable Extremal Regions. In: *Proceedings of the British Machine Vision Conference*, 2002, 384–393.

35 R. Baeza-Yates, B. Ribeiro-Neto, *Modern Information Retrieval*. ACM Press, 1999.

36 D. Nistér and H. Stewénius, Scalable Recognition with a Vocabulary Tree. *IEEE Computer Society Conference on Computer Vision and Pattern Recognition*, 2, 2006, 2161–2168.

retrieval instead of constantly using one frame per second to force better query results (these key frames are solely used for object detection purposes and not for the navigation purposes described in section 3.1.2). When a new key frame of the movie is observed, each stable descriptor of the frame is assigned to the nearest visual word. The benefit of this casting is that matches are effectively pre-computed so that at run-time, frames can be retrieved immediately by matching the features with the visual words in the vocabulary. Because very few visual words are common with many entries and many visual words only have a single entry, the application of a so-called 'stop list' is highly recommended, where those visual words in the vocabulary are deleted. This implies a reduction of the vocabulary size without any loss of performance in terms of accuracy.

In the retrieval stage, the defined region of interest contains low-level features which are used to match the visual words in the vocabulary. Every key frame which is retrieved by a successful match gets a vote and is inserted into the hit list. This hit list of key frames is finally ranked by the number of votes and presented to the user.

Figure 2 illustrates the implemented application. The image on the left shows the video player with which the user can navigate through the video and mark interesting objects with a rectangle, the so-called 'region of interest'. After the selection, the search process can be started and within a few seconds all key frames found are listed in a ranked hit list as shown in the right image. If an image that was found does not match the requirements of the user, its checkbox can be unmarked. After verification, all key frames marked as correct results can be annotated in the video by the application automatically. It is also possible

*Figure 2: Left Image: Video player with object to search for in the region of interest. Right Image: Hit list with retrieved key frames. The correct key frames are marked for later annotation.*

to jump directly from a key frame in the hit list to the position in the video player to perform another search and to come across more similar occurrences of this object.

## 3.2 Manual Video Annotation

As soon as the automatic analysis of a video is completed, the produced metadata description can be displayed, edited and extended by the Media-Annotation tool (see Figure 4). This tool has a number of views which enables quick and easy navigation in the video. Through the key frames and the stripe image, the user is provided with a quick overview of the video content. There are two time lines, one for the whole video time and one which shows only a selected time period (time zoom). In the time lines, the shot boundaries and the dissolves are displayed and they can also be edited. There is also the option of structuring the video depending on the video content. For example, shots can be grouped into scenes; scenes can be combined to build chapters and so on. This structure yields a table of contents and is displayed by a separate view (see Figure 4). Depending on the selected structural element, different textual annotations are possible. These are, for example, the title of the structural element, content description, remarks, and specifications about time, location, and persons. At the shot level, shooting settings like camera motion, camera angle, or view size can be documented (see Figure 3).



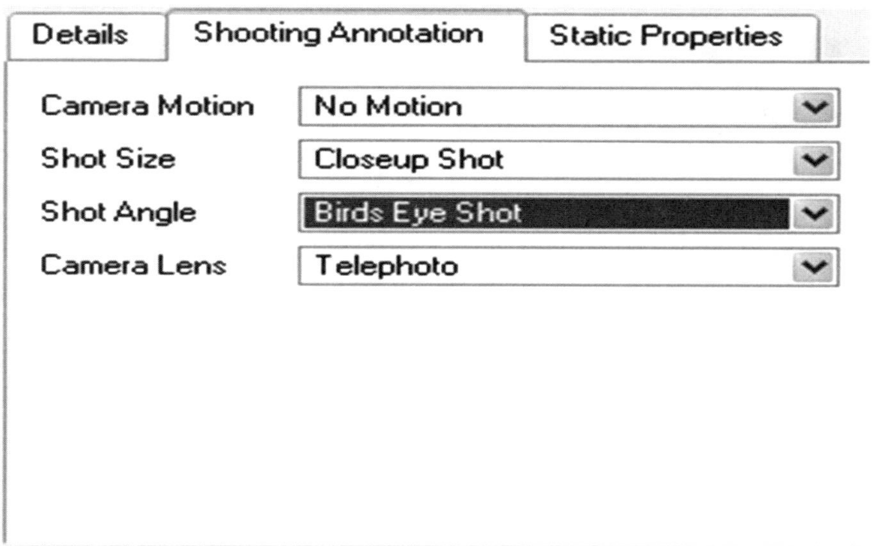


*Figure 3: Possible annotation of the shooting settings*

The integrated video player has drawing functionalities for the annotation of regions or objects. Once an image region is specified (see white rectangle at the left side in Figure 4), it is possible to start an automatic search for a similar

*Figure 4: Semantic Video Annotation Tool (SVAT)*



region in other frames of the video. For this, the pre-calculated SIFT feature values are used (see chapter 3.1.5). Objects which do not change their visual appearance and shot locations (background regions) can be redetected. The search result is a list of key frames which include the detected regions. This list can be manually edited and is used to assign textual annotations of objects, persons, locations, etc. (which have to be specified only once) to several shots, scenes or any other structural unit.

# 4. Conclusions and Outlook

We have presented the video and film annotation tool SVAT, which enables film analysts to efficiently annotate video content. In comparison to existing annotation tools, which in most cases only allow global annotations, SVAT allows for temporal and spatial annotations. Hence, objects moving in time (e.g. a person moving from one point to another) can be annotated as well as single objects within one frame. SVAT also supports the transformation of spatial into temporal annotations by means of automatic tracking. The user marks a certain object and SVAT automatically tracks the object forwards and backward, thereby generating an automatic annotation of it. Moreover, the tool offers innovative mechanisms for navigation by several configurable views such as a shot, key, and stripe image view. With regard to structuring, the user can individually and hierarchically group parts of the film (e.g. shots, scenes) together, starting from a frame level.

With respect to object recognition, we presented an approach based on Difference-of-Gaussian key points and computed SIFT descriptors as local low-level features for every frame in the video. These key point locations are very precise, repeatable, and also highly scalable. Therefore, it is possible to add more local feature detectors and descriptors. The big advantages of our specific approach are that the user does not waste time with interactive training and it is possible to preprocess every video without any technical knowledge. After the offline preprocessing task, which may take a few hours, the video is immediately ready for use. There are no limitations on the underlying video format and it is possible to use black-and-white videos should any color features be required.



The presented tools enable and facilitate the description, structuring, and analysis of a video. Of course, the result should be reusable for further analysis steps with respect to the video itself but also in relation to other annotated videos. As for the annotation tool, additional functionalities are required for generating statistics and reports. A database for managing the video metadata as well as a database search tool have already been implemented. The extension of these tools is planned, with specific functionalities which should facilitate the analysis and comparison of different videos.

In order to facilitate the interpretation of symbols in media products, a database is developed which should link traditional symbols of Christian iconography with those used in media. Keeping in mind the technical advancements in object recognition, as well as its current technical limitations, we will consider it as important to develop an algorithm that is able to link objects in videos to those database entries.

## Acknowledgments

Parts of this work were funded by the Austrian Science Fund (FWF) and the European Union as part of the research projects PrestoSpace (IST-FP6-507336) and GMF4iTV (IST-2001-34861).

Christian Wessely

# Theological Film Interpretation

## Some Approaches to a Better Understanding of 'Moving Images'[1]

Without exaggeration, one can talk of an omnipresence of religious and quasi-religious elements in the age of multi media. It might be surprising at first view that the religious takes up such space in the media culture of a secularised society: be it films or TV shows which have religion explicitly as their topic and make it accessible to the masses (e.g. THE PASSION OF THE CHRIST), or which represent a religious/quasi-religious conglomerate (e.g. THE MATRIX), or that just play with religious motifs in their titles (e.g. THE DEVIL WEARS PRADA).[2]

### 1. To Begin With: Three Scenarios



*A film sequence:* an older woman is hanging up the washing to dry, a young man picks hazelnuts. He gives her some of the nuts and helps her with her work. The sun is shining, the setting is idyllic. The glances exchanged between the two suggest wordless understanding, they aren't interrupted by distracting synchronisations or dialogues. The wash dances in the breeze, the weather is beautiful – obviously, there isn't much to say. The two go back to the lady's house, not much more talkative than before.[3]

*A video clip:* a man picks fruit. On the acoustic level, there is a wordless singing and a harmonic sound space is set up, arhythmic at first, then with a soft groove. The man is tired, sits down in the grass, falls over backwards. In the following sequences, important moments of his life[4] pass by and each is associated with an agricultural theme (sowing, growing, harvest). The sequences are arranged backwards, the last scene showing a baptism. In this image, the water drips from

1 Translation by Stefanie Knauss and Barbara A. Emmel.

2 Stefanie Knauss / Alexander D. Ornella, "There are no angels in america"? Eine fundamentaltheologische Annäherung an religiöse Phänomene in der Medienkultur, in: Christian Wessely (ed.): *Kunst des Glaubens – Glaube der Kunst. Der Blick auf das unverfügbare Andere*, Regensburg: Pustet 2006, 384–396, here: 384 (translation S.K. and B.A.E.).

3 Robert Bresson: L'ARGENT (F/CH 1982), Yvon and the woman who offers him shelter, just before the final scene.

4 Represented in the respective *rites de passage*.

the baby's head back into the bowl of the baptist. The lyrics say: "This is not the beginning of the end, it's the return to innocence!" In this clip, the music has a rather supporting function; the viewers' attention is concentrated on the information conveyed by the images.[5]

*An advertisement:* in a cloister, a monk is asked: "Father, is this fasting in your view?" The monk takes a taste from a cup of "Fasten-Jogurt" (low-fat yogurt). He replies: "No, because fasting means renunciation. But this tastes a bit too much like sin." The voice-over says: "The new fasting. Works like fasting, tastes like sin." The image shows the yogurt cup with a waist around which a measuring band is tied. This band becomes a snake at the right side of the frame. Again, the priest is shown reading the text on the cup and commenting on it: "0.1 % fat?" He holds up his index finger: "Thou shalt not lie!"[6]

## 2. Religious 'Signatures'

These widely different clips from various genres – feature film, music video,[7] advertisement – are my starting point for thinking about the presence of religious signatures in unexpected places, and the meaning they carry. Not because each

and every example above contains religious allusions, but because these clips illustrate so well the complexity of the question of the presence of religious[8] signatures. All of these phenomena have one thing in common: they relate to something which exceeds the viewers' immediate life in the here and now of the film-viewing experience, they are defined by the *impact* they have, which transcends the limits of the film. And this means, vice versa, that traditional religious symbols no longer have to be understood as such: a cross on the wall does not necessarily have to have more meaning than any other prop; a tree appearing out of the mist, by contrast, can takeon a religious dimension.[9]

5 Enigma, RETURN TO INNOCENCE, Germany 1994 (Virgin).

6 ORF 1, 1.4.2006, 20:05. Cf. Wiener and Löhnert's article in this volume.

7 For a basic introduction to the theological interpretation of music videos, I recommend: Ilse Kögler, *Die Sehnsucht nach mehr: Rockmusik, Jugend und Religion. Informationen und Deutungen*, Graz: Styria 1994; Ilse Kögler, Clip-Hits: Eminem "Stan", in: *Katechetische Blätter* 126 (2001), 204f.

8 'Religious' in this context includes a wide variety of phenomena and is not restricted to the Christian tradition.

9 Cf. the reality TV show BIG BROTHER, produced for six seasons so far by Endemol Entertainment between 2000 and 2006, in which there's a cross on a wall in at least the second season which, however, has apparently no meaning for the people living in the container; the counter example is Theo Angelopoulos' LANDSCAPE IN THE MIST (GR 1988); in the final scene, the children's hope and perspectives on their lives culminate in a tree appearing out of the fog.

10 This is quite essential given that even http://www.wikipedia.de distinguishes between 15 different meanings of the German word *Signatur*.

What does 'signature' mean in this context?[10] I will approach a definition using the example of an artist's signature on his or her painting. Usually, paintings are unobtrusively signed in a small corner; some ideotypical marks characterise the work as that of a particular artist. The accumulation of colour on some material – whether abstract or representative – is put in a specific biographical context by the signature and gains a market value which serves, beyond purely aesthetic criteria, as a fairly reliable parameter for an evaluation of the work. Thus, the signature puts the work in a new context and framework of interpretation aside from the value it has in and of itself. This understanding of the signature is useful for our purposes: a signature is a determinating factor, an indicator of that which puts the product as a whole into a new context, potentially changing its meaning in a fundamental way. But this does not say anything about its form and place yet. The question is: how can such a determinating signature not only be discovered, but also be classified in a way that is comprehensible to others, and how can one avoid inappropriately forcing an interpretation onto the work, and instead use a careful and adequate hermeneutics?

For our purposes, it is also important to distinguish – following Umberto Eco – between *using* a text and *interpreting* it. According to Eco, an *interpretation* is potentially already there in the material waiting to be discovered; the number of possible interpretations is therefore limited by the possible ways of reading the text in a logically consistent way (even though there will be more than one possible and consistent interpretation). The interpreter interacts with the texture, in fact, he or she *has to* interact with it because the text follows the rules of its own language game and uses its own symbols and codes. The interpretation has always to be legitimated by and be based on the text. When using a text – according to Eco – the reader/hearer/viewer freely deals with the text, makes a choice which can be motivated by his or her interests and not necessarily by logical consistency.[11] According to Peter Hasenberg, one can classify a text as 'religious' by defining a number of characteristics which have to be contained in the text: concepts and definitions, but also metaphors, allegories, symbols or formal characteristics, and only if these characteristics can be found, can the text be labeled as 'religious'.[12] In the following, I offer some reflections based on the possibility of interpreting – not using – media products.



11 Cf. Umberto Eco, *Lector in fabula. Die Mitarbeit der Interpretation in erzählenden Texten*, München: dtv 1990, in particular 65ff.

12 Cf. Peter Hasenberg, Der Film und das Religiöse. Ansätze zu einer systematischen und historischen Spurensuche, in: *Spuren des Religiösen im Film. Meilensteine aus 100 Jahren Filmgeschichte*, Mainz: Grünewald 1995, 13f.

## 3. The (Para-)Religious Dimensions of Media Culture?

Media industry claims to offer something *essential* and *substantial* to its consumers; this claim becomes obvious in the way this sector advertises and promotes the purchase of its products. Now this 'essential and substantial' offer does not consist of – or at least not only of – the *content* of the offered products, which is in most cases fairly trivial and thus cannot contribute to an increase in knowledge or offer help in dealing with one's life and making sense of it. It can be rewarding, therefore, to take a look at the underlying *structure* in such cases.

Many advertisements attach, to a product, a simple, often gnostic-dualistic world view which can contain characteristics of the religious. Far from assisting in finding the ultimate meaning of contingent human existence, these advertisements provide a quasi-religious, but completely distorted message: for example, the biblical comment "Do not be afraid!" has shown up in several advertisements in recent years[13] It is a word of consolation which becomes a promotional message in this context. The product is supposed to take away fear – but fear of what?

Fear *(Furcht)* – in contrast to anxiety *(Angst)* – is related to an object, something concrete that one is afraid of. The message of the advertisement insinuates – even strongly suggests – that the viewers are full of fear. And here, the media industry offers a consolation it cannot provide in reality: the essential questions of one's own existence, most of all, of one's own contingence, can perhaps be covered up, but are not answered by it. The biblical "Do not be afraid!," in which the *cause* of fear has been outweighed by the promise of grace and salvation, is replaced by media industry's "Do not be afraid!" which counteracts the *effect* of fear, and it's message is: "If you consume my products, you shall not have to be afraid anymore, because you shall be so overwhelmed."



It is a well-designed system which provides fast and easy options of meaning-making to those who doubt ('those who are afraid'), but such options cannot help in bearing the burdens of a real crisis. They do, however, succeed in camouflaging the consumers' real problems and existential questions and thus herald a renaissance of classical and naively Christian images of God(s): by defining guilt and responsibility as always being on the other's side, a person can feel relatively guilt-free; because of the anthropological imperative "This is how you should be/look/smell/organise your life," one is absolved from developing one's own goals in life.

13 This phrase (cf. Mt 14:27; 17:7; 28:5; 28:10; Mk 6:5; Lk 2:10; 12:7 and Joh 6:20), has been used variously in advertisements in the last few years (with the appropriate pseudo-sacred setting), e.g. by the chain for electronic appliances, Media Markt ("Do not be afraid! I come!"), and the A-Card ("Brothers and sisters, do not be afraid!").

But this comes at a high price: behind the beautified and smooth facade of a sense of orderliness contained herein, the essence of violence is hidden and causes new ruptures in the seeming order, which then have to be covered up again. In contrast to those arts which are often called 'serious' and whose works require real involvement on the side of the recipient because of their challenge to the viewers' receptive capabilities, commercial art also claims to be an indicator of a religious need,[14] but fails to communicate ultimate meaning in its realisation of this claim.

This quasi-religious rationale, but also obvious quotations (in iconographic details, textual citations, relationships and connections), challenge the theologian to critically analyse the potential of a given product. There is no doubt that media industry does not aim at being a 'first philosophy'[15] or foundational theology (and this is not asked for by the consumers, either); but this makes the question even more urgent as to why notions that are essential to both spheres are in principle present in media.

## 4. The 'Objectivity' of Interpretation

One might say that film is a medium of deception *per se*: it pretends that there is continual movement even though there are just individual frames; it shows persons and actions that do not occur in reality and pretends that they are realistic ones; it offers problems and often potential solutions; and most importantly: it changes the viewers' perception of time and space. The apparent immediacy of the audiovisual impression is just that: *apparent*. This illusion, however, bears the risk of a misinterpretation, namely that the relevance of media is either completely underestimated (mere entertainment) or overestimated (the essential social role of 'cult films'). In fact, there is no film that is pure entertainment for its two hours of run time and whose impact is left behind in the cinema when the audience leaves; also, there is hardly a (feature) film to be found that negates the aesthetic forms of mainstream films completely (apart from most experimental films).



As in literature, a strictly objective interpretation is not possible in the field of audiovisual media: whether productive or analytical, it is guided by subjective interests. Nevertheless, an attempt at a comprehensible and productive

14 Cf. Gerhard Larcher, Vom Hörer des Wortes als „homo aestheticus“. Thesen zu einem vernachlässigten Thema heutiger Fundamentaltheologie, in: Gerhard Larcher, Klaus Müller, Thomas Pröpper (eds.), *Hoffnung, die Gründe nennt. Zu Hansjürgen Verweyens Projekt einer erstphilosophischen Glaubensverantwortung*. Regensburg: Pustet 1996, 103.

15 "Erste Philosophie," in the sense in which Hansjürgen Verweyen uses this phrase, cf. Verweyen, Hansjürgen, *Gottes letztes Wort.* Düsseldorf: Patmos 1991, in particular 196–203.

interpretation is possible, as long as one is aware of the intentions behind each analysis and interpretation. Thus, similar hermeneutical rules are as valid for the interpretation of media products as for 'classical' texts: the researcher's cognitive interests cannot be bracketed, but instead need to be defined and taken into account right from the beginning.

The hermeneutical situation of a film interpretation, and in particular a theological one, is most of all a perceiving interpretation: it assumes that film is an independent work of art which is in and of itself and above all able to produce truth and also to make statements that are true. The work states 'a truth' about a particular way of viewing humans and their world(s) which has – in a first approach – to be taken seriously. Possible ruptures – ironical or involuntary ones – in the text on the part of the producer or director, are of marginal interest. In the end, an approach that takes the work itself as its starting point is what is required: interpretations that are provided or intended by the producers are secondary to the work's own impact on the audience.



The interpreter has to question and interpret this claim of truth in relation to his or her own world view, but has to resist the theological 'mortal sin' of using the film for one's own ends and purposes: confrontation is necessary, but compatibility is not. The search for theological starting points (and possibly 'religious signatures') happens within one's own world view and not within the framework of the producer's world view – which, however, is no less reasonable, as the completely 'other' is ultimately an object of theological reflection which can make itself heard here and there. Yet, even if producers place obvious religious content in their products, it should be treated as every other class of content in the process of interpretation. It is not without reason that a theological hermeneutics attempts "to comply with the contextual conditions of the present time."[16]

In talking about 'signatures of the totally other' – i.e. signatures of the religious – in media products or when looking for them, several levels where these can be found have to be differentiated:

a) Elements on the audiovisual level of content: the priest eating yogurt, the young priest drinking Coke, a priest in an advertisement for a pizza chain, the mystical-esoterical chants in the video of "Return to Innocence" or religious symbols that apparently just happen to be in the set and therefore in the frame. These elements are obvious, and are simply there. Producers, however, often like to use religious symbols because they have long been filled with meaning and are thus completely inculturated und accessible to

16 "[...] den grundlegenden kontextuellen Bedingungen der Gegenwart [...] entsprechen" (Siegfried Wiedenhofer, Art. Hermeneutik, systematisch-theologisch, in: *Lexikon für Theologie und Kirche* Vol. 5, Freiburg: Herder 2006, 7, translation S.K. and B.A.E.).

viewers at first sight.[17] The recipient cannot avoid their connotations, even if he or she thinks of herself as religious or as an atheist. Religious symbols are a part of the social and cultural system, at least historically, but also for many in the specific context of their biography. Clerics in particular carry archetypal roles: 'the priest' is conflated with trustworthiness and authority (comparable to 'the doctor') and these qualities are passed on to the product he manufactures (a cordial) or tastes (pizza).[18]

b) Iconic and semantic elements on the level of form and content, all of which have to be analysed closely: iconographical details that appear in image or sound – archetypal images that require contextual interpretation (water, tree, wind, fire), as well as the architectural design of the setting – the connections produced technically or simply evident in the image, but also the language ('text' in a narrow sense) of the film, the message of the advertisement or of a music video. Text and image can diverge or converge, or be fairly independent from each other.[19]

c) The action and the interaction between subjects and between subjects and objects. In particular in music videos, it is not always clear whether those characters in addition to the protagonist are actual subjects or simply being used as props. If minor characters are shown in an advertisement for skin care products, for example, they are not really subjects, but rather props: they serve merely to illustrate the promoted effect of the product.[20] On this level, themes such as protection, pleasure, security, and gain of time can be found.



d) The technical level: this is at least as important and expressive as the other levels. The type of lense, filter, colour balance, set and decoration (directly related to the architectural design mentioned in section b above), such as camera angle, pans, tracks, cuts, rhythm – all of these are extremely expressive formal elements that have to be taken into account in any analysis. Reinhold Zwick has shown that the connection of form and content is particularly important to a theological analysis of filmic material,[21] and here it is indeed possible to discover undercurrents and hidden allusions.

17 On the possible changes in the meaning of religious symbols due to their use in advertisement cf. Rafael D. Wiener, *Religiöse Bildsprache in der gegenwärtigen TV-Werbung*. MTheol. thesis, Graz 2006, and Wiener's and Löhnert's article in this volume.

18 Cf. Carl G. Jung, *Archetyp und Unbewusstes*, Olten: Walter 41996 (=Grundwerk Vol. 2).

19 Cf. Christian Wessely, Akustische Apokalypse, in: Gerhard Larcher (ed.), *Gott-Bild. Gebrochen durch die Moderne?* Graz: Styria 1997, 344–350.

20 Cf. the advertisement campaign of L'Oreal on prime-time TV in May and June 2006.

21 Cf. Reinhold Zwick, Pfade zum Absoluten. Zur Typologie des religiösen Films, in: Walter Lesch (ed.), *Theologie und ästhetische Erfahrung. Beiträge zur Begegnung von Religion und Kunst*, Darmstadt: WBG. 1994, 88–110.

e) Finally the central question: which view of the human person does the media product generally and as a whole convey? What is presented as good, beautiful, right, desirable (if such categories are presumed at all), and to what degree are existential situations in human existence represented realistically and without straining for dramatic effect?[22]

## 5. The Awkward Question of Analysis

Much has been written about film analysis.[23] My intention here is to support – at least to some extent – the often despised structural analysis as being an essential instrument and support to any interpretation of a media work.[24] Knut Hickethier has pointed out that any analysis is ultimately a deconstruction of the product 'film' which, however, is unavoidable given the need to interpret the filmic texture.[25] Thus, one does not necessarily become familiar with the *film* if one knows the outcome of the analytical process of interpretation; for this purpose, a (simple) re-telling is more useful than a sequence analysis and the conclusions drawn from it.[26] To make substantiated and well-founded arguments about a media product, one necessarily has to commit to the effort of undertaking a detailed analysis. There are various approaches for such a task, each with its own strengths and weaknesses, each best suited for a particular field, and neither ever exhaustive. The analytical work can always be refined and advanced. The more detailed the analysis is desired to be, the more effort one has to put into it, and thus the choice of method always depends on the aim of



22 One might imagine that these moments in human existence (death, illness, pain etc.) are left out in advertisement or music videos, because they carry negative connotations. Far from it: they are used as a foil to the perfect world of the film, not only in advertisements for pharmaceutical products, but also in other clips and music videos. The example by Enigma mentioned above, however, is somewhat unusual in its soft and lyrical treatment of death.

23 Without claiming to be exhaustive, I would like to reference some of the better known approaches: Knut Hickethier, *Film- und Fernsehanalyse*, Stuttgart: Metzler ³2001; Werner Faulstich, *Grundkurs Filmanalyse*, München: Fink 2002; James Monaco, *How to Read a Film. The World of Movies, Media, Multimedia: Language, History, Theory*, Oxford: Oxford University Press, ³2000; Robert Stam, *Film Theory. An Introduction*, Oxford: Blackwell 2000; Jaques Aumont et al., *Aesthetics of Film*, Austin: University of Texas Press ⁵2004.

24 Cf. Faulstich, *Grundkurs*, 60ff.; Hickethier, *Film- und Fernsehanalyse*, 36ff.; Kanzog, Klaus (ed.): *Einführung in die Filmphilologie*, München: diskurs film 1991, 135.

25 Cf. Hickethier, 27f.

26 A good example for that is the treatment of the film WOLFZEIT (M. Haneke, A 1997) by Astrid Polz-Watzenig in Wessely, Christian / Larcher, Gerhard / Grabner, Franz (eds.), *Michael Haneke und seine Filme. Eine Pathologie der Konsumgesellschaft,* Marburg: Schüren 2005, 337–346. Thís essay reflects the content and atmosphere of the film well, but its conclusions are not binding because of this approach. Alfred Jokesch's approach, in contrast, is more analytical, but remains limited with regard to recounting the film (cf. …und wer ist schuld?, 315–336 in the same volume). Thus, each approach has its own strengths and weaknesses.

the analysis. However, any statement about a particular world view in a media product can have only as much insight and depth of meaning as it is based on a structural analysis. This has two elements: the *background* of the work (production history) and the *structural elements* of the work (quantitative analysis).

## Production History

Each media product is defined and made accessible through its history and context.[27] Even though it is true that the finished work has to be read as apart from any possible interpretative frameworks given by the producer, one has to take into account the intentions of the producers on the one hand, and the context in which the work was produced on the other hand. Apart from the conditions of the production of the work, the biographies of people involved in the making of the work are noteworthy (even if they should not be used as the main guideline of interpretation). Thus, Leni Riefenstahl's films about the Olympic Games 1936 in Berlin[28] could not be interpreted adequately either as a whole or in their parts, if one did not take into account the Nazi regime of the time; nor could Riefenstahl's innovative technique and creativity be appreciated properly without knowledge of film history and iconography before 1936.[29]

Faulstich shows that two things are indispensable for a serious film analysis: on the one hand, a personal and legitimately emotional encounter with the film; and on the other hand, the use of existing materials (e.g. script or story board which are sometimes published or can be requested from the production companies) or one's own written and more or less extensive transcript of the film, which becomes the foundation for all further interpretative work on the film: "In the film transcript, the transitional aspect of the film is ideally transformed into something linear […] its enormous potential is exhausted only very rarely."[30] This can – depending on the requirements and research questions pursued – comprise all levels of intensity and detail, from a complete transcript to a list of sequences.[31] All these forms have one thing in common: they require a careful cost-benefit evaluation.



## Quantitative Analysis

The necessity of a quantitative analysis (structural analysis) is not uncontested: "Insisting on the written transcript of films sounds weird to many," observes

27 Cf. Paul Portmann-Tselikas, Mit Worten bewegen durch überzeugende Versionen von Welt, in: Esterbauer, R.; Ebenbauer, P.; Wessely, Ch. (eds.): *Appelle und Parolen* (in print).

28 FEST DER VÖLKER and FEST DER SCHÖNHEIT (both Germany 1938).

29 For example in representing the fencing competition by filming the shadows of the fencers instead of the persons themselves.

30 Faulstich, *Grundkurs*, 63 (translation S.K. and B.A.E.).

31 Cf. Hickethier, *Film- und Fernsehanalyse*, 210–223.

Hickethier.[32] On an ironic note, he writes that many might hope "to have understood the aesthetic structure of a film fully by means of the film transcript."[33] Hickethier underestimates the possibilities of a structural analysis, or perhaps more accurately put: he assumes that the considerable workload of a structural analysis does not pay off by revealing enough new aspects to legitimate the invested time. But in fact it turns out that the hope he shrugs off so easily is often fullfilled, because not only are all parts of a film exactly and definitively located according to comprehensible, traceable criteria through the structural analysis, but also the structure in most cases reveals complex interrelations between scenes that are invisible to the viewer on first and second sight. These are not only formally and aesthetically interesting, but also provide the material for an interpretation of the particular meaning of the film.

The film transcript is usually a list of the shots or sequences of the film (in chronological order, including notation of duration), with more or less detailed comments on setting, action, formal aspects etc. (depending on what the analysis aims at). While for a shot analysis, the criteria are clear (a shot refers to the film material between two cuts), the definition of a sequence can vary: often, the same setting, characters, or a particular object in a series of shots define a sequence, but this depends to a large extent on the desired exactness of the transcript and on the analyst's interests.



Although a sequence transcript is most useful for a feature film,[34] short and complex products such as advertisements or music videos require a shot analysis in order to be able to do justice to the multiple *topoi* condensed in just a few seconds of run time. Such a transcript should include time, duration, setting, characters, action and any information on the acoustic level.[35]

In addition to the systematic correlation of visual and acoustic codes along a temporal axis and to each other, a structural analysis also provides insight into the rhythm of the editing, the principles of the montage, moments of particularly intense action and not least into the connections between characters and iconic motifs. Sometimes coherences or contradictions between form and content are thus discovered which might relativise or completely change the interpretation of a film 'at first sight'.

32 Hickethier, *Film- und Fernsehanalyse*, 37 (translation S.K. and B.A.E.).

33 Ibid. (translation S.K. and B.A.E.).

34 For an example of a functional sequence analysis, see: Christian Wessely, *Von Star Wars, Ultima und Doom. Mythologisch verschleierte Gewaltmechanismen im kommerziellen Film und in Computerrollenspielen*, Frankfurt: Lang 1996. In this work and with the help of sequence analyses, I have traced parallels between the STAR WARS trilogy by George Lucas and mythological narrative structures.

35 A copy of the original, which includes the timer, helps to avoid inexactness and makes the job easier.

Since a quantitative analysis requires an enormous amount of time depending on the chosen model of analysis and the desired precision, yet is of considerable use for the analytical and interpretative work, one of the main objectives of the research project "Theology in a Media Society," conducted at Graz University in 2004–2007, was to automatise these analytical processes as much as possible and thus to reduce the time and effort needed to compile a transcript. Former computer-based solutions were unsatisfactory in various degrees:[36] they were either manually controlled or worked with a very simple algorithm that produced an automatic division of the material shot by shot, but used only differences of light and contrast in the image material and thus produced material that was inexact and of little use to the researcher. In contrast to this, the analytical tool developed in this project makes suggestions with regard to the division of the material into sequences, but the final decision is made by the user. Most importantly, it is possible to annotate individual sequences according to a well-defined system.

Given that the beginning and end of a sequence is marked by a cut (in rare cases, a sequence and a shot can be the same), and that an intelligent image recognition program should be able to recognise the change from one shot to the next, as well as distinguish changes in the content of an image, a program was developed, in cooperation with Graz University of Technology and the research institute Joanneum Research, which is able to recognise sequences and shots in digitalised film material and to develop automatically a possible division of the film into shots and sequences.[37] It is also able to recognise sections of an image and save them in a database which also includes material from films analysed before, for subsequent searches. For example, a section of an image containing a full moon can be defined, and the program searches automatically in this and all previously analysed films for this object, listing the shot time and annotations. User interaction is still required, but reduced to the exclusion of misunderstandings and the refinement of the suggestions by the software. In the next stage it is planned to plug the image recognition into a iconographic database, which includes not only films run by the software, but also other image material from art history, so that recognised patterns can be linked to classical icons, signs or symbols.

The results of working with the software are encouraging so far. Even though manual adjustments are still necessary, the time required for compiling a sequence transcript has been reduced from four weeks[38] to not quite two days.



36 Vgl. Hickethier, *Film- und Fernsehanalyse*, 41.

37 For more details on the technical aspects of this cooperation, cf. Baier et al.'s article in this volume.

38 Faulstich, *Grundkurs*, 72f. mentions this time frame.

This, however, does not include the time needed for digitalising video material, which takes about twice the amount of the real time of the film (for recording and then for rendering on a fast computer). However, this does not require the continual presence of the researcher. All annotations are done in the user interface and can be exported as a list if required.[39]

The flexible attribution and organisation of annotations makes possible the distinction of individual shots or sequences in the different threads of the action, depending on the requirements of the material and the analysis. In particular, feature films often use different time levels (flashbacks and flash forwards) which are edited in complex sequence structures. These different levels can be represented clearly by the automated analysis. The alignment of characters and objects furthermore helps to discover symbolic relations which might go unnoticed in a purely manually compiled sequence transcript, simply due to the mass of material that needs to be dealt with. The search function for objects of the software, finally, offers a further level for the analysis of important objects and their context, not just in a film that is currently being analysed, but also in others that were already rendered and run by the software.



Potentially, this program is a powerful tool for a substantiated and well-funded interpretation of film material because of its use for the quantitative structural analysis of the material.[40] However, it is merely a *tool*: it does not replace the interpreter and his or her interpretative and analytical work on a film or his or her ability to enter hermeneutical processes which form the basis of all film interpretation. And, as before, any film analysis itself is shaped by the 'cinematographic literacy' of the viewer and the analysist's individual associations, all of which play an important role in the analytical outcome.

## 6. Conclusion

Why should a film be analysed at all? Faulstich has four answers to this question which complement each other well and offer a general perspective on the problem:[41]

- Films do not *have to be*, but they *can* be analysed, in so far as scientists who think about film professionally deal with a film in a way that is both reflected and guided by their interests, and thus have to produce results that are comprehensible by others.

39 Further work on this list is possible in e.g. Excel, and also allows for drawing diagrams and graphs.

40 Right now, it is available in a beta version; in the future work of the research project, it will be further developed and then made available to the scientific community.

41 Cf. Faulstich, *Grundkurs*, 15–19.

- Films can be analysed because they can be seen as a specific form of literary code. They have, therefore, multiple meanings and are polyvalent, and thus open to interpretation; this interpretation, however, has to satisfy certain criteria.[42]
- Film is a process of communication between producer and recipient in which particular relations are expressed in particular ways. The medium of this communication is a product which is 'made' in a particular way. The analysis discovers formative structures behind what appears obvious, which are used to transmit a specific message. Thus, potential dimensions of meaning are opened up by a film analysis.
- Films can be analysed because they are a collective dream in their experiential character in which "the repressed: fears, desires [which grow out of] renunciation, suppression of base instincts, deferral of satisfaction" is expressed.[43] Film analysis makes conscious the process of working with dreams.

From a theological perspective, it also should be clearly stated that films also function as human expressions about life and are thus based upon the experiences of life (on the side of both producers and consumers) and, as such, contain central messages about the essence of human existence, humans' needs and relationships to the world. And it is not only the 'wrapping' which is new and different in each film, but the content which changes, as well: society and its members are determined by media in a significant way, and change accordingly. Therefore, Christian, and in particular Catholic, theology whose task it is to recognise the signs of the time, has to find its way in relation to the products by which society and people – who form the 'kingdom of God' – are shaped and determined. Only by doing so can we critically confront our own message and the forms it takes with those products. This critical confrontation which can (and should) result in an open-minded, self-reflective critique, is the central intention of a film analysis from a theological perspective.[44]



42 Cf. Eco, Umberto, *Einführung in die Semiotik*, Stuttgart: UTB 1972, 250–261.

43 Faulstich, *Grundkurs*, 20 (translation S.K. and B.A.E.).

44 It should be added that the Catholic Church has a remarkably open approach to these issues; cf. the Second Vatican Council's "Inter mirifica", the Papal Encyclical "Redemptoris missio" (1990) and the Apostolic Letter "The Rapid Development" (2005), both by John Paul II. It remains to be seen whether Benedict XVI will devote the same care to such 'burning questions' as these.

# Authors and Translators

*Werner Bailer* (1979), M.Sc. He graduated in 2002 with a diploma thesis on "Motion Estimation and Segmentation for Film/Video Standards Conversion and Restoration" at the Institute of Information Systems and Information Management at Joanneum Research, Graz (Austria), where he has worked since 2001 as a research engineer. His main research interests are algorithms for video content analysis and digital film restoration, metadata description of audiovisual content (with a focus on MPEG-7) and system architectures of media processing systems.

*Horst Bischof* (1967), MSc, PhD in applied computer sciences from Vienna University of Technology (Austria). Currently, he is professor at the Institute for Computer Graphics and Vision at Graz University of Technology (Austria). He is also senior researcher at the K+ Competence Center "Advanced Computer Vision" where he is responsible for research projects in the area of classification. He has received an award from the Pattern Recognition Journal in 2002, for the paper "Multiple Eigenspaces."

*Barbara A. Emmel* (1948), MFA, PhD in rhetoric and composition. She regularly publishes poetry and essays, as well as academic articles in the field of rhetoric and with a focus on the role that values play in our communicative processes. Recently she has been selected for a fellowship at the Atlantic Center for the Arts in Florida to finish a book of poetry. In addition to academic articles, she is currently working on a book of essays regarding culture in Germany, as well as a series of essays regarding her travels in Egypt, where she also takes part annually in a Christian monastic archeological project.



*Robert M. Geraci* (1976), PhD in religious studies from the University of California, Santa Barbara (USA). He is Assistant Professor of Religious Studies at Manhattan College in Riverdale, NY. He has published several articles on religion and science, including "Spiritual Robots: Religion and Our Scientific View of the Natural World" in *Theology and Science* and "Theological Implications of Artificial Intelligence: What Science Fiction Tells Us about Robotic Technology?" in *Zygon: Journal of Religion and Science*.

*Charlotte Haines Lyon* (1972), BA Hons, MA. She is a freelance writer and has written for publications including the Guardian Online, The Tablet and www.surefish.co.uk. A BA Honours in Informal Education and a Masters in Philosophy and Religion helped develop an interest in ethics and how society builds a moral framework. Papers: "A Discussion on the Morality of the State Imposing a Particular Model of Citizenship," 2000, Heythrop College, London University. "KILL BILL 2, A Worthy Film for Meaning Making," 2007, Edinburgh Film Audiences Conference, Film House, Edinburgh.

*Michael Hölzl* (1975), Dr. theol. He studied chemistry, theology, and philosophy in Graz (Austria) and Berlin (Germany). He has taught at the University of Manchester (UK) since 2003; since 2005, he has been a Lecturer for Philosophy and Religion.

*Leo Karrer* (1937), Dr. theol. He studied theology and psychology in Vienna (Austria), Chicago (USA), Munich and Münster (Germany) and worked together with Karl Rahner. Since 1982 he is a professor of Pastoral Theology at Fribourg University (Switzerland). He is the former president of the European Society for Catholic Theology. Publications on questions of ministry and the role of laypersons in the church, biographical pastoral theology etc.

*Stefanie Knauss* (1976), Dipl. theol., Dr. theol. Studies in Catholic theology and English language and literature at Freiburg University (Germany) and Manchester University (UK). Doctoral thesis on "Transcendental Bodies: Reflections on the Importance of the Body for Filmic and Religious Experience" at Graz University (Austria). Currently research fellow at the Fondazione Bruno Kessler – Centro per le Scienze Religiose, Trento (Italy) with a study on film, sex, and religion, and lecturer in Religious Studies in Graz. Publications on film and religion/theology, gender studies, Jewish studies.

*Florian Kröppel* (1980), Mag. theol. from Graz University (Austria). Finished his degree in theology with a dissertation on the initiation of heros in commercial film. Currently writing his doctoral thesis on "Branding Catholicism" at the Institute of Foundational Theology, Graz. Member of SIGNIS (Graz) and jury member at international film festivals. Publication of film reviews and papers on film and religion.



*Gerhard Larcher* (1946), Dr. theol. Professor for Foundational Theology at Graz University (Austria). He is the former president of the European Society for Catholic Theology. Research and publications on the interaction of art, culture and theology.

*Markus Löhnert* (1977) worked at customer services before studying Catholic theology at Graz University (Austria). In his master's thesis, he looks at religious diversity in the US and its influence on how characters in popluar TV-Series like *Smallville* are constructed.

*Gerard Loughlin* (1957), BA, MA, PhD. He is Professor of Theology and Religion at the University of Durham, UK. He is the author of *Telling God's Story: Bible, Church and Narrative Theology* (1996) and *Alien Sex: The Body and Desire in Cinema and Theology* (2004). He is also editor of *Sex These Days: Essays on Theology, Sexuality and Society* (1997) and *Queer Theology: Rethinking the Western Body* (2007). Among his current projects is a theological study of the films of Andrei Tarkovsky.

*Clive Marsh* (1959), BA, MEd, DPhil. He works in a national post in the Methodist Church in Great Britain, and lectures in theology and film at the Department of Theology and Religious Studies at the University of Nottingham. He co-edited, with Gaye

Ortiz, *Explorations in Theology and Film* (Blackwell 1997), and his more recent writings include *Cinema and Sentiment: Film's Challenge to Theology* (Paternoster Press 2004), *Christ in Focus: Radical Christocentrism in Christian Theology* (SCM Press 2005), *Christ in Practice: A Christology of Everyday Life* (DLT 2006) and *Theology Goes to the Movies* (Routledge 2007).

*Birgit Meyer* (1960), Dr. phil. She is professor of Cultural Anthropology at the Department of Social and Cultural Anthropology at the Free University Amsterdam (NL). She has conducted research on missions and local appropriations of Christianity, Pentecostalism, popular culture and video-films in Ghana. Her publications include *Translating the Devil. Religion and Modernity Among the Ewe in Ghana* (Edinburgh University Press, 1999), *Globalization and Identity. Dialectics of Flow and Closure* (edited with Peter Geschiere, Oxford: Blackwell, 1999), *Magic and Modernity. Interfaces of Revelation and Concealment* (edited with Peter Pels, Stanford University Press, 2003), and *Religion, Media and the Public Sphere* (edited with Annelies Moors, Indiana University Press).

*Helmut Neuschmied* (1967), PhD. Studies of telematics (information technology) at Graz University of Technology (Austria). PhD thesis: "Analysis of endoscopic images of cyclical combustion processes in engines" at Graz University of Technology. Since 1998 research engineer at the Institute of Information Systems and Information Management at Joanneum Research, Graz. Main fields of activity: Project leader of the European project "RAA" (Recognition and Analysis of Audio), design and development of distributed software systems and development of matching algorithms for image, image sequence and audio data.



*Sandra Ober* received her BSc and MSc degrees in computer science from Graz University of Technology (Austria) in 2003 and 2004, respectively. Currently she is a PhD student at the Institute for Computer Graphics and Vision, Graz University of Technology. Her main research interests include computer vision, object recognition, and video content analysis.

*Alexander D. Ornella* (1977), MMag. theol. Studies in theology at Graz University and telematics at Graz University of Technology (Austria). Currently, he is working on his PhD thesis on subjectivity in modern media society and its theological implications. Teaches classes on religion and media at Graz University. Publications on media theory and theology, film and theology.

*Herwig Rehatschek* (1969), MSc, PhD. Studies in telematics and technical sciences at Graz University of Technology (Austria). PhD thesis on "Design of a Distributed Planetary Image Data Archive Based on an ATM Network" at the Graz University of Technology. Currently working at Joanneum Research (Graz) with a main research focus on digital media, digital content analysis and media monitoring applications.

*Sebastian Schlöglmann* (1977), Mag. theol. Studies in history and theology at Salzburg, Vienna and Graz (Austria). Master's thesis on manga and their religious symbolism. Publications on film and theology. He now makes his own films and video installations.

*Wolfgang Johann Schöffmann* (1982) studies theology at Graz University (Austria). In his master's thesis he attempts to find parallels between iconoclasm and modern media theories.

*Sofia Sjö* (1977), ThD from Åbo Akademi University (Finland). She has recently defended her doctoral thesis *Spelar kön någon roll när man räddar världen? Kvinnor, kvinnligheter och messiasmyter i SF-film* (Does gender matter when you save the world? Women, femininity and myths of messiahs in SF-film). Her main fields of interest are religion and film, and religion and gender. She has directed much of her studies towards science fiction and has, among other things, written articles on religion and science fiction for Finnish SF-fandom. Currently she is planning to continue her research in the field of religion and film concentrating on questions of gender.

*Graham Ward,* Head of the School of Arts, Histories and Cultures and Professor for Contextual Theology at the Department for Religions and Theology at the University of Manchester. He was formerly the Dean of Peterhouse, Cambridge. His publications include *Cities of God* (2001), *True Religion* (2002), *Cultural Transformation and Religious Practice* (2005)and *Christ and Culture* (2006).



*Christian Wessely* (1965), Ing., Dr. theol. Associate Professor for Foundational Theology at Graz University (Austria). Research and publications on new media, film and theology.

*Rafael Donner Wiener* (1981) studies theology, philosophy, psychology and pedagogics at Graz University (Austria) and is active in the production of audiovisual media (planning, script, camera, editing).

**Theologie – Kultur – Ästhetik**
Grazer fundamentaltheologische Schriftenreihe
hrsg. von Prof. Dr. Gerhard Larcher und Dr. Christian Wessely (Universität Graz)

Gerhard Larcher; Karl M. Woschitz
**Religion – Utopie – Kunst**
Die Stadt als Fokus
Religion scheint heute säkularistisch ersetzt, ästhetisch beerbt oder fundamentalistisch vereinnahmt zu werden. Das alles wirkt sich lähmend auf bzw. gefährlich für die Entfaltung visionärer Ideen in Gesellschaft, Kultur und Politik aus. Gibt es also einen Zusammenhang zwischen der gegenwärtigen Utopienflaute bzw. Gedächtnislosigkeit der Weltzivilisation und dem Schicksal der Religion in der realisierten Moderne? Und wie könnte Religion als Kulturfaktor, gefiltert durch kritische Rationalität, offen für Pluralismus und Dialog, wieder impulsgebend werden? Überlegungen hierzu aus Anlaß des Kulturhauptstadtjahres (Graz 2003) bestimmen diesen Band.
Bd. 1, 2005, 216 S., 17,90 €, br., ISBN 3-8258-7724-8

LIT Verlag GmbH & Co. KG Wien – Zürich

Auslieferung Österreich: Medienlogistik Pichler-ÖBZ GmbH & Co KG
IZ-NÖ Süd, Straße 1, Objekt 34, A-2355 Wiener Neudorf, Postfach 133
Tel. +43 (0) 2236 / 63 535 - 236, Fax +43 (0) 2236 / 63 535 - 243, e-Mail: bestellen@medien-logistik.at

Auslieferung Deutschland: Fresnostr. 2 48159 Münster
Tel.: 0251 / 620 32 22 – Fax 0251 / 922 60 99
e-Mail: vertrieb@lit-verlag.de – http://www.lit-verlag.de

Gerhard Larcher
**Annäherungsversuche von Kunst und Glaube**
Ein fundamentaltheologisches Skizzenbuch
Die Kunst hat "auch jenseits ihrer typisch religiösen Ausdrucksformen eine innere Nähe zur Welt des Glaubens, so daß sogar in den Situationen eines größeren Abrückens der Kultur von der Kirche gerade die Kunst weiter eine Art Brücke zur religiösen Erfahrung hin darstellt. Als Suche nach dem Schönen, Frucht einer das Alltägliche übersteigenden Einbildungskraft, ist sie ihrer Natur nach eine Art Anruf an das Mysterium."
Papst Johannes Paul II Brief an die Künstler (Ostern 1999)
Bd. 2, 2006, 120 S., 14,90 €, br., ISBN 3-8258-9183-6

LIT Verlag GmbH & Co. KG Wien – Zürich
Auslieferung Österreich: Medienlogistik Pichler-ÖBZ GmbH & Co KG
IZ-NÖ Süd, Straße 1, Objekt 34, A-2355 Wiener Neudorf, Postfach 133
Tel. +43 (0) 2236 / 63 535 - 236, Fax +43 (0) 2236 / 63 535 - 243, e-Mail: bestellen@medien-logistik.at
Auslieferung Deutschland: Fresnostr. 2 48159 Münster
Tel.: 0251 / 620 32 22 – Fax 0251 / 922 60 99
e-Mail: vertrieb@lit-verlag.de – http://www.lit-verlag.de